THOMAS F. WALSH

MINING THE AMERICAN WEST

Boomtown Blues: Colorado Oil Shale
ANDREW GULLIFORD

Hard as the Rock Itself: Place and Identity in the American Mining Town
DAVID ROBERTSON

High Altitude Energy: A History of Fossil Fuels in Colorado
LEE SCAMEHORN

Industrializing the Rockies: Growth, Competition,
and Turmoil in the Coalfields of Colorado and Wyoming
DAVID A. WOLFF

The Mechanics of Optimism: Mining Companies, Technology,
and the Hot Spring Gold Rush, Montana Territory, 1864–1868
JEFFREY J. SAFFORD

Silver Saga: The Story of Caribou, Colorado, Revised Edition
DUANE A. SMITH

Thomas F. Walsh: Progressive Businessman and Colorado Mining Tycoon
JOHN STEWART

Yellowcake Towns: Uranium Mining Communities in the American West
MICHAEL A. AMUNDSON

SERIES EDITORS

DUANE A. SMITH
ROBERT A. TRENNERT
LIPING ZHU

THOMAS F. WALSH

PROGRESSIVE BUSINESSMAN AND COLORADO MINING TYCOON

John C. Stewart

UNIVERSITY PRESS OF COLORADO

© 2007 by the University Press of Colorado

Published by the University Press of Colorado
5589 Arapahoe Avenue, Suite 206C
Boulder, Colorado 80303

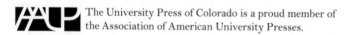 The University Press of Colorado is a proud member of
the Association of American University Presses.

The University Press of Colorado is a cooperative publishing enterprise supported, in part,
by Adams State College, Colorado State University, Fort Lewis College, Mesa State College,
Metropolitan State College of Denver, University of Colorado, University of Northern
Colorado, and Western State College of Colorado.

∞ The paper used in this publication meets the minimum requirements of the American
National Standard for Information Sciences—Permanence of Paper for Printed Library
Materials. ANSI Z39.48-1992

Library of Congress Cataloging-in-Publication Data

Stewart, John C., 1947–
  Thomas F. Walsh : progressive businessman and Colorado mining tycoon / John C. Stewart.
    p. cm. — (Mining the American West)
  Includes bibliographical references and index.
  ISBN 978-0-87081-870-7 (hardcover : alk. paper) 1. Walsh, Thomas F. (Thomas Francis),
1850–1910. 2. Businessmen—United States—Biography. 3. Colorado—Gold discoveries. 4.
Gold mines and mining—Colorado—History. I. Title.
  HD9536.U52W35 2007
  338.7'6223422092—dc22
  [B]

                                                                    2007008034

Design by Daniel Pratt

16   15   14   13   12   11   10   09   08   07   10   9   8   7   6   5   4   3   2   1

The era of Thomas F. Walsh and the present era are separated by one long lifetime. In my case, that lifetime belonged to my mother, Mary Elizabeth Putman Stewart, who was born in 1910, the year of Walsh's death, and passed away in the early morning hours of New Year's Day 2006. This book is dedicated to my mother, who reviewed early drafts, offered much encouragement, and just missed being able to read her son's work (although she witnessed and accomplished many other things in her ninety-five years).

CONTENTS

FOREWORD

In Colorado mining lore, three men—Horace Tabor, Winfield Scott Stratton, and Thomas Walsh—leap out from the pages of history and legend as the epitomes of striking the "big bonanza." Their careers stretch across the entire saga of nineteenth- and early-twentieth-century mining in Colorado, and each in his own way fulfilled the dream of many who had come west to get rich from mining.

Of the three, Irish immigrant Thomas Walsh was the last to make his big strike, but what a strike it was—the famous Camp Bird Mine near Ouray. He might have been the last of the group to find his fortune, but Walsh was no fortunate prospector who just happened to stumble onto a rich gold lode. The immigrant had become a well-versed mining man.

The twenty-one-year-old Walsh arrived in Colorado in 1871 to start his odyssey. Like many of his generation, he was a wandering man. He traveled through several historic mining districts before securing his bonanza. His travels took him to Colorado's beautiful San Juan country first, then to the Black Hills, Leadville, and finally back to the San Juans and eventual fortune and fame. Along the way, he learned about mining, with its hard work and danger. His is the story of the mining West in the years following the Pike's Peak rush of 1859.

From his humble beginnings, Walsh came to exemplify Ben Franklin's all-American success story of rising from poverty to wealth and then becoming involved in the world beyond mining. While he did not particularly enjoy the limelight, he became the friend of politicians and titled nobility and the spokesman of progressive ideas. With the leisure time and philanthropic potential that came with Camp Bird's millions, Thomas Walsh donated one library in Ouray, another in Ireland, and a research fund for the Colorado School of Mines. He supported irrigation projects and served as president of the Colorado Humane Society. Nationally, he led the Trans-Mississippi Congress and served as a U.S. commissioner to the 1900 Paris Exposition.

Wealth and celebrity did not always bring happiness, as Walsh and the other two Colorado mining millionaires found out. A dark side soon appeared that included blackmail and a host of lawsuits. Nor did his wealth bring joy to his family after his death in 1910.

This is Tom Walsh's story, finally successfully researched and told. So welcome to a world not too long ago in time but epochs away from twenty-first-century Colorado.

DUANE A. SMITH
PROFESSOR OF SOUTHWEST STUDIES
FORT LEWIS COLLEGE

ACKNOWLEDGMENTS

My personal search for Tom Walsh began in the most logical place, Ouray, Colorado, where Tom found his fortune and is probably more honored today than in any other place. I am greatly indebted to Ann Hoffman, executive director of the Ouray County Historical Society, and to her staff for their time and effort in opening their fine collection to me. They led me to Ouray historians Doris Gregory and Tom Rosemeyer, who shared their own writings and research and generously reviewed drafts of my work (as did Ann Hoffman).

My next research site was Ireland. I quickly learned that the Irish, even those not familiar with the Tom Walsh story, love to hear about a local youth who found a fortune in the United States. The Rotary Club of Clonmel stopped its regular business to hear my tale and then sent one of its members, Jim Trehy, to help me find graveyards in the Lisronagh area that might be the final resting place of Tom's family. The staffs of the County Tipperary Library in

Thurles, as well as of tourist information centers in Waterford and Carrick-on-Suir, were a great help in researching the Walsh story and ultimately locating the Walsh graves in Kilmurray Cemetery.

I am also greatly indebted to members of the Walsh family for their help and support. Dublin author Mary Ryan, who is descended from Tom's younger sister Margaret, shared her knowledge of Irish history and Tom's upbringing in their native land, not to mention her own book, *Hope*, a fictional account of the Walsh story. Her brother, Michael Ryan, and their cousin in France, Sean Dior, were likewise valuable sources of information and encouragement. They put me in touch with cousins Michael O'Brien of Clonmel, Ireland, and Kathleen O'Brien of Worcester, Massachusetts. Kathleen sent me the unpublished family history and other information on the Massachusetts branch of the family, as well as copies of Irish records and newspaper articles. Tom Walsh's great-great-grandson Joseph Gregory and his coauthor, Carol Anne Rapp, who updated *Father Struck It Rich* into *Queen of Diamonds*, generously shared their research. Carol opened the extensive and well-organized records in her St. Louis home for my review.

The largest collection of information on Tom Walsh and his family is found at the Library of Congress. Through a total of nearly two weeks of research time, the staff of the Manuscript Division ably showed me the ropes of working with a large collection. The assistance of Fred Bauman and Dr. Alice L. Birney particularly stands out. Dr. Birney also led me online to the little-known collection of Walsh papers at Syracuse University, where Diane Cooter and her staff copied and boxed the entire collection and sent it to me in Denver. Ratmoko Ratmansuyu of the Press and Information Division of the Indonesian Embassy gave me a very informative tour of the old Walsh Palace at 2020 Massachusetts Avenue in Washington, D.C.

My research led me to many more libraries and collections and the valuable assistance of their staffs. Locally these include the Western History Section of the Denver Public Library, the Colorado Historical Society, and the Colorado State Archives. At the Colorado School of Mines, archivist Bob Sorgenfrei showed me the informative Camp Bird Mine collection. Lorena Donahue of the Littleton Historical Museum found valuable pictures and other archives of the Wolhurst estate. In Deadwood, South Dakota, Arlette Hanson, Raul Ponce de Leon, and the rest of the staff of the Adams Museum located references to Walsh's stay in their town, while Leann Paananen of the Hearst Library in nearby Lead provided newspaper articles. Black Hills historians Orval Van Deest, Bob Otto, and Mark Wolff also provided valuable assistance. In Wisconsin, mining historian Mark Langenfeld of Madison gave me the names of his Lafayette County contacts, Dorothy Beckwith and Marian Howard, who, together with Darlington historian Charlie Sleep, informed me about the area's history and the fact that Darlington is proud to be the home of Carrie Walsh.

As a lawyer with a background in land titles, I turned to a valuable but often overlooked source of history: county land records. Many thanks to the dedicated employees of the various clerk and recorder's offices in Colorado, South Dakota, and Wisconsin that are noted in my sources.

With all my research in hand, my work first saw life as a master's thesis at the University of Colorado–Denver. I owe a great deal of thanks to my friend, mentor, professor, and author Tom Noel, who approved the Walsh topic for a paper in his Western History class and then recommended that I develop it into a thesis. The other two members of my thesis team were Professors Jay Fell and Jim Whiteside, both accomplished Western History authors, and they proved of invaluable assistance. Professor Duane Smith of Fort Lewis College looked over the thesis and told me what it would take to turn it into a book. He ended up reviewing it at least twice more and then graciously agreeing to write the Foreword. Mining historians Maury Reiber, Ed Raines, and Stan Dempsey added comments. Ed graciously took the mining and geology sections of the book and helped me turn them into a product that is scientifically accurate and quite accessible to the general public.

Last and most important, I thank my wife, Carol, and my daughter, Emilie. Carol helped me with typing and editing, and they both enjoyed the ups of having an author in the family (such as riding horses in Ireland while I researched) and the downs of the long hours and my tying up the best computer in the house.

A host of others added help and encouragement. When a project is this long and also this enjoyable, it reflects the kindness and generosity of many contributors. I will never adequately name all of you, but rest assured that you are in my heart.

THOMAS F. WALSH

INTRODUCTION: IN SEARCH OF TOM WALSH

It is a sad thing to happen to Colorado. He was always one of the most valuable citizens of this state, generous to a fault, ready to help in any enterprise for Colorado's advancement. His kindness will be remembered by thousands, the people will miss him more than they would any other citizen. Ten years ago I worked in Washington and found him always ready to help the Colorado delegation. In spite of all his wealth and riches, he had a strong sympathy for the poor and love for the masses. There was no question concerning them but what found Walsh upon the side of the common people.

Colorado governor John F. Shafroth eulogized Thomas F. Walsh in the April 9, 1910, edition of Denver's *Rocky Mountain News*. Another old friend and politician, former governor and future U.S. senator Charles S. Thomas, later noted in his memoirs the passing of "one of our most noted mining characters, a tall warm-hearted Irishman of florid complexion, genial to a fault, lovable and generous." Friends and acquaintances throughout the nation added their praise. Tom Walsh, as he was known by nearly everyone, had passed away the previous evening at his mansion in Washington, D.C. In just over sixty years of life, Walsh had risen from Irish commoner to millionaire and philanthropist and was Colorado's unofficial man in Washington. Denver's newspapers joined many others nationwide, offering accolades in a series of articles over the coming days. The coverage detailed the life and career of a man little known before he acquired Colorado mining wealth at age forty-six.[1]

This reporting included many Tom Walsh stories, for the "Colorado Monte-Cristo" had become a national legend. Like Shafroth and Thomas, the journalists assured their audiences that the wealthy Mr. Walsh possessed a most unassuming character, welcoming "common" friends from his hard-rock mining days as readily as new friends from among the elite. Although living in style in Washington, he had still nostalgically accepted the gift of his old carpenter's tools, entrusted to a friend long ago in the Black Hills. Others tried in vain to fill in the many gaps in the forty-six years before fame arrived. Tom had once turned down a chance to own half of the rich Homestake Mine (a story that is false). He made an earlier fortune and retired to the East Coast, only to go broke in the Panic of 1893 (also false). So little was known about his Irish childhood that the press described it in a broad range, from abject poverty to relative prosperity.

Today, Tom Walsh and his prominent family are more likely to be remembered for one particular way they used his wealth. The year after Tom's death, his daughter, Evalyn Walsh McLean, purchased the world's largest blue diamond, the Hope, and with it, supposedly, an ancient curse. Evalyn later became a well-known Washington figure in her own right and was the only member of the family to pen a book about their lives. In 1936 she published the aptly named *Father Struck It Rich*, a Depression-era tale of a rich family's joys and successes followed by sorrow.[2] Although most of the public blamed her diamond for that sorrow, in her book Evalyn blames wealth instead. The book is her autobiography, not her father's biography, and is in keeping with a time when the rich (or formerly rich) laid bare their guilt to an eager national audience. While concentrating on her Washington social life, Evalyn struggles to recall a distant childhood. She was approaching age fifty when she wrote the book, and no close family members were alive to support her often faulty memory. She portrays the father who made it all happen as the ultimate straight shooter, tall and dignified, fair and honest. Possessor of an Irish temper, Tom Walsh had an even stronger degree of Irish charm.

Evalyn's character assessment of her father seems close to the mark, but she fails in other respects. Some names, dates, and relationships are wrong, while important facts are strained or omitted. In the end, however, researchers must make a truce with Evalyn, for she is often our only source of information about the Walsh family. Moreover, she is a very accurate source regarding her own childhood feelings. She can remember the pained look of a parent under stress, even if she does not remember the cause of that stress. She assures us, and we believe, that newfound wealth never disturbed the love among members of a close-knit family, nor did the tragic death of her brother. Descriptions of childhood play and pranks often override historical events. What was really happening at the 1900 Paris Exposition while Evalyn escaped from a convent? What did Tom accomplish when Theodore Roosevelt sent him to settle a Colorado labor dispute? What we really want to know is how Evalyn's father managed to achieve such high standing and influence in such a short time (and just how influential he really was). Nonetheless, *Father Struck It Rich* holds an enduring charm because its author never left her childhood behind. Evalyn buys the Hope Diamond on a lark and defines her one continuing problem as deciding "what amusing thing can I do next?" Important primary sources such as mine and business records, family letters and diaries, and some public records have disappeared over time. *Father Struck It Rich*, however, remains in print.

The search for the true Tom Walsh presents a formidable but rewarding challenge. The sixty-foot-long Evalyn Walsh McLean collection, donated by her executors to the Library of Congress, is the single best source of information on the man. Evalyn may never have read all its contents. Had she done so, she would have discovered missing friends and relatives. Perhaps she wanted some of them to remain missing. The fragments of some events, from business deals to close personal relationships, are rendered meaningless, if intriguing, by the passage of time. Could Evalyn have provided missing material? Many details do remain about Tom's heartrending lawsuit against the father of one of her friends. Did Tom hide the fact from Evalyn, or did she choose to forget? The Denver papers of his old friend Charles Thomas infer that the normally placid Walsh may have died angry over the remarks of a Durango publisher. Once again, Evalyn remains silent on the subject.

In the end, most parts of the Tom Walsh puzzle do fit. They confirm the highly decent and upright man portrayed by the adoring daughter and appreciative friends, although they also lead to undiscovered territory. They paint a portrait of an American businessman in keeping with his era, one in which the excesses of the Gilded Age passed, somewhat reluctantly, into the awareness of the Progressive Era. Ready wealth awaited those who worked and studied hard, encountered a little luck or good timing along the way, or had a personal

manner that led to acceptance and influence. Walsh had all of these characteristics. Many of his successful contemporaries shared his common origin overseas, with no formal education. As new American millionaires of the Gilded
Age, they filled their mansions with artwork and other finery and raised their
children to expect luxuries. Tom Walsh was no different. He also engaged in
philanthropy, by then viewed as the obligation of the very rich. However, in an
era when an entrepreneur could run his business in nearly any manner he saw
fit, Walsh ran his with skill and integrity. He did not abuse the trust of partners or investors. He kept his wealth until his death and spent his last years
striving to do good works (and entertain lavishly), rather than building more
financial capital. His finest trait, noted in many eulogies, was that Tom Walsh
always seemed to look upon those less fortunate not just as recipients of charity
delivered from a distance but rather as fellow citizens.

ORIGINS IN IRELAND

Thomas Francis Walsh had the good fortune to live in some of the world's most beautiful places. The first of these was his birthplace. Lisronagh, County Tipperary, Ireland, was and remains a small crossroads settlement just north of the larger town of Clonmel, which lies along the north bank of the River Suir as it flows along the county's southern boundary.

Richard Dowling, a nineteenth-century writer raised in the area, describes how "from the very bank of the river rose a long, low line of hills, and beyond this another and a higher range, and still further back, a third and loftier. Beyond the third the settled order ceased, and was succeeded by a chaotic confusion of heather heights which rose and fell for many a good long Irish mile, and finally once more marshaled themselves into order and descended in long undulating lines down to the ocean." Lisronagh sits in a fertile and productive area. Yet for much of its human history this land did not bestow commensurate prosperity on its Irish farmers. This fact was especially true during Tom Walsh's childhood.[1]

With a common name like Walsh, it is difficult to tell when Tom's ancestors reached County Tipperary. A name with a distinctly non-Irish origin, Walsh is now the fourth most common surname in Ireland. It means "Welsh," which is its pronunciation in Ireland. The Walshes have been in Ireland for at least eight centuries. They followed in the wake of twelfth-century invaders from the east, led by Normans based in Wales.

A Massachusetts cousin named Margaret Kennedy wrote what is probably the only history of this branch of the Walsh family. It could be the story of many Irish American families. She begins with Tom's great-grandfather Michael and grandfather John, who bought an abandoned rocky field on the outskirts of Clonmel "for a song" and then cleared it for a farm. The land's previous occupants were itinerant Gypsies. It was the time of the American Revolution, when owning such a parcel was the best hope for an Irish Catholic family. During the eighteenth century the Irish owned only one-tenth of their land, and no Catholic could become a physician, a soldier, or a lawyer or openly practice his or her religion. Soon thereafter, in 1798, the Irish attempted their own revolution, only to see it swiftly put down, with more rights taken away. To our knowledge, none of Tom Walsh's ancestors joined the rebellion. Like the majority of their Catholic neighbors, they were content to work hard, avoid trouble, and make the best of a less-than-ideal situation. The British punished them by implementing the 1801 Act of Union and moving all parliamentary functions to London.[2]

In the case of Michael and John Walsh, hard work paid off with a flourishing farm, praised in the family history as one of the finest in the county. If correct, the father and son were well ahead of most Irish Catholics of their time. As the story goes, John inherited the land from his father and added a passenger ferry across the River Suir. This brought the family more income, for a steady clientele needed to reach the growing town of Clonmel, with its churches, marketplace, and county fairs. John Walsh married, although his wife's name is lost. Two daughters arrived over the next few years, Catherine in 1808 and Bridget in 1811. A son, Peter, was born in 1812. The fourth child, Tom's father, Thomas K., followed in 1820. He showed a talent for music, and John could afford to buy him a violin.[3]

For a while, the area around Clonmel prospered as a result of British agricultural policies. Corn Laws, a form of tariff, protected Irish grains so they could be sold in Britain and on the Continent. High demand during the Napoleonic Wars led to relative wealth for men such as Michael and John Walsh. When there was peace in Ireland, the presence of English soldiers was an economic boon. Clonmel's army post bought supplies from local merchants and contributed to musical and sporting events.

The two Walsh daughters married two brothers named Power; Bridget married Laurence and Catherine wed James. The Power families settled in the village of Nine Mile House, northeast of Clonmel. Here the family history tells us they raised fine horses to sell to British soldiers and gentry. Their home, called Rock View, still stands.[4]

A CHILDHOOD WITH FEW ADVANTAGES

As an adult, Thomas K. Walsh leased a farm in a rural area called Baptistgrange, just outside Lisronagh. Five acres was the average for Irish tenant farmers of the time, but Thomas's holding may have been larger, for he was able to elevate his family above simple peasant status. However, economic conditions prevented him from duplicating the success his father and grandfather had enjoyed. He married Bridget Scully, a native of nearby Ballyneale Parish. As the two began raising a family in the early 1840s, their land's prosperity, which had been ebbing for some time, finally evaporated. Irish farmers exported their grains and turned to the potato for sustenance. Potato blights were common in Europe, but in 1845 a particularly severe blight struck the country most dependent on the crop—Ireland. Moreover, in 1846 British free trade advocates convinced Parliament to abolish the Corn Laws, leaving Irish grain unprotected. Thus the two firm pillars that had supported Irish farm life toppled almost simultaneously. The Potato Famine raged until 1850, killing at least 1 million Irish and sending even more to new homes overseas. The Walsh family and their Tipperary neighbors fared better than many. They usually had just enough money to buy meal, and only the nearby mountain districts experienced great want and starvation. The majority of the deaths occurred in the poorer lands to the north and west, in counties such as Clare, Galway, and Mayo. However, very few people in any part of Ireland considered themselves fortunate.[5]

The worst was over when young Tom Walsh entered the world on April 2, 1850, but the land and its people experienced a very slow recovery. Welcoming the newborn were his parents, Thomas K. and Bridget, along with John, age six; Michael, four; Mary (or Maria), almost three; and Patrick, age one. They had escaped the famine, but personal tragedy soon followed. When Tom was two, his younger sister, Alice, and his mother, Bridget, died within the course of a few months. The cause of their deaths is not known. Bridget Scully Walsh passed away on October 12, 1852, at age thirty-three. The family laid her to rest a few miles from their home in Kilmurray Cemetery, Ballyneale Parish. They could afford only a simple marker. Later, Tom made certain that his mother and other family members were honored with a more impressive monument.[6]

Others in the family had left Ireland. The entire families of the two Power brothers and two Walsh sisters sought new opportunities in Worcester, Massachusetts, departing in 1850 but staying in close touch. Still, the Thomas K. Walsh family remained in Baptistgrange. Thomas K. married a woman named Margaret Cunningham, and in time two daughters were born, Kate and Margaret. Writing eighty years later, Evalyn remembered few stories about her father's childhood. She describes Thomas K., the grandfather she never knew, as a farmer popular for his violin playing. No doubt his talent helped break the gloom of the times. Evalyn tells of a trip back to Baptistgrange in 1899, although she does not name any Irish relatives she met. The place where her father was born and raised had a whitewashed, thatch-roofed house. Chickens pecking in the mud seemed ordinary to her, but to her father they were "creatures in a chain of life that had touched his long before."[7]

Tom himself passed down few childhood memories. We can imagine him growing up in the small farmhouse, shared with his family in what we would consider cramped quarters. Hard manual farm labor, church, and school probably took up all his waking hours. If any time remained for leisure, he spent it at church-related social events or fairs. Later, Tom provided a rare glimpse into that world. By then he was a renowned world traveler and after-dinner speaker. Reporting on the fair in Seville, Spain, he stated that the sight of a young boy seeking gingerbread from a street vendor reminded him that "I too was once a little ruddy-faced boy back in Ireland, waylaying the walking peddlers of gingersnaps and cookies as they passed on the road near our house on their way to the patron of Fethard, Tipperary, feeling wealthy in the extremest sense if I had a plurality of pennies, which was seldom the case, but happy and contented if I had even one." The quote displays Tom's tendency to describe himself as poorer than he really was. One relic that remained in the family was a crucifix owned by Bridget, his mother. It was made of handsome mother-of-pearl and inlaid wood. Even in a land of devout believers, it seems unlikely that the woman who owned the crucifix was living in dire poverty.[8]

EDUCATION AND TRAINING

Tom received as good an education as could be expected for the time and for his place in society. While the few public schools educated the British upper class, Catholic merchants in the Clonmel area had endowed the private education of their poorer brethren. Young students received religious training and learned the "3 Rs" and handicrafts. Even if taught by Irish masters, all students had to recite the same daily rhyme, which went, "I thank the goodness and the grace, that on my birth has smiled, and made me in these Christian days, a happy English child." Tom's only surviving tale of his school days proves that from an early age he wanted to climb the social ladder and escape this oppression. As he later told Denver friends, "I knew when I was a boy that some day I would be rich, and that my riches would come out of the earth. So when a mere lad going to an Irish school with the children of the poor families of Tipperary, I took great interest in the study of geology, of rocks and soil, and one day when the teacher had been away and came back bringing a block of granite for us to look at and study I felt I had come into my own."[9]

His formal education was over by age twelve, when Tom became an apprentice millwright. The fact that he received the apprenticeship was something of a privilege, proof that Thomas K. Walsh was a farmer of sufficient means to afford the fee for the training. He must have recognized a special talent in his youngest son, granting him the rare opportunity to enter the skilled trades. Tom probably started in the town of Fethard, just north of the family farm, and later moved to the larger town of Clonmel. He is said to have worked for and lived with a prominent Clonmel Quaker family named Grubb. He would have been exposed to what were liberal ideas for the time, for the millwrights had a tradition of political activism. In 1844 they had led a large yet peaceful demonstration on behalf of the great Irish reformer Daniel O'Connell. Many of the same millwrights must have become Tom's co-workers and mentors.[10]

THOUGHTS OF LEAVING

Walsh soon realized that his millwright's trade, with its carpentry skills, was a line of work he could take to a new location, even to a new land. Milling was on the decline in Clonmel. It had never recovered from the 1846 Corn Law repeal and soon faced a new threat from U.S. competition. Other lines of work were diminishing as well, leaving Clonmel to survive as a regional administrative center. However, the service sector could not provide enough new jobs to absorb the losses in other areas. In the countryside, where many members of the Walsh family lived, unemployment was high and eviction of tenant farmers frequent. The result was growing discontent and violence.

Typical of the times was an 1868 incident at Ballycohey, a small settlement northwest of Clonmel. A less-than-popular landlord named William Scully sought to evict tenants, not for the first time. This time the tenants were forewarned, and they planned an ambush. In the melee that followed, Scully was seriously injured, and two of his supporters were killed. Ballycohey was much on the minds of the British Parliament when it passed the Irish Land Act of 1870, granting more rights to tenant farmers. William Scully was already planning his alternatives and had purchased large tracts in the United States. Eventually, he became one of the largest landowners in his new country. To establish residence and citizenship, Scully purchased a large home in an affluent neighborhood of Washington, D.C. Eighteen-year-old Tom Walsh of Clonmel no doubt heard about the incident at Ballycohey and may have considered it one more factor weighing against his future in Ireland. He could not have imagined that just over thirty years later he would be William Scully's Washington neighbor and friend.[11]

It is not known if Tom kept his millwright job to the end, but he became firm in his resolve to leave Ireland for America. He was not alone. Evalyn tells us the pivotal moment came in 1865 when Tom's older brother Michael left to join the U.S. Army and fight Indians in the West. Maria remained unmarried and must have felt her prospects for finding a husband were better across the ocean. Ireland did not lack single young men, but most of them were very poor and without land, so they often remained lifelong bachelors. Tom and his brother Patrick did not want to accept that fate. For Tom, it came down to the vision inspired by his teacher's granite block. Ireland did not possess mineral riches to match those of the United States, and the Crown owned most of those it did have. Any fruits of mining labor would likely pass to Queen Victoria, not to the miners. Tom Walsh wanted to live in a place where a miner might find and keep a fortune.

In 1869, four members of the Walsh family of Tipperary set out for a new home across the sea. Patrick left first, followed by Tom, Maria, and Thomas K. The father, age forty-nine, felt the same urge as his children. He was now estranged from Margaret. John, twenty-five and recently married, decided to stay behind and run his father's farm. Kate and young Margaret remained in their mother's care. It was not unusual for Irish emigrant families to leave others behind, especially young children, in hopes that they might later join their now-successful family members in the United States. In this instance, however, the oldest and the two youngest Walsh children lived out their lives in Ireland.[12]

TO AMERICA AND THE WEST

CHAPTER TWO

A SUPPORTIVE FAMILY IN WORCESTER

Tom, Maria, and their father traveled in steerage and landed at the port of Boston. Thereafter, the family separated. While Evalyn tells us that all three immigrants settled in Worcester, Massachusetts, the tradition of the Power family in that city purports that only Tom lived with them. Thomas K. and Maria probably headed straight for the Colorado goldfields. This is an early indication of Tom's cautious and prudent nature, choosing better employment opportunities and life with settled family members in Worcester. Gold could wait until he got his feet on the ground and became accustomed to his vast new homeland.

Tom arrived with $50 in his pocket and moved in with his Aunt Bridget Power's family. Their home was a Worcester "three decker," a typical three-story residence of Irish families that housed many relatives. Tom's cousins

Catherine, Joanna, and Sarah cleaned up the young Irishman, taught him how to dress, and instructed him in his new community's expectations. He would never forget their kindness, years later calling them "my three sweethearts." In keeping with the style of a Victorian gentleman, he remembered, "I worked at my trade in Worcester getting $3.50 a day.... I went to live with my relatives, among whom were young men and women. They were Christian people. On Sunday they took me to church and through their influence I joined the Father Matthew Abstinence Society. While other young carpenters were drinking whiskey on Saturday nights I was at home with my cousins or calling on friends. God has been good to me since I came to America."[1] Looking back on his start in the same era, another successful U.S. businessman made a similar declaration. John D. Rockefeller Sr. remembered, "How grateful I am that these associations were given to me in my early boyhood, that I was contented and happy with . . . the work in the church, with the work in the Sunday school, with the work with good people—that was my environment, and I thank God for it."[2] Rockefeller and Walsh both succeeded in the Gilded Age, despite their vastly different business practices. Nonetheless, they agreed that abstinence and self-discipline, not to mention keeping the right company, were the keys to that success.

Tom held several jobs in Worcester, and like many immigrants he started at the bottom. In his case, the term applied both literally and figuratively. His first job was in the city's sewers, but even there he showed the tenacity that would later make him famous. Soon he became a sewer contractor and then a carpenter. Years later, a building contractor named McElroy told Tom's cousin Katherine Kennedy how much he had appreciated the work of a young man who volunteered to climb to the top of a church steeple in nearby Leominster. He was happy to hear that this was "the Mr. Walsh of whom so much has been written."[3]

Only a few years after the Civil War, the Irish as a whole were still a despised group of newcomers in a nation yet to see its greatest influx of immigrants. Catholics in a Protestant-dominated land, they were different and disrespected. The Irish draft riots in New York during the Civil War were not forgotten in the northeastern United States, despite the number of Irish who had served the Union cause with distinction. However, Worcester was a heavily Irish town, and Tom found himself in a prominent ethnic group with roots dating back to well before the Potato Famine. Tom probably suffered little, if any, discrimination. He seems to have been very happy with his extended family, and he always had a job. Nevertheless, in two years' time he was ready to move on.[4]

RAILROADS AND GOLD IN COLORADO TERRITORY

Tom's family in Colorado could have told him tales of mining wealth, even if they themselves had not found it. There were also plenty of job prospects in another locale where the Irish had achieved some respect. One of those jobs required a carpenter to build trestles for the new Colorado Central Railroad in Golden. Feeling secure with his savings of $300, Tom bid goodbye to Worcester and headed west in 1871, at age twenty-one.

Walsh was, if anything, a latecomer. Gold seekers and their supporting cast had flooded into Colorado since 1858. The first wave, the so-called Pikes Peak rush, was centered in the new settlement of Denver City. Here streamed gold was found in just enough quantity to attract easterners fleeing economic recession in their part of the country. Soon they found lode deposits in the Colorado mountains that eclipsed the meager streamed (or placer) deposits, and Denver City became a jumping-off place. The Central City boom started in 1859, and Idaho Springs, Georgetown, Fairplay, and Oro City (later Leadville) soon shared the enthusiasm. The early booms waned within a few years because the richest ores near the surface were soon mined out. Miners left to fight the Civil War, and when they returned, better technology followed them. New smelting processes meant the lower-grade ores then being mined could be processed right in Colorado, not in the faraway places once required.[5]

All this meant that Colorado's transportation system needed to improve quickly. Denver (with "City" now dropped) was frantic to get a railroad, one that, it was hoped, would go straight west to the Pacific. Some of the loftiest peaks in the country stood in the way, however, so the builders of the first transcontinental railroad chose a lower route through Wyoming. As Denver struggled not to lose its supremacy to Cheyenne, it discovered another threat closer to home. The little town of Golden boasted that it was as close to Wyoming as Denver and even closer to the goldfields. Led by William A.H. Loveland, a promoter, mine owner, and politician, Golden pushed its Colorado Central line. Denver responded with the Denver Pacific, and the race was on. Led by such early civic leaders as former territorial governor John Evans, Jerome Chaffee, and David Moffat (later a close friend of Tom Walsh), the Denverites won. The first Denver Pacific locomotive rolled into the small city in June 1870. By August of that year, Denver gained a second line when the Kansas Pacific arrived from the east.[6]

Undaunted, Loveland and his supporters continued to promote the Colorado Central, although the line never made much money. It did, however, create opportunity for young carpenters like Tom Walsh. Tom's 1871 journey from Worcester to Golden was much easier than the one many of his contemporaries had endured only a few years earlier. When David Moffat arrived in 1860, the stagecoach ride from Omaha took twenty-nine days. Now the railroad cut the trip all the way from Worcester to as little as six days. The cost probably consumed no more than forty dollars of Tom's savings, plus meals and overnight accommodations. While a decided improvement over the older stagecoaches and wagons and even travel by foot, the ride was by no means relaxing. Another new railroad employee of the era described a long and rough journey on hard seats. A wood-burning stove heated each coach, nearly roasting those nearest it while leaving others at the far end of the car shivering in misery.[7]

Tom arrived in time for the Colorado Central's 1871 thrust west up Clear Creek Canyon toward the gold camps and Loveland's dream of a Continental Divide crossing at Berthoud Pass. The line had been promised the proceeds of a Gilpin County bond issue if it reached the town of Black Hawk by May 1872. With this incentive, Loveland increased the number of his workers from 150 to 500 men, each earning an average of $3.25 per day. Despite their best efforts, the Colorado Central fell far short of its goal. It finally reached Black Hawk in December 1872, earning $100,000 for doing so. The figure would have been three times that amount had the May deadline been met. Financial problems for the Colorado Central continued into the next year.[8]

For Walsh and his fellow workers, the job was long and hard, nearly all of it performed in steep mountain canyons. After completion of the line to Black Hawk, work commenced on a branch leading toward Idaho Springs and Georgetown and, it was hoped, a Continental Divide crossing (prevented in the end by the steep grades needed to reach the high-altitude passes). In the meantime, the financial panic of 1873 brought everything to an abrupt halt on this and many of the nation's other railroads. While Evalyn tells us Tom left the Colorado Central because he caught "mining fever," the simple truth is that he must have lost his job. With no railroad work, why not try to look for gold?[9]

Walsh followed his first gold rush to southwestern Colorado in 1873. His strategy, which he would follow for some time, was to seek carpentry work first and look for gold on the side. He made the town of Del Norte his headquarters, building during the winter and prospecting in the warmer months. Riches did not follow, and by the next year Tom was back in the Denver area. It would be interesting to speculate on what might have happened had he stayed. Del Norte was another jumping-off place that in time was surrounded by bonanzas. At the time of Walsh's stay, the new excitement lay farther to the west. Evalyn thought her father may have prospected near the Arizona border, which probably placed him in the San Juan Mountains. What might have happened if he had stayed a while and met such prospectors as William Weston and Andy Richardson? Both men were destined to explore a beautiful and remote San Juan basin, where they dreamed of wealth and encountered only frustration. Had Tom joined them, he could have arrived at the scene of his greatest success twenty years earlier. Instead, he spent those twenty years becoming thoroughly schooled in the pain and rewards offered by mining. Without that education, he might have died in obscurity after his exhaustive work failed to hit pay dirt, the experience of many other miners.[10]

POET, REPORTER, CARPENTER, AND MINER IN THE BLACK HILLS

A short stay in Colorado's Central City district was next for Tom. Site of one of the territory's earliest booms, the camp still provided riches for some, but not for Tom Walsh. Little is known of his time in Central City. He once again combined mining and carpentry. Tom must have conducted his mining ventures through unrecorded documents such as leases or bonds, for his name does not appear in the public records. He lived in Nevadaville, a small town with many Irish residents. One source has him supervising construction of some of Central City's principal buildings. The town needed the help, for it suffered devastating fires in both 1873 and 1874.[11]

At some point in 1875, what might be called the nation's worst-kept secret reached Central City. By the terms of the 1868 Fort Laramie Treaty, the Black Hills of Dakota Territory were to remain in the hands of the Sioux (or Lakota) tribe, which considered this land one of its most sacred places. Nevertheless, by 1874 the Grant administration in Washington had become curious about what might lie in these rugged hills surrounded by plains. Lieutenant Colonel George Armstrong Custer led a military expedition to find out. While the official mission was to locate a site for a new fort, a few scientists accompanied the soldiers to study the hills' natural properties. They soon found glittering metal in a stream. According to his orders, Custer was to protect his scientific findings with the utmost secrecy. Since the expedition had to return a considerable distance to Fort Lincoln in what is now North Dakota, the commander felt it wise to send the findings to a closer point, Fort Laramie in Wyoming Territory.

Before Custer and his men even caught a glimpse of Fort Lincoln in the distance, word of the gold discovery had reached the outside world. Soon prospectors were outfitting for the latest boom and then striking their way into hostile Indian territory. Travel in groups was the norm, and even the larger numbers suffered attacks in broad daylight. Tom Walsh was soon caught up in the excitement, joining a number of Central City citizens to look for a bonanza. He deemed these men experts in gold extraction. On their journey, Tom's party fared better than most. Their only encounter with the enraged displaced owners of the land came when some Lakota stampeded their horses.[12]

Tom and his party first explored in the Custer area of the Black Hills, site of a short-lived boom. Then in early 1876 they joined the next wave of excitement, heading fifty miles north to what would soon become Lawrence County, with its legendary county seat, Deadwood. Tom first appears in the local press as T. F. Walsh, mine reporter, presenting a September 9, 1876, report on the Sand Creek Mines to the editor of Deadwood's *Black Hills Daily Times*. The account credits others with developing the promising district, failing to mention what reporter Walsh's role might have been. However, as this excerpt shows, Tom was gaining valuable early experience as a booster of both his community and the West:

> When I came to Deadwood last April, I was told this country was a "bilk." This is not so. We have hundreds of gulches here that will pay from three to four dollars per day. Our streams are pure as crystal, our valleys are decked with choice fruits and flowers, and are bursting with vegetation; our hills are covered with quartz. These features which this section of the hill possesses . . . will draw hither numbers of our fellow citizens that are eking out a miserable existence in the crowded cities of the states.

In a time of great fear, Walsh was not above the bigotry that infested the area. While he personally took no part in retribution against Native Americans, his next remarks may have ignited a passion in others:

> The leaves of autumn are appearing, which reminds us that this camp is now one year old. How many a noble life has been extinguished during this eventful year. There is scarcely a portion of our hills that is not sacred to the memory of "someone's darling," murdered by the Indians. And yet in the face of all this the news comes as a mockery that a new batch of these sanctimonious hypocrites are on their way to Red Cloud to sanction by their presence, acts and words the hellish butcheries of those red fiends. We should seek out a terrible revenge for our murdered brothers.

Tom carries the same theme into a new arena he had not demonstrated before, that of published poet. His work entitled "Long Ago" closes his report:

> Away up in the Black Hills,
> Where bears and Indians roam,
> As I sit beside the camp-fire,

In my log cabin home,
I'm wafted back on memory's wing
To where the shamrocks grow,
To other scenes and other days—
The days of "long ago."
The days of childhood's innocence,
When naught of care I knew,
Nor how the world would change with me
As I to manhood grew.
The little cot, my mother's smile,
That ever welcomed me,
As oft from school I bounded home,
So gaily, gaily free.
My childhood's home I can't forget,
Though far from it I've strayed;
Nor time can ne'er efface these scenes
By memory's pen engraved.
As I sit beside the camp-fire
It sets my heart aglow,
To ponder on these happy scenes
And days of "long ago."
If my scalp escapes the treachery
Of those cruel Indian bands;
If fortune smiles upon me
In these, the golden lands
I'll take a trip to where I played,
With the boys I used to know;
I'll visit all the dear old haunts
And scenes of "long ago."[13]

Tom soon made another effort as a poet, this time in the October 1, 1876, *Black Hills Pioneer.* His work entitled "Early Friendships" carries the same nostalgic theme, probably brought on by lonely days in an isolated cabin. This time, however, Native Americans are mercifully left out. By March 1877 Walsh emerged as secretary of the Strawberry Gulch Mining District, just a few miles south of Deadwood. His July 6, 1877, report to the *Pioneer* is entitled "Gleanings from the Strawberry Beds of the Buttes." He lists prominent men and their rich mines discovered in the past season and adds, "I have tested rock from all these mines, and as an uninterested party I must say they all prospected well. An express route is being constructed to connect the camp with Galena, six miles to the northeast. . . . The express to Galena will travel over it, so you see we then will be able to procure copies of the *Pioneer* without walking eight or ten miles, and if we have any bitter spite against a neighbor we can have our sweet revenge by reading, or endeavoring to read to him the latest dispatches from the Turkish War." Tom's last plea is for a Strawberry Gulch post office.[14]

Walsh soon followed the express route, and by December 1877 he showed up as a resident of Galena. In her history of the area, Mildred Fielder credits him as the only millionaire to come from Galena, adding that his wealth was acquired later. Writing in 1976, she also reports that locals called a rustic cabin on the small town's main street "the Tom Walsh cabin" (as it is still known today). Galena was an exception in the Black Hills, a silver camp. Walsh, in turn, sought an exception to the exception, gold. He formed a partnership with Jerry Daly, who would be a longtime associate. Crediting Black Hills legends, Fielder tells us they located the Anchor Mountain gold mine. Supposedly, the two men argued over how to work the mine, although their friendship was not affected. Walsh favored digging for quartz lode deposits, while Daly wanted to work surface streams for their placer gold. The disagreement was settled when Walsh let Daly run the mine his way. Tom also sought carpentry work in Deadwood.[15]

It is not known exactly when Tom Walsh, carpenter, began his Deadwood career. He worked in the muddy boomtown around the same time as his sojourns in the outlying camps. Fielder tells us that his shop was back of the Starr and Bullock hardware store. Others give him credit for erecting many of the town's trademark false-front buildings. If so, Tom's creations did not last long. A September 1879 fire wiped out much of the wood-constructed town, including its public records. Deeds, mining location certificates, and other records filed after the October 1 opening of the new courthouse provide no evidence of Tom's stay in Lawrence County.

At least two stories do place Walsh in Deadwood's community life, however. On one occasion he offered advice to a young shopkeeper named Albert Gushurst. The man had encountered a common problem in the West, miners digging up the street in front of his store. Asserting that their mining claims predated the platting of the town, they asked for $500 to make the problem go away. The price was too steep, so the young shopkeeper turned to "an older man by the name of Walsh who had been in other mining camps and had had a lot of experience." Walsh suggested raising the money from the town's sawmills, which also found their paths blocked by the miners. The fund-raising idea worked, and Gushurst was able to carry on his business. He later remembered that this Mr. Walsh became very wealthy and that his family owned the famous Hope Diamond.[16]

Evalyn remembers a Washington meeting many years later between her father and Captain Jack Crawford, the long-haired and flamboyant figure known as the Poet Scout of the Black Hills. Crawford recognized Walsh as a fellow member of the posse called together to hunt for the murderers of Preacher Smith, presumed to be Lakota. Henry Weston Smith, Deadwood's first man of the cloth, met his demise on August 20, 1876, while traveling between his preaching duties in Deadwood and Crook City. Custer's defeat at the Little Big Horn, less than 200 miles away, was a recent and fearful memory, so Native Americans were obvious suspects. The posse was unsuccessful in its mission, but at least one later historian has suspected that Smith was killed by whites who, for whatever reason, resented the Methodist's presence and knew who could be framed for his murder. Smith had not been scalped, a common practice of the Lakota. Jack Crawford was one of Walsh's many new Deadwood friends. Another was the "lean and gray-sheriff Seth Bullock." Later, Walsh and Bullock shared a friendship with a man who had not yet arrived in the Dakota Territory. His name was Theodore Roosevelt.[17]

A LEARNING EXPERIENCE

According to family and friends, one event in 1876 Deadwood marked a water-shed in the early career of Tom Walsh. An old prospector named Smoky Jones needed to have some carpentry work done, and he approached Tom, who invited him to stay for lunch. A friendship developed, and Smoky dropped by for many future visits. By Tom's recollection, under Jones's outer shabbiness "there dwelt a charming and lovable personality." The old-timer soon wanted to share some information. His prospect in the hills looked very promising, and he needed a partner to develop it. Might his carpenter friend be interested? Tom turned to the advice of the experts from Central City who had accompanied him. Their response was ominous. No slate formation could possibly bear gold. Look only for a true fissure vein in granite. Sadly, Tom turned Smoky down on the partner-ship. The friendship probably lasted, but Jones had to seek support elsewhere. As the story goes, he found it, and the result was the richest and longest-lived of all U.S. gold mines. Tom Walsh had supposedly turned down a half interest in the Homestake Mine, which produced millions of dollars' worth of ore until closing in 2001.

Most other sources cast doubt on the Smoky Jones tale, particularly the part about Walsh being offered half of what became the Homestake. The most recent account, author Duane Smith's 2001 history of the Homestake, credits Moses Manuel with discovering the Homestake Ledge (or Lead) on April 9, 1876. Manuel formed a partnership with his brother Fred, Alex Engh, and Henry Harney. All they lacked was development capital. The following year

California capitalists, led by George Hearst, purchased the mine and made a fortune. Earlier accounts bear out these facts, including the one discovery notice found in the post-fire records of the Lawrence County recorder. According to this document, recorded in January 1880, Moses Manuel and H. C. Harney affirmed their location of the Homestake Lead on April 27, 1876. The two men added that their intention was "to show present ownership, title and claim, and to cover any illegality that might attach to making mining claims upon an Indian Reservation." Moses Manuel's personal account of the discovery, told later to a Homestake Mine superintendent, does not mention a fellow discoverer named Jones.[18]

Smoky Jones was real, for early Black Hills historian Richard B. Hughes describes the old prospector as a colorful local character who could howl like a wolf. Hughes adds that Smoky was fortunate enough to have discovered a valuable mining property and to have disposed of it for a considerable sum. Later in his book, Hughes credits the Manuel brothers and Alex Engh with discovering the Homestake. If Smoky Jones had been involved, Hughes would have told us. The county records consumed by the fire, not to mention the common name of Jones, make his property impossible to locate. Possibly, Jones's mine was later incorporated into the Homestake property. Even if this is the case, any interest Walsh might have owned in the entire mine would have been considerably less than half. Tom knew he had made a mistake, but he also loved to tell tales with a moral to his family and friends (even ones in which he was the victim). In this one, he missed a handsome reward by failing to think independently. Over time, abetted by Walsh himself, the story stretched from poor investment decision to colossal missed bonanza. Other Deadwood tales, such as one in which Tom knocked away the gun of his would-be murderer, probably fall into the same category of a good story overriding the facts.[19]

Tom Walsh left the Black Hills for good in 1878, perhaps a little heart-broken over his missed opportunity but definitely not broke. Evalyn credits her father's prudence in sticking to the building trades as the reason he left with between $75,000 and $100,000. Others report him selling Black Hills properties for close to $100,000. These figures are no doubt exaggerations. A more credible story is told by one Denver newspaper in Walsh's obituary and is later picked up by Mildred Fielder in her Galena history. Tom's partner, Jerry Daly, grew tired of working the Anchor Mountain mine by himself and leased it to a German named Asmus. Daly then left for Colorado, leaving Walsh to deal with Asmus when the lease expired. Walsh was ready to leave the area himself, so he offered Asmus $30,000 in gold dust for the property. The German quickly accepted, and Tom left the Black Hills with what was a large sum for 1878, half of which belonged to Daly. He also carried carpentry earnings of about $10,000. Evalyn states that her father used Black Hills gold to pay for the impressive cross on his mother's Irish grave. However, Tom erected the cross years later when he had far more money from a different mining source. What is true in the stories told by others is that the Black Hills provided Tom with a good learning experience. At any rate, he was wealthy for the times.[20]

LIFE IN THE SILVER BOOMTOWN OF LEADVILLE

CHAPTER THREE

PROPRIETOR OF THE GRAND HOTEL

Later in 1878, Tom Walsh found Jerry Daly in the next great boomtown, Leadville, Colorado. Early prospectors in the area had found gold, leading to the short-lived Oro City and California Gulch bonanzas of the 1860s. Then they met a frustration common to their brothers working Nevada's Comstock and other western mines. A thick bluish-blackish substance kept getting in the way. Late in the 1870s the miners learned that the "damned blue stuff," or "black cement," was actually carbonate of lead, rich in silver. The now highly regarded substance gave Leadville its name, and the area had a second boom. At more than 10,000 feet above sea level, it was one of the highest mining camps in the United States (although several in Colorado were higher). Reporting in early 1879, the Colorado representative of the *Mining Record* of New York City found that "[i]t is not too much to say, that California and Nevada in their palmier days never knew such an excitement as is raging here, nor did the Black Hills. . . . Out of a comparative wilderness, a little over a year ago, has arisen a town, of now nearly ten thousand people, some very handsome buildings, three banks, several churches, and an organized fire department."[1]

Shortly after his arrival, Walsh joined Daly and another old Black Hills friend, Felix Leavick, in purchasing the Grand Hotel. Already considered by some the premier place of lodging in the growing town, the imposing two-story Grand had just undergone renovations. George Harris, its previous owner, hosted a grand opening on July 4, 1878, and then offered it for sale. The Black Hills trio offered him $14,120, which Harris readily accepted. Their new venture was so successful that they paid Harris off by December. Lack of better competition at the time meant the proprietors could offer their finest first-floor rooms at $7–$10 per night, while a guest willing to stay in the garret could get by for $3. It was a shrewd real estate move as well, in a town of skyrocketing land values. The building had additional space for business offices. A young and prominent Denver attorney, Charles S. Thomas, took one of these offices for his firm's Leadville branch. The future Colorado governor and U.S. senator began a lifelong friendship and professional relationship with Walsh. For Tom, business was good, and pursuit of silver remained a sidelight.[2]

MARRIAGE PRESENTS A RELIGIOUS DILEMMA

Tom arrived in Leadville a bachelor. He enjoyed good music, which was increasingly available in the growing metropolis. A particular singer caught his eye. It may have been at the June 1879 presentation of the top local talent before the Knights of Robert Emmet, an Irish group Tom proudly joined. Here, "Miss Reed, but recently arrived in our city, a lady whose musical culture is of the highest order[,] played her own accompaniment upon the piano." It might also have occurred when the young Catholic Irishman ventured into a Protestant church one Sunday and heard her voice in the choir. Yet another version has her staying at the Grand Hotel upon her arrival. Carrie Bell Reed and Arabella, her mother, had journeyed to Leadville to see if the boomtown might benefit from Carrie's teaching talents. Since it was also the home of many overnight millionaires, the mother and daughter probably felt life at 10,000 feet could be bearable if it meant finding Carrie the right husband. For Tom, it was love at first sight. Evalyn reports that her father's immediate reaction was "[t]hat's the girl I'm going to marry." She adds that he won the heart of one of the town's most eligible young women, who had "a figure that men would turn to stare at" but who was also "one of the most refined women I ever knew."[3]

Nine years Tom's junior, Carrie was born in 1859 in the little southwestern Wisconsin town of Darlington. She and the family passed along few tales of her childhood. The county's 1881 history lauds her father, Stephen S. Reed, as Darlington's first merchant, in partnership with J. S. Fassett and offering an unknown stock, but one that "consisted of such articles alone as were needed to supply the real wants of the settlers." Stephen Reed, a native of Vermont, married Arabella Beckwith, an early Darlington schoolteacher born in Ellsworth, Maine. Arabella was nearly eighteen years younger than her husband. By early 1859, anticipating the birth of Carrie, their first child, the Reeds purchased a stone house on Cornelia Street, not far from downtown and a few blocks east of the Pecatonica River. The seller was Fassett, Reed's business partner. Carrie's first home survived for many years, until taken down to make way for the town's new fire station in 2002.

The Reed family grew with the additions of young Stephen in 1864 and Lucy in 1868. Sometime after 1870 the family moved to Birmingham, Alabama, where the elder Stephen had a brother in the florist business. The probable reason for the move was the senior Stephen's poor health, with his financial health suffering as well. The Reed family's net worth decreased between 1860 and 1870 (from $5,000 to $3,600 per the censuses), while Darlington itself was growing. Evalyn recalls a kindly but frail grandfather with lung problems. The cold Wisconsin winters had no doubt taken their toll on the longtime merchant. Carrie also left few memories of the family's time in the post–Civil War South, although she and Tom later spent time in Birmingham.

The Reed family moved to Denver in the late 1870s. Arabella had some notable relatives in Colorado. Her brother George was a prominent Denver citizen, and her two first cousins, Elton and Edwin Beckwith, ran a very successful cattle ranch in the Wet Mountain Valley west of Pueblo. Elton parlayed his success into election as a Colorado state senator. Stephen S. Reed needed the West's dry air for his lungs, as well as any assistance his wife's relatives could provide. However, he could tolerate no altitude greater than Denver's mile-high location. He stayed in the city with the two younger children while Carrie and Arabella made the climb to Leadville.[4]

The wedding of Thomas F. Walsh and Carrie Bell Reed took place on October 7, 1879, and was considered one of Leadville's most prestigious events of the time. It was strictly a private affair, for the bride's and groom's friends were too numerous to be housed in any Leadville establishment. The newspaper notice advised "that none may have occasion to be blighted, it has been wisely concluded to issue no invitations whatsoever." Attendees were "Judge Murphy, Mr. J. Daly and Colonel Leavick, the two business partners of the groom, Mrs. Reed, the bride's mother, and Miss Marie [Maria] Walsh, a sister of the groom." The Catholic Tom and Presbyterian Carrie worked out an interesting religious compromise. The service took place at the home of Carrie's mother, with Father Henry Robinson of Leadville's Annunciation Catholic Church presiding. However, as the attending society reporter noted, the priest presented his remarks and was dressed so that one would not guess he was of the Catholic faith. The simple service was followed by an elegant reception at Tom's hotel, under the supervision of Michael J. Welch, "the steward and head waiter at the popular Grand, who is in his profession a very prince." Banquet fare included oysters (raw and stewed), brook trout, venison with currant jelly, tongue with calf's foot jelly, malaga grapes, pears, apples, cream cake, and champagne.[5]

While Maria attended her brother's wedding, the rest of the Catholic Walsh family did not. Thomas K. Walsh and Tom's brothers Michael and Patrick lived in Colorado at the time, yet none went to the wedding. Signs of religious friction within the family continued for some time. At least from this time forward, Tom showed little attachment to the Catholic Church, later even joining the Masonic Order. Evalyn tells of overhearing talk of a family scandal because she was being raised a Protestant. Her family rarely visited the homes of her Uncle Michael and Aunt Maria, who lived in Denver. For the rest of his life Tom kept a close relationship with his family in both the United States and Ireland, yet Carrie and the children seem to have been left out. Tom's father lived in Denver during the last years of his life, passing away in 1883. Little is known about the life of Thomas K. Walsh in Colorado, apart from a short reference in one family letter. Tom did not have a close relationship with his father at this time, and religion seems the likely reason for the rift. Evalyn never mentions that her Grandfather Walsh lived in Colorado. Although Tom later placed an impressive memorial on his mother's grave in Ireland, he made no such provision for his father's grave in Denver's Mount Calvary Cemetery, burial place for the city's Catholics and located only a few blocks from his future home on Vine Street.[6]

Love was probably not the only reason Walsh strayed from the traditional religion of his family and homeland. As the proprietor of a prominent hotel, real estate developer, and soon a successful mine developer, Tom was rising within the business world. He had to be paying attention to the paths of success for U.S. business leaders. Protestants dominated, with Catholics often found within the working classes. John K. Mullen, Denver's wealthy flour miller, was another Irish Catholic immigrant of this era who succeeded in Colorado. Mullen staunchly held to his religion and openly supported Catholic charities, an asset when dealing with his largely Catholic millworkers. However, Mullen also had to deal with anti-Catholic antagonism from many leading Denver citizens and Protestant wheat farmers. Catholics at every level of society suffered harassment from the Ku Klux Klan and other nativist organizations, which were becoming a vocal force in Colorado and the rest of the nation in the late nineteenth and early twentieth centuries.

Not all U.S. Irish Catholics were as bold as John Mullen, even those who became wealthy and prominent. Some hid their religious beliefs altogether. New York publisher Robert J. Cuddihy rose from poverty to make millions from his *Literary Digest.* Cuddihy secretly supported Catholic causes while keeping a religious-neutral position in his editorials. So few of his friends suspected his beliefs that when one presented him with a book of anti-Catholic propaganda, Cuddihy merely accepted the gift and thanked the man. Known Catholics, even among the richest residents, were banned from exclusive social clubs or were admitted on a quota system. When on vacation, they sought out Catholic resorts. They remained Democratic, the "people's party of Jefferson." Even so, the "lace curtain" Irish who advanced in U.S. society often found themselves at odds with their working-class counterparts. Wise leaders like Mullen learned to straddle the fence, making Protestant friends and even joining the Republican Party.

Throughout his career Tom Walsh sought lofty goals, including social acceptance at the highest levels, while incurring as little personal animosity as possible. He was usually, but not always, successful. Since Tom displayed only the normal amount of religious fervor for his time, he probably decided early on that he could afford to abandon the religion of his birth if doing so smoothed the path to success. The long hours required by mining and other ventures provided a convenient Sunday morning excuse. He did not abandon being Irish, but he avoided the more militant and religious-based Irish causes. "Irishness," to the American mind of the time, also included positive traits of ambition, courage, fighting spirit, and, most important, charm. Walsh noted this as well.[7]

SOCIAL STRATA OF A FRONTIER TOWN

Carrie helped Tom run the Grand, which soon was theirs alone. In early December 1879, Tom obtained financing from a former Memphis banker named Thomas Fisher and bought out his partners, Leavick and Daly. The latter two wanted to work their mining interests full-time, and Tom continued as their part-time mining associate. The local press regretted the loss of the "genial faces" of the departing partners but found that "[t]he new firm will be a most acceptable one to the patrons of this excellent house, Mr. Walsh having few equals and no superiors as a host, and having a large acquaintance all over the mountains." One Leadville historian praised their efforts for attracting as clientele "the sober and respectable," adding, "Although the Walshes do well enough from roomers and boarders they [did] not attain bonanza rank during this boom."[8]

Who did attain bonanza rank? In January 1880, the *Leadville Chronicle* conducted a survey of sorts to find the richest of the rich. A search for local owners of diamonds turned up 130 "happy possessors." Few could top Horace A.W. Tabor, silver millionaire and lieutenant governor of Colorado, reported as "decked with diamonds, wearing elegant and costly studs and sleeve buttons." Tom's former partner, Felix Leavick, owned "a solitary stud that sparkles as merrily as his eyes." Near the end of the article the name of Thomas F. Walsh appears in a group of twelve "other men who owned magnificent, handsome or elegant diamond studs." Carrie did not make Leadville's list of "silver ladies." In fact, the newlyweds' personal home seems a bit sparse for their position. Tom owned claims in Sowbelly Gulch, soon christened St. Kevin's by his bride. This area was located about six miles northwest of Leadville, just west of the open expanse known as Tennessee Park. Finding no suitable dwelling in town, Tom moved a boxcar into the gulch and fixed it up into a better-than-acceptable home by Leadville standards. Carrie was evidently happy there, for later in life she always smiled when telling the story of this home.[9]

Leadville had developed several distinct levels of social strata. At the top stood the legendary Tabor. His mines, such as the Little Pittsburg and Chrysolite, brought the former Vermont stonemason untold riches, and his jewels were only part of his ostentatious lifestyle. Silver money helped build his Bank of Leadville, the city's largest (although Tabor found banking a boring sideline). A man plying Walsh's old trade, carpenter Winfield Scott Stratton, lived in a lower stratum. Stratton is said to have first met "Silver King" Tabor when he built a large silver dollar for the top of Tabor's bank. Later, when Tabor's fortunes crashed along with the price of silver, the now-wealthy Stratton tried unsuccessfully to pull him out of the doldrums with the sum of $15,000. Stratton intended it as a gift, Tabor insisted it was a loan, and no one knows where the money went. Horace Tabor was never again successful in mining. Meanwhile, Tom Walsh progressed through fits and starts from somewhere in the middle of Leadville society to the top of national society. It is not known whether these three men, prominent at different times in Colorado history yet living in the silver boomtown of Leadville at the same time, were acquainted at the time. Stratton's biographer, Frank Waters, describes a meeting of the three on a Leadville street after completion of the bank's silver dollar. Waters is probably conjecturing to make the point that passersby could not have guessed they were beholding "the three greatest mining men that Colorado was to produce in all its years of fabulous strikes." However, their examples of western reversal of fortune are very typical.[10]

FULL-TIME MINING

Evalyn and others tell a story that proves that Tom's mining knowledge, gleaned from part-time activities, was beginning to pay dividends. He was prospecting along the Frying Pan River, west of Leadville and over the Continental Divide, when he found an abandoned claim and cabin. The miners had dug a pit, found only worthless rock, and departed. Walsh was also tempted to leave, but his curiosity told him to look further. Inside the cabin he found gold-bearing quartz poking up through the clay floor. Tom found the owners, paid their low asking price, and went to work. In only a short time he netted a handsome profit, estimated at close to $75,000. The claim is never given a name, although Evalyn identifies it as a large gold producer a quarter of a century after its discovery. In the public records, Walsh's name does not appear on any claim in the Frying Pan District. However, he may have taken the claim under an unrecorded document such as a lease or a bond. Perhaps his deed or location certificate became the victim of shoddy record keeping. The story must be relegated to the status of a "Tom Walsh legend," like so many told after he became famous, but it could well be true.[11]

Soon Tom felt confident enough to try full-time mining. His financier for the hotel, Fisher, had died, and Tom placed his business up for sale. In April 1880 he sold the Grand to James Street and Howard C. Chapin. Walsh's earliest mining properties were near his home, an area now known as St. Kevin's Mining District. A local landmark nearby is still called Walsh Hill. Tom's brothers Michael and Patrick worked with him, along with Arthur Lafferty, their sister Maria's new husband. A former Leadville policeman, Arthur probably found mining a more peaceful profession, judging from Evalyn's tales and the town's lawless reputation. In time, Walsh added other partners. One was S. Vinson Farnum, a Denver real estate developer who grew so close to the family that Tom and Carrie named their son after him. Another was David Wegg, a Chicago lawyer and businessman who became a lifelong friend and associate. The group's success does not place them among the legendary Leadville fortunes of Tabor, Moffat, Chaffee, and Guggenheim. Still, if one newspaper account is true, Tom's returns were impressive. The Griffin Group, his best property, provided income as high as $95,000 during some months. The Shields Mine netted a profit of $45,000 on sale. Tom's half interest in the President Mine brought combined income and sale proceeds of $50,000.[12]

At the same time, Walsh would have had more than one chance to view Leadville mine promoters operating under a cloud of suspicion. Perhaps the most infamous was the Little Pittsburg affair. Two miners named George Hook and August Rische found that rich silver vein after they were grubstaked by Horace Tabor. Eventually, Hook and Rische sold out, and in 1878 Tabor joined David Moffat and Colorado senator Jerome Chaffee in a partnership. They combined their holding with three neighboring mines, the Winnemuck, Dives, and New Discovery, to form the Little Pittsburg Consolidated Mining Company. Then they capitalized their venture at an astonishing $20 million. Such capital was not available locally, so the promoters turned to eastern investors. By this time investors on the East Coast and even in Europe had developed a fascination with mining in the West, forming many investment clubs. A good example (and arguably one of the most gullible) was New York's Bullion Club, which boasted British prime minister William E. Gladstone as an honorary member.

Moffat, Tabor, and Chaffee outfitted a special train from the East designed to unite these eager investors with their dream. The travelers enjoyed a pleasant journey to Leadville, accompanied by fine food, wine, whiskey, and cigars. The group included speculator Ulysses S. Grant Jr. (Senator Chaffee's son-in-law), newsman Charles H. Dow (later cofounder of Dow Jones & Company), and the editor of the *Engineering and Mining Journal*, Rossiter Raymond. When they arrived in Colorado, the promoters gave them a surprisingly low-key sales pitch that was nonetheless effective. After all, mine profits of $519,000 over a six-month period were hard to turn down, not to mention that the Little Pittsburg had declared a January 1879 dividend of $100,000, followed by $125,000 in February. Raymond claimed the ore in sight was worth $2 million, with another $1 million in "probable yield." Dow went even further, valuing the mine at a staggering $54 million, with enough high-grade ore to continue the $100,000 dividends for another three to four years. Only the *New York Times* reporter found anything suspicious. Noting an "unwholesome similarity to previous Colorado booms," he warned his readers that "there is nothing new in this method, and we apprehend that the result will be equally as stale."[13]

Still, investors swallowed the bait, and stock sales soon overtook mining profits as the prime moneymaker for the Little Pittsburg. In September 1879, Horace Tabor sold out to his partners for a handsome profit. He escaped most, but not all, of the ensuing notoriety. Moffat and Chaffee remained firmly in control and continued the promotion. They sold 50,000 shares of Little

Pittsburg Consolidated at $20 each, then another 3,000 shares at $25 apiece. As a further inducement, Moffat and Chaffee pressed for rapid production of the richest ore. All told, they brought in over $2 million in revenue before the stock offering was even complete. The Little Pittsburg has been referred to as one of the most successful speculative mining operations in Colorado history, simply because it was more of a financial than a mining transaction.[14]

Sadly, by early 1880 the operation no longer lived up to its inflated expectations. Back in April 1879, James Hague, a respected engineer, had inspected the Little Pittsburg Mine and its two neighbors, the Winnemuck and New Discovery. He reported that even on a speculative basis, the three mines together were worth no more than $1 million. Hague's report had convinced his buyer client that this was not the time to purchase, but it was shoved aside by others in the early optimism. Now the charge arose that the promoters had deliberately hidden the report from prospective investors. The intense, profit-seeking operations were rapidly exhausting the mine's valuable ore pockets. In an interview, Chaffee admitted that the rich Little Pittsburg vein had come to an end, or "pinched out" in mining terminology. What is undisputed is that Moffat and Chaffee got out at the right time. Most of the 85,000 shares of stock sold in February and March 1880 belonged to the two Coloradans. Stock in a mine once touted as being as "strong as the Bank of England" collapsed, falling from $30 a share in January to $5 in mid-May. The investors were resentful, disgruntled, and looking for a scapegoat. At first it was engineer Raymond, who quickly defended himself by pointing a finger at the mine's developers and their policy of rapidly removing the highest-grade ore to pay large dividends and continue inflating the stock price.[15]

One irate eastern shareholder brought suit against the two Colorado developers in the Supreme Court of New York. The suit dragged on until 1885, when a jury found Moffat and Chaffee not liable for willful misrepresentation. The two men had Moffat's Leadville manager, Oliver H. Harker, to thank. The night before the trial, Harker entertained key witnesses—including the mine's former laborers—with dinner, whiskey, and cigars. The resulting testimony disclosed no wrongdoing by the mine's two Colorado operators. In two letters following the trial, Harker sought reimbursement from Moffat for his "entertainment" expenses. Beyond this and the rather suspicious timing of the events, there is no solid evidence that Moffat and Chaffee were engaged in any fraud. Nonetheless, their venture brought considerable disrespect to Colorado mining promotions. Jerome Chaffee died in 1886. David Moffat continued for some time in his role as a major promoter of Colorado's mines and railroads and of Denver's public utilities. He amassed a large fortune. His state's citizens generally viewed

Moffat in a positive light, although he was never completely above suspicion. Later, as will be seen, he made one last great promotion that doomed his vast personal empire.[16]

Tom Walsh probably had the Little Pittsburg and many similar western mining ventures in mind when he later reiterated to a promoter that he was "not in the mining stock business." He did become a lifelong friend of David Moffat's. Walsh was rising in the mining field at a time of great prosperity and in time attracted the attention of its leaders. His rise could not be attributed only to on-the-job training, nor was it based on the hit-and-miss luck of many western prospectors. Lacking formal schooling, Tom gave himself a thorough education in mining, metallurgy, and geology. He studied the particulars of ore body deposition and the development and treatment of mining products. He read everything available, met people with knowledge of the field, and asked penetrating questions. All this would soon pay dividends.[17]

DENVER, SMELTING, AND THE SILVER CRASH

CHAPTER FOUR

PROMOTER, INVESTOR, AND FAMILY MAN

Tom Walsh had always wandered, and in his first year of marriage his new bride begged him to make one more move. Carrie would always suffer from living at altitude. As her earliest known letter to Tom shows, by June 1880 she had sought relief. Writing from Cañon City, Colorado, with its lower altitude and mineral springs, a relieved Carrie had just learned that Tom had returned safely to Leadville: "I just received your first letter. What a hard trip you must have had. You left here Monday afternoon and I did not get one dispatch from you till Wednesday afternoon. I began to think you were sick. I am so glad you feel well. I am almost like myself once more. Thank God."

Carrie then implored Tom to include her brother Steve in his mining ventures with Felix Leavick and Jerry Daly in Gunnison County. She offered Tom hope and encouragement in his hard work. She closed, "Take good care of yourself and write every day. This is the fourth letter I have written to you. I think I am very good considering my eyes, but they are most well. Don't worry about me or fret about your business. From your true Loving Wife, Carrie B. Walsh."

Tom was unsuccessful in his attempts to reform his wayward brother-in-law, Steve Reed. Evalyn later vilified her Uncle Steve as a "dark-eyed fiend, always in trouble, frequently drunk." Tom once promised to pay for Steve to take the cure, apparently to no avail. Tom paid for his brother-in-law's tombstone when he died in Chicago at age thirty-eight.[1]

Carrie does not mention in her June 1880 letter that she is six months' pregnant. Their daughter, Vena Francis, was born September 2. Her birthplace is unknown but was probably either Leadville or Denver. Sadly, the little girl lived only four months and twenty days, passing away in Denver the following January. Her simple funeral announcement in the *Rocky Mountain News* states that the service would take place "from 422 Glenarm Street corner of Seventeenth, on to-day (Sunday) at 2 o'clock." Her parents held Vena's funeral at their part-time Denver home, in a residential neighborhood that later became the heart of the growing city's business district. Vena may have been sick from the start of her short life, something not uncommon for babies born or raised at high elevation. Taking her to a place 5,000 feet lower in elevation made good sense, and Carrie hoped the move would be permanent. Evalyn, the next child, born nearly six years later in Denver, remembered her parents being terrified at the thought "that I was going to follow my little sister into oblivion."

Tom and Carrie found a supportive family in Denver. Carrie's parents, Stephen and Arabella Reed, lived nearby, as did Carrie's sister Lucy and her husband, businessman Samuel Lee. Evalyn later recalled having a close relationship with that side of the family. Tom's family soon followed. His brother Patrick formed a partnership with brother-in-law Arthur Lafferty in 1884–1885 to run a downtown Denver saloon. In the warmer months, however, Tom, Patrick, Arthur, and their other partners continued to mine near Leadville. Reports in 1882 and 1883 show Tom operating quite successfully at the Griffin Mine. Public and newspaper records of the time show he was active in the area at least until 1886.

Nonetheless, the growing metropolis of Denver was the place to be. According to the city directory, the house at 422 Glenarm became the Walsh family's permanent residence in 1882. Tom's success with the Grand Hotel property encouraged him to invest in the booming Denver real estate market. He turned to Vinson Farnum, his developer friend, for valuable advice. He acquired downtown business properties at Champa and 22nd and on Arapahoe between 16th and 17th streets. His mining investments took on broader scope as well. Tom invested in the great copper camp of Butte, Montana, and also in cattle ranches.[2]

The Walsh family began to grow. On August 2, 1886, the *Daily News* proclaimed, "The home of Mr. and Mrs. Thomas F. Walsh, 124 South Fourteenth Street, was made happy yesterday over the arrival of a fine baby girl weighing eleven pounds. Mother and child are doing quite well." Although not announced in the paper, her parents had named her Evalyn Lucile. Her first memories are of adoring and protective parents, although Carrie was ill for some time after giving birth. A nurse hired to help seemed adept at soothing Evalyn's cries until it was discovered that she did so with the aid of morphine. Grandmother Reed took over the baby's care, and the two developed a strong bond.

It was an era when every successful man, and his family and friends, wanted a son to carry on the family name. Soon, Tom got his wish. The *Denver Evening Times* of April 9, 1888, trumpeted:

> The happiest man in Denver today is Thomas F. Walsh, the popular mining man of Denver and Leadville, whose friends are numbered by the thousand all over the state. The occasion of so much unalloyed joy is the arrival of a little boy in the Walsh family this morning at half-past 8 o'clock, and as the mother is progressing finely, the causes for joy and happiness are double. Master Walsh begins life with a name which at once stamps him as a thoroughbred gentleman, being named after Mr. Vinson Farnum, who is Mr. Walsh's intimate friend and business partner. Vinson Farnum Walsh will be recognized from the start as Tom Walsh's boy, he will not lack for the sweets of life. That he may grow to manhood and ever be a pride and comfort to his fine parents will be the wish in many a heart today.

Evalyn recalls a childhood of frequent moves, with the family's only visits made to her father's mining properties in the Colorado mountains. From 1886 to 1889 the family lived at three different Denver addresses and at two others in 1892–1893. Although never mentioned by Evalyn, Carrie later told of frequent stays in the East, especially at Atlantic beaches, as well as a short stay in Birmingham, Alabama, where Tom invested in rental real estate. These departures from Denver must have taken place in the years 1884–1885 or 1890–1891, when the name Thomas F. Walsh does not appear in the city directory. As two July 1888 letters from Tom to Carrie attest, on this occasion Tom had gone east for both health and business reasons. Both letters are written on the stationery of a Massachusetts beach resort. Tom and his business party had visited Chicago on the way out, with plans to stop in St. Louis during the return trip "to see the stockholders there, and try and arrange with parties to take up our option later on." He also reported, "When I reached Chicago I weighed 156 lbs. Today I weighed 160 lbs. You can see I was somewhat reduced, and I have reason to congratulate myself for my trip on my health's account at least." He added, "I feel as though I am too selfish, to be here loafing and you working. However dear wife I shall endeavour to make up for it, if I live." Evalyn describes her parents living comfortably at the time, but her father was not well.[3]

The Walsh family lifestyle seems modest for the times, especially considering the extravagant lives led by others who succeeded in mining. The Walsh home for the last three years of their stay in Denver, 1343 Vine Street, was and remains an imposing two-and-a-half-story red brick Queen Anne–style residence in the Wyman neighborhood. At the time, 1894–1896, the area attracted the upper middle class and lay well to the east of the mining barons' mansions on Capitol Hill. The Walsh home was one of the last designed by a gifted yet tragic architect named William A. Lang (discussed later in the chapter). Considered Denver's greatest residential architect of the nineteenth century, as well as its most eclectic, Lang created more than 150 houses from 1888 to 1893, including the Pennsylvania Avenue home of the "unsinkable" Molly Brown. After years of living in mansions, Evalyn would later look back on "our little house on Vine Street." The family hired a young Scottish woman named Annie MacDonald, who remained with them for a long time. Their summer accommodations in the mountains were even simpler than those in Denver. Neither Carrie nor Tom had known riches, and they were not ready to begin a lavish lifestyle—a fact very much to their benefit.[4]

SMELTING IN THE TEN MILE DISTRICT

By the early 1890s, the focus of Tom's mining business had shifted to ore refining. He formed a partnership with his old friend David Wegg and San Francisco inventor William L. Austin. Austin had created and patented a new refining technology, and Wegg held the license to implement that technology in Colorado. The Austin process was potentially very economical, as it required little fuel to process low-grade sulphides, a type of ore prevalent in the Colorado high country. The fuel sources were only required to heat the ores to the combustion point, after which the sulphides themselves provided enough additional heat to complete the smelting process. The Austin process was first used in Colorado in 1891 at the Bi-Metallic smelter run by David Moffat and Eben Smith in Leadville. Early runs were encouraging, so Wegg and Austin teamed with Walsh to expand their operations. Walsh was to look for promising mining properties, and he soon acquired silver mining leases near the town of Kokomo in the Ten Mile District. Located northeast of Leadville over Fremont Pass, the district took its name from the lofty section of the Continental Divide to its southeast. It would go down in history as a land of some overnight successes but even more broken dreams, as Tom and his partners were about to discover.

Tom also formed a friendship with another businessman with whom he shared an office in Denver's Boston Building. Arthur Redman Wilfley, described by his biographer as "blessed with an innovative spirit," was a successful mining entrepreneur who would enjoy a long and rewarding business career. His discussions with Walsh soon disclosed that each man's goal could be achieved if the two worked together. Wilfley's White Quail Mine in the Elk Mountain section of the Ten Mile District held low-grade iron and lead sulphides with some silver content. However, he needed a smelter nearby, for it would be uneconomical to transport his ores very far for processing. He had learned of the Austin process and was happy to hear that Walsh was its representative. Their meetings soon led to the formation of the Summit Mining and Smelting Company. Wilfley and his partner Ethan Byron contributed the White Quail Mine, and Walsh's Union company contributed its leases and the Austin process. Tom's job was to construct a pyritic smelter at Kokomo. He completed the job in early December 1892, and the initial test runs looked promising. Walsh added an innovative feature to his new smelter, an electric dynamo to light the plant for around-the-clock operations.[5]

The organizers of the Summit company named Wilfley president and Walsh vice president. S. Vinson Farnum joined his old friend to become a director, as did Tom's Denver brother-in-law, Samuel W. Lee. However, family strife ensued when Tom hired his other brother-in-law, Arthur Lafferty. The former policeman and miner did have smelter experience in Leadville, but he soon ran afoul of Lee, his supervisor, who dismissed him. Tom received a stern letter from his sister Maria, complaining of the treatment her husband had received and requesting that Tom find him a new job. Whether he complied is not known, but Tom hated to be part of such animosity. In September 1892 he arranged, with Farnum's assistance, to be the anonymous guarantor of a Denver bank's loan to Lafferty.[6]

The Kokomo smelter soon suffered from more than a family feud. The developers had been too hasty in applying the Austin process in a new setting. In July 1892, Farnum warned Walsh that Leadville newspapers were declaring the process a failure at the Bi-Metallic smelter. Soon thereafter, Austin himself addressed the problem. Responding to Walsh's question about problems with ores containing zinc, the inventor first praised the mechanical ingenuity displayed by the developers of both smelters. However, both had disregarded his warnings that his system would not necessarily work for all pyritic ores. Now radical alterations were needed to handle the ores from Wilfley's property. Austin's advice could not be implemented, for there were no profits to support the necessary work. By late December the new smelter was losing money, and the main reason was a drop in silver prices. The trend continued into 1893.[7]

THE SILVER CRASH BRINGS ECONOMIC DEVASTATION

Tom Walsh, his partners, and many other miners and investors did not foresee that the bottom was about to drop out of silver. Since 1881, Colorado had led the nation in production of the metal. Silver had many uses, but the most important were for coinage and as a reserve backing paper money. Therefore, Colorado needed a favorable attitude in Washington to keep up the demand for its product. There were many opponents, chiefly in the East. With passage of the Bland-Allison Act of 1878, Congress had at least been willing to compromise on the issue. This act, passed over President Rutherford B. Hayes's veto, provided for coinage of $2 million to $4 million worth of silver each month, the exact amount to be set by the secretary of the treasury. Mint price of the silver would equal current market price. Coloradans were generally pleased with the legislation, although it fell short of their demand for unlimited free coinage. However, secretaries of the treasury tended to favor price deflation and to coin only the minimum amount required. Pressure from Colorado, Nevada, and other silver states led to the passage of the Sherman Silver Purchase Act in 1890. The law required Treasury to purchase 4.5 million ounces of silver per month. Prices rose to a dollar per ounce in late 1890, but then a decline set in. The act had fallen far short of the westerners' goal.

The year 1893 was a gloomy time of international economic crisis, known in the rest of the United States as the Panic of '93. In Colorado it was simply called the year of the Silver Crash. The price of the metal dropped to eighty-three cents an ounce in June, and then India announced it would no longer coin silver. Within four days the price had plummeted to sixty-two cents an ounce. When Congress repealed the Sherman Act in August, Colorado's economy already lay in ruins. In July twelve Denver banks had closed, while around the state, mines and smelters stopped running and real estate values dropped through the floor. A September 1 report of the Colorado Bureau of Labor Statistics found 377 business failures, 435 closed mines (nearly half of which had been producing a year before), and 45,000 persons out of work.[8]

The toll on the state's residents, rich and poor, was devastating. Leadville's Silver King, Horace Tabor, had become one of Denver's richest citizens. With his second wife, Baby Doe, he owned many prized personal possessions, as well as Denver's Tabor Block and Tabor Grand Opera House. However, too much of his fortune lay in silver properties and other unwise investments that soon dropped in value. Tabor's material wealth passed to creditors' sales or was used up supporting his family. The Tabors soon were living a very simple existence, while Horace tried many schemes to recoup his former glory. Nothing worked, and debts piled up. Finally, concerned Denver friends found Tabor a job as the city's postmaster. The relief was short-lived, for he died of peritonitis in April 1899, just over one year after taking the job. Baby Doe lived a sad and poverty-stricken life for many more years.

Other Colorado citizens and their businesses felt the effect of the crash, even if they were not involved in silver mining. One such casualty was William Lang, the architect who designed the Walsh house on Vine Street. The halt in new home construction ruined Lang's practice. By 1895 he was in dire financial straits and was also suffering from alcoholism and mental illness. He fled the state and surfaced two years later in Illinois, where he was arrested for drunken and disorderly behavior. Soon thereafter, a passing train killed Lang as he walked along its tracks. Even Walsh's first Colorado employer, William A.H. Loveland, did not escape financial problems. Loveland's fortune was seemingly safe and well diversified, for although he invested in mines, his money also went into railroads, banks, land, and newspapers. Nonetheless, he died poor in 1894. He left impressive holdings, including a coal mining company and about half the land that would become the city of Lakewood, Colorado. In the year following the Silver Crash, however, the properties were of little value.[9]

Tom Walsh was more fortunate, and he had Arthur Redman Wilfley to thank. The astute Wilfley persuaded his partners that a new gold mining district west of Colorado Springs looked promising. The Summit company bought three claims named the Deer Horn, Deer Horn No. 2, and Pride of the Rockies. As the rest of the state neared the crash, the Summit group earned $45,000 from these claims in the first half of 1893. The local camps had been called Hayden Placer and Fremont, but now they went by the name Cripple Creek. For the next few years, the district would be a rare shining light in the darkness of Colorado mining (although labor problems soon followed). The area's first millionaire, Winfield Scott Stratton, would never again need to help build a bank for someone else.

The Summit Mining and Smelting Company eventually sold its Cripple Creek holdings for another $45,000 profit. Tom's share in the venture was only $^3/_{32}$, but nonetheless he had some money in his pocket at a time when many others in Colorado did not. By this time he had soured on business in eastern Colorado. After some negotiations, Tom sold his interest in what was left of the Kokomo smelter venture to Wilfley and Byron. He was not done with Cripple Creek, although his earnings from the district never approached those of Stratton and the twenty-seven other millionaires it helped create. Walsh continued to lease and operate two Cripple Creek mines, the Deer Horn and Summit, both of which were now owned by Stratton. Here Tom noticed a certain type of rock that he called "pink spar." An unusual mineral for the area, it bore gold, yet it brought him little wealth from these claims. It did provide one more bit of geological knowledge, which Tom decided to take elsewhere. He was still affiliated with Wegg and Austin, and they had an idea for a smelter much farther west, in the San Juan Mountains. Tom had abandoned the area more than twenty years before. Perhaps it deserved a second look.[10]

A BONANZA IN THE SNOWY SAN JUANS

CHAPTER FIVE

REMOVING THE UTE INDIANS

Tom Walsh once again prospected and developed business opportunities after the region's Native Americans had been moved out of the way. This time he could do so in relative safety, for the Ute tribe, longtime residents of the San Juan region, had been banished years before. Like others, he benefited from what they knew and passed on to the newcomers. From their hundreds of years in the mountains, the Utes knew the area's natural properties well. One of the things they found was of little use to them: a soft, shining metal found in the rocks and sometimes in the hot springs. It had no functional value, and the Utes looked elsewhere when they wanted ornaments. If this useless material was all the whites wanted, the Utes would let them have it. Eighteenth-century Spaniards such as Don Juan Maria de Rivera were the first whites to locate San Juan gold, followed by the Charles Baker expedition in 1860–1861. Soon, however, too many whites wanted too much gold. Their leaders sought treaties with the Utes. While the tribe was sometimes warlike, most Utes wanted only peace. An 1863 agreement gave the San Luis Valley to the whites. Another treaty in 1868 pushed the line farther back while still leaving the Utes one-third of Colorado Territory.

About this time two leaders emerged, one a Ute chief, the other a young immigrant from Russia. Ouray (the "arrow") had a Ute mother and an Apache father. By tradition he joined his mother's people and became one of their chiefs. Ouray spoke Ute and Apache, fluent Spanish, and understandable English. Nearly all whites who met him were impressed. Some mistakenly thought he led all the Utes. In fact, he led only his band, known as the Tabeguache, while receiving respect from others of the tribe. Ouray was a peace chief, and he formed a friendship with Otto Mears, a skillful businessman and interpreter. Mears had arrived penniless from his native Russia at age twelve, only to find that his sponsoring relative in the United States was nowhere to be found. He overcame the deficit and while still a young man had earned the title "Pathfinder of the San Juans" for his road building, which opened up the area. He met Ouray as his path encroached on Ute land. Mears was extremely tactful and quickly learned the Ute tongue, so arrangements to continue his work were easily made.

Grateful that they had finally met a white person they could trust, Ouray and the Utes made Otto Mears their spokesman. The Del Norte gold rush, whose numbers included Tom Walsh, threatened to consume more of their land. Ouray and Mears met the whites at the Brunot Treaty negotiations in 1873. Otto spent long hours explaining the needs of his Indian clients. In the end, the whites received the entire San Juan mining region, with the Utes settling for annual gifts of food, clothing, and supplies for their shrunken reservation. Ouray received a house and an annual salary of $1,000. Mears was perhaps the ultimate winner. The whites paid him $2 per head for each Ute who signed the treaty. Later he was accused of various financial schemes while acting as chief transporter of supplies to the tribe. He probably wished them no ill will; Otto Mears simply knew what it took to succeed in his world of business. He learned to make his roads no steeper than railroad grade, so a fortune awaited with the arrival of the iron rail. The Utes may have suspected Mears's motives all along. Their continuing friendship with him proves one point: Otto Mears was still the white man they could trust the most.[1]

By 1881 the Utes had been forced out of the San Juan region altogether. While Ouray's Tabeguache band lived in peace with the whites, troubles began farther north with the White River band. The U.S. government assigned an agent named Nathan Meeker to their reservation in 1878. An agrarian utopian, Meeker dreamed of turning the nomadic Indians into farmers. He found few followers, so the next year Meeker threatened to plow up the Utes' racetrack to make his point. Enraged by this and by the approach of white troops in support of the agent, the Indians killed Meeker and his male employees and kidnapped the three white women at the agency. A fight with the advancing troopers resulted in a bloody standoff. Tom Walsh, getting his start in Leadville at the time, probably heard some of the exaggerated reports that the Utes were about to overrun the entire mining district. Even though Leadville was more than 100 mountainous miles from the site of the Meeker Massacre, its newspapers sounded the same cry heard throughout the region. An October 1879 issue of the *Leadville Chronicle* warned, "[T]he savages are sweeping through the outlying settlements of the State, murdering miners and ranchmen. . . . Some man is needed who will out Chivington [John] Chivington—some man who will duplicate Sand Creek. . . . Murder is the Indian game. Give them enough of it."[2]

In fact, Ute warfare did not spread. Ouray and his wife, Chipeta, were among those who convinced the White River Utes to give up their hostages and surrender. The whites now had the perfect pretext to convince any doubters that "the Utes must go!" It was too late for Ouray's negotiating skills to make any difference, and he was also very ill. The peace chief died on August 20, 1880, soon after returning from the Washington meeting that sealed his tribe's fate. While his band had not taken part in hostile action, its members were still banished to a Utah reservation along with their White River brethren. Chipeta went with them. Only the Ute Mountain and Southern Ute bands remained in Colorado, on reservations well south of the San Juans. The mountains were now free for all the mineral exploitation whites might want to undertake.[3]

THE TOWN OF OURAY AND THE IMOGENE BASIN

One of the numerous mining towns that sprang up in the San Juan country in 1876 took the name of the great Ute leader, even though its newspapers and public were as vocal in calling for the tribe's removal as those anywhere in the region. For natural beauty, Ouray's founders could not have picked a better spot. Later called the Switzerland of America, the town site lay amid high mountains, with waterfalls cascading down nearby canyon walls. Hot springs valued by the Utes awaited the settlers. For accessibility, however, Ouray was one of Colorado's worst locations. The sheer walls of the Uncompahgre Canyon led south to Red Mountain Pass. These barriers challenged even the resourceful Otto Mears. He succeeded in building a toll road that literally hung from the side of the canyon but he failed in his struggle to convert the route into a railroad. To the north, a less daunting canyon still presented a barrier to the construction of the railroad, which finally arrived in 1886. To the southwest, the shortest route to another boomtown, Telluride, passed over the rugged, 13,000-foot summit of Imogene Pass. Arriving in 1895, nine-year-old Evalyn Walsh remembered, "Ouray was wonderful. A child first glimpsing that valley from the mountain trail scratched in the rocks high above it could look down upon a toy town the few streets of which were cross-hatched as if a giant had chalked on the basin's floor the pattern for a couple of games of tick-tacktoe."[4]

Ouray's fortunes rose and fell with its minerals. To the south, the Red Mountain district produced a silver bonanza, then joined the rest of the state in a major decline after 1893. The high Imogene Basin, just below the pass of the same name, saw much activity and an equally large level of frustration. Its early explorers were certain its potential lay in silver, not gold. The area's discoverer, Andy Richardson, named both basin and pass, honoring his wife. However, an Englishman named William Weston brought the greatest early attention to the basin. Weston had just arrived to explore the West when the Kansas Pacific Railroad paid him to return to London and promote the line to traveling Europeans. Then a friend in Del Norte, Colorado, told Weston about rich silver strikes in the San Juans, especially in an area called the Mount Sneffels Mining District. Weston dropped the railroad promotion and enrolled in the Royal School of Mines for a six-month assaying course.

William Weston reached Del Norte in September 1877, put all his supplies on a burro, and crossed Stony Pass and Commodore Gulch to arrive at the Imogene Basin. It was part of the Mount Sneffels district, where riches should have awaited him. He formed a partnership with another Englishman, an experienced miner named George Barber. They built a log cabin and began staking claims. The seven they staked that fall were named the Gertrude, Una, Crusader, Conqueror, Monument, Emily, and Norma. Only two were destined for success, the Gertrude and Una, although not for the Englishmen. They located both claims at a lofty altitude, just under 12,000 feet, meaning their holdings would be covered by snow much of the year. Weston honored his family in England with the claim names. "Gertrude" was his sister-in-law, Mrs. A. Johnstone Campbell of London; "Una" was his niece, Una Weston of Brighton. Weston knew how to assay his own ores using an outfit he had brought with him. For the Una and Gertrude claims, gold values ran in the range of $12 to $20 per ton. At the time it cost $35 per ton to pack the ore and ship it to the Greene smelter in Silverton, then another $45 per ton to treat the ore, so something in the range of $100 per ton in value was necessary to make a clear profit.

By 1879 Weston and Barber had exhausted their limited resources, with no tangible results. The partners then hired mining engineer brothers Hubbard and Caleb Reed to develop their claims. The Reeds were to drive a 50-foot adit along the line separating the Gertrude and Una (see Appendix A for the definition of "adit" and how it differs from the more commonly used term "tunnel"). This adit would supposedly intersect the vein 150 feet below its surface outcrop. The adit could be used by the owners of either claim, and as compensation for their time and effort, the Reeds could choose one of the two claims to keep. They chose the Una.[5]

Still, they found only low-grade ores. The Reeds drove farther into their new claim, the Una, but found nothing of commercial value. However, as fate would have it, the Reeds' original adit between the claims had crossed a high-grade vein at a dead spot, or "pinch," where no ore in paying quantities was exposed. A mere directional change of ten feet could have made them all very wealthy, for the vein's great gold deposits lay in scattered pockets called "shoots," not in a continuous line.

The following year an Illinois mining engineer named W. C. Coman examined the area for Orrin Skinner, a New York lawyer. Coman liked what he saw and recommended a purchase. In February 1880, Weston and Barber sold the Gertrude claim to Skinner for $50,000. Skinner then organized the Allied Mines Company to develop the property. His backers among the shareholders and directors included many prominent easterners. Perhaps foremost among them was Skinner's father-in-law, Orville Hickman Browning, of Quincy, Illinois. A close friend of Abraham Lincoln, Browning, a lawyer, had served as a U.S. senator and secretary of the interior. Sadly, he placed great reliance on his son-in-law, loaning him large sums of money for the development of Allied Mines. However, Skinner's scheming and incompetence soon wrecked the company, leaving Browning (who died shortly thereafter) and other family members penniless. Weston, who stayed on as mine manager, was highly critical of Skinner's insistence on building a mill much too large for the size of the operation. Skinner did drive a new adit thirty-eight feet into the Gertrude claim but then neglected to take any samples of the exposed ore. Soon Allied Mines declared bankruptcy, and creditors seized all of its equipment.

Next in line was a Maine corporation, the Cosmopolitan Mining Company, which achieved little more success than its predecessor. In 1884 the company ordered its workers to complete the final twelve feet of the Gertrude adit, left unfinished by Allied. The chief reason was to perform enough labor to qualify for a mineral patent of the claim. The work was completed, but once again no sampling was done, this time because a great snowstorm drove the laborers off. Cosmopolitan ended up in receivership, and the Gertrude was written off as unprofitable. Had that final twelve feet been sampled, the story would have been vastly different, for rich ore was exposed in the adit. William Weston, who had left Allied when he could no longer pay his men, still believed in the Gertrude and the Una. He felt only his lack of personal funds prevented great success. It was not to be, for in the words of Denver columnist Frances Melrose, "Gertrude was not a fickle lady, she just had one suitor in mind." At the time, that suitor was in Denver.[6]

One day in 1879, Ouray received a claim to fame that did not come out of the earth. David Frakes Day had earned a Civil War Medal of Honor for heroism at Vicksburg when he was only sixteen. The experience gave him supreme self-confidence. Now the flamboyant Day arrived in Ouray and set up the presses of the *Solid Muldoon*. He was somewhat evasive as to the source of the name, finally declaring that "muldoon" was the Zulu word for virgin. However, Day was not evasive in his opinions on all other matters. Rival towns suffered his barbs, as did Republicans, the town's other newspaper, mine owners, and any public official who did not fully support his positions. His small paper received state, national, and ultimately world attention. Queen Victoria is said to have been an avid *Solid Muldoon* reader.

Vintage reporting by Day included the misinformation that "Telluride has seven lawyers and two dance halls, 0 churches and 000 school houses. Mercy what a wicked village."[7] Day is said to have been named in forty-seven libel suits and to have won them all (or at least to have never paid his opponents a penny). He had a wide reputation for honesty, often of the brutal variety. He even challenged Judge Theron Stevens to a duel, after the latter objected to being called "a liar, a scoundrel, a hypocrite and a dirty dog." The two men later settled their differences.[8]

However interesting the other topics of the time, mining fraud reigned supreme as Day's favorite subject. He attacked one mining company after another, especially if he suspected the venture was merely a scheme to make money through the sale of stock. He liked to brag that capitalists looked first to his paper before investing. Typical was his coverage of the Osprey Consolidated Mill and Mining Company. Bold print in the November 21, 1879, edition of the *Muldoon* warned that the company "is an infamous and damnable fraud, and on behalf of the countless thousands of good and meritorious mines in Ouray Co., that the press of Colorado denounce it as such and credit THE SOLID MULDOON . . . [which], while possessing a name that is rather suggestive, is nevertheless the tiger that scoops the San Juan 'wild cat.' Beware of the OSPREY!" As grounds for this accusation, Day quoted from an ad in the *New York Mining Record* purporting that Osprey stock "[i]s full paid and non-assessable—fine fix to be in. The company has in the treasury 40,000 shares of stock which will be sold at $1 per share 'when the price will be advanced'—heap much taffy." Day knew for a fact that the Osprey property in Ouray County was not worth $1,000 and that "Mr. Bouton, a mining expert and strictly honorable gentleman, says that the highest assay he obtained from the osprey was 3½ ounces—pass 'em around."

The following week's paper displayed an Osprey sonnet (in "middling long meter") from Day's pen. By December 5 he could report that the capital stock of

> this giant fraud is placed at $1,250,000. This company claim [sic] to have six full grown mines near the town of Ouray, and upon examining their diagram, we find the six namely: Rachel, Wakarusa, Osprey, Haslam, White House and the Michigan lode. . . . We will state, for the benefit of those who have to view the purchase of Osprey stock, that one thousand dollars would be an exorbitant price for the entire mess. They are not mines, but merely prospect holes, and miserably poor ones at best.

The day after Christmas, Day found at least three favorite targets in one, as he lampooned rival Ouray editor Henry Ripley: "Elder Henri Riplie crawled out of bed Christmas morn to take a peep at his sock. Santa Claus had been around. There was [sic] two shares of Osprey, a beautiful editorial from the pen of Judge Cutler, four onions and a box of concentrated lie, which will answer for a trade-mark."

The Osprey was not to be Ouray's Little Pittsburg. In only a few months' time, it passed out of existence. Day was positive that his persistent attacks were the reason. As he informed the *Muldoon*'s March 26, 1880, readers, "The Osprey Mill and Mining fraud we learn has turned its toes to the daisies. Thanks to the MULDOON's tow-line for ridding Ouray county of one base and infamous fraud."

The Democratic Day gave unequivocal support to the common man who worked the mines. Even as silver prices fell, he announced that "the *Muldoon* will oppose any and all attempts to reduce the wages of miners. A good miner earns every dollar he receives in this country." He contrasted their vital role with that of others for whom he found no real demand: "preachers, lawyers, book agents, tramps or ornamental nuisances."[9]

The era of the *Solid Muldoon* ended in 1892, brought on by Day's earlier misjudgment of how far the Denver and Rio Grande Railroad could reach.

Guessing it could never navigate the canyon to the north of Ouray, Day invested in the nonexistent town of Ramona (later Chipeta), north of the canyon. He was not alone, for other investors included Otto Mears, Ouray's 1883 mayor John Jardine, and at least one prominent banker. However, mine owners and other prominent citizens rose in solid opposition. Some withdrew advertising from the *Solid Muldoon*, while others exhorted the railroad to reach their town. Rio Grande president David Moffat bowed to the pressure, then astonished Day and his supporters by switching to the opposite side of the canyon and pushing the tracks straight into downtown Ouray in 1886. The townspeople forgave Day for some of his other shortcomings but always felt he would remain loyal to them. His local popularity plummeted, and in 1892 he packed his presses and moved to Durango. His *Durango Democrat* allowed Day's rancorous voice to be heard in southwestern Colorado until 1914. However, he never achieved the fame and notoriety of his stay in Ouray. Would-be investors in Ouray area mines, not to mention the miners themselves, had lost a champion. Some would find a new one in Tom Walsh.[10]

A TROUBLED START FOR WALSH IN OURAY

Tom Walsh missed not only the area's Native Americans but also Otto Mears (who left in 1896 to build railroads in the East) and the Ouray tenure of David Day. Still, he felt the effect of both men. But for Mears's ingenuity and tenacity, Tom would have lacked a way to carry out the ores from the bonanza he would one day find. Day left a legacy of miners who were aware that they were entitled to at least some rights as human beings. Walsh wholeheartedly agreed. However, he would later encounter Day in a totally different setting, and not to his pleasure.

Starting in the early 1890s, Tom first explored the San Juan area, then chose Ouray for his base of operations, as it was situated in the midst of his new interests. He was manager and also part-owner of another pyritic smelter employing the Austin process, for David Wegg owned the patent rights to the process for southern Colorado. Walsh took over and refurbished the old Martha Rose smelter in Silverton, south of Ouray over the formidable Red Mountain Pass, completing the work in July 1894. Tom also acquired mining interests in Rico, another San Juan boomtown. The best of these was the Black Hawk Mine, a consistent producer that helped pay for his other operations and which later sources consider a major building block for the bright future he would soon achieve. Tom looked into the potential of the Ouray area and Telluride as well. He found promising results in the Ben Butler and San Bernardo mines.

However, for Tom and his investors, overall profits were inconsistent, and the glory days of the 1880s could not be repeated.[11]

The Walsh family seemed in dire straits compared with its well-to-do status during the 1880s. Tom's once valuable Denver real estate did not sell and was heavily mortgaged. His Birmingham, Alabama, investments faltered. Yet in the end, he would recoup something from these ventures. Evalyn paints a picture of a father under great stress. Any childish transgression could bring out his Irish temper at full capacity. She recalls a father with "piercing blue eyes that could be as gentle as forget-me-nots or cold as a blizzard wind." The faithful Annie MacDonald was kept on as a servant, but in most other respects the Walsh household appears Spartan. Their first home in Ouray was the Geneva Hotel, remodeled and refitted as a dwelling (probably using Tom's own carpentry skills) for the summer of 1895. The family sold the house on Vine Street in Denver in 1896 and settled into year-round life in the small town. Their first permanent home was a modest two-story residence. Evalyn's description of her childhood at the time seems typical of the way any child would look for excitement (often in the form of pranks) in a small town that provided few luxuries for its residents. Her father worked hard and was often absent for days.[12]

A letter dated August 2, 1895, to business partner Wegg is a study in desperation and is quoted by Evalyn in her book. The Chicago partner had likely questioned why greater (or any) profits could not be realized from his investments. In a seven-page response, Walsh agonizes in phrases such as "I have no money, not even enough to pay my life insurance. I have not spent any on myself nor family beyond our support. . . . I gathered you would like to get completely out of the mining interests. . . . Now Dave, don't think I have my Irish up or that I have any grievance against you. . . . P.S. Of course if there is any way for me to keep on and hold on to our lease I will do it. In any event, I will do nothing until I hear from you first."

Tom did hear from David Wegg in the form of a check for $1,000 and other statements of support. By the end of August, Tom's communication to Wegg is more optimistic, noting that Red Mountain still held great prospects for their venture. In a letter dated March 25, 1896, however, despair has returned. Commenting on the final demise of the Kokomo smelter (and perhaps feeling underappreciated), Walsh laments, "Without stating it in a complaining mood I have given a good deal of my time to the Austin process. Within myself I feel even though no one else agrees with me that I recovered victory from defeat at Silverton, made what was a lost investment worth something. Kokomo was ruined by the drop in silver. I am very poor, I have nothing to look forward to, and it is but natural that I should desire to have some plan mapped out by which

I should get a definite sum that once more would place my family in an humble manner above want."

Tom probably did not receive that sum, at least not from Wegg. Their business together continued for at least one more year, although much of it involved closing up affairs in southwestern Colorado. The letter of May 29, 1897, states, "[Y]ou and I have had a final adjustment and separation in all mines in which we were interested together, as well as all other interests including the Silverton smelter." However, most of the letters from Walsh to Wegg also convey warm personal and family messages. Their friendship survived long after their business dealings ended.[13]

As the Walsh family settled and made Ouray acquaintances, the John Thompson family stands out most in Evalyn's memory. The two families had known each other in Denver, where Walsh allowed Thompson to use a desk in his office free of charge. Faith Thompson became one of Evalyn's best friends, as did her mother, Ella, with Carrie. John, the father, held himself out as a mining expert, although as recently as 1888 he had worked in a Michigan post office. Prior to meeting Walsh, his only mining venture had been a failure. He quickly sought to curry Tom's favor. Walsh suspected that John Thompson knew more about mining stock than about the mines themselves. Nonetheless, he accepted the gesture of friendship, with the possibility of developing a mutual and profitable business. Later, under far different circumstances, he stated that he had only accommodated Thompson because their wives were such close friends.

The two men took frequent trips together into the mountains for four or five days, investigating mining property. No lasting commercial mining developments resulted from the trips. In 1894 Walsh, Thompson, and others leased various claims, including the Ben Butler, in the Eureka Mining District of San Juan County. Walsh knew something about the district, for nearly ten years earlier he had examined a nearby claim with David Wegg and Vinson Farnum. Once, in June 1895, Walsh helped Thompson locate mining claims for the benefit of mutual friends. Tom kept no interest in the claims, later assigning them to Thompson and his company. The two were briefly partners in the Last Quarter Mine near Cripple Creek, their only joint venture, but Walsh left Thompson to run the mine. Beyond this, Tom later strongly asserted, the two men had no business dealings whatsoever. An associate recalled Walsh's assessment of Thompson as good socially but otherwise tricky and unreliable. Yet John Thompson must have been impressed with Walsh's knowledge and his willingness to share (perhaps incorrectly seen as gullibility). If Thompson could not find quick riches in a joint mining venture, maybe there was another way to tap Walsh's expertise.[14]

DAUGHTER, I'VE STRUCK IT RICH

Tom's Silverton smelter needed low-grade gold ore for flux in processing. He thought the Imogene Basin might be a good source, and so in early 1896 he began to explore the area. By this time it held many abandoned mines and prospect pits dating back to the earliest days of exploration by Weston and Barber. Tom soon became friends with the area's discoverer, Andy Richardson. Evalyn remembered Andy as a frequent guest at the house, an old prospector who wore a coat turning green at the seams. He had thick calluses on his hands and great tufts of hair growing out of each ear. He fell in love with Annie MacDonald, never mind that he had a wife, Imogene. Andy had worked the basin for years without major success, and now the low price of silver had severely depressed its values. He still remained loyal to the beautiful place he had named for his wife, and he greatly respected Walsh because he too was interested in the area. Andy did not believe the Imogene held any gold values, but Tom had strong reason to disagree. He recognized what he thought to be the same pink spar in a pyrite porphyry that he knew was an indicator of gold in the Deer Horn and Summit mines near Cripple Creek. Mining engineer T. A. Rickard later wrote that he thought Walsh had actually confused fluorite at Cripple Creek for either rhodonite or rhodochrosite in the Imogene Basin.[15]

However, as it turned out, Tom could easily dismiss that error. He put in long hours and was able to buy much of the basin from owners happy to part with their claims. He purchased several others, including the Gertrude, at tax or sheriff's sales as a result of defaults by prior owners. In July 1896, Walsh and Richardson took a memorable trip to look at Tom's newly purchased Hidden Treasure Mine, which Andy strongly felt could live up to its name. The two men rode as far as they could and climbed the rest of the way on foot. The steep trail ran high up the side of the mountain. About three-fourths of the way up, they found a slide of the misidentified pink spar, which immediately attracted Tom's attention. Tom took samples from the slide and, over Andy's usual protest that there was no gold in the basin, had them assayed. They contained gold valued at two dollars to the ton, confirming his suspicion. Tom owned one claim located at about the same altitude and 300 feet from where he sampled the slide. He had never seen the inner workings of this claim because a snowfield that never melted covered the mouth of the claim's adit. However, he suspected that the claim's vein passed through or near the slide and that it also carried gold values. The claim was the Gertrude.

Walsh knew he was on to something, but he abruptly came down with another bout of the mining-related lung ailment that had plagued him for years.

His doctor recommended a visit to a resort with mineral springs, and Tom left for Excelsior Springs, Missouri, near Kansas City. Before leaving, he asked Richardson to clear an opening in the Gertrude's snowfield and take mineral samples. His new project was so crucial to Tom that he violated the doctor's orders, returning to Ouray after only two weeks while still suffering from the illness. The next morning a feverish Walsh mounted his horse and started off for the cabin he had built in the Imogene Basin. Richardson waited there with two or three sacks of samples, feeling they were the best the Gertrude had to offer. Tom was ready to accept the results, but then he remembered how long Richardson had been operating in the basin without finding gold.

Still sick and weak, Tom made the reluctant Richardson help him up on his horse, and the two men rode as close to the Gertrude adit as possible. A strenuous hike brought them to its mouth. The rocks, now freed from their snow cover, did not surprise Tom. The claim's dump held the showy galena, sphalerite, and chalcopyrite (lead, zinc, and copper minerals) he had just seen in Richardson's samples. Inside the adit he found a vein with an eighteen-inch-wide zone of these same minerals. The vein, however, had more than one ore zone. Between the base metal zone and the hanging wall lay about three feet of milky quartz. By Tom's later recollection, "[I]t had none of the adjoining mineral in it and looked so barren that the average miner would consider it no good; but as I examined it closely I saw little specks and thread-like circles of glistening black mineral all through it which experience told me was gold in the tellurium form." Tom suddenly forgot he was sick. Richardson begged him to slow down. He also kept pointing to the ore Tom knew to be low grade, feeling his companion was looking for the pay streak in the wrong place. Tom replied, "Never mind, Andy; I always assay everything in a vein." He took the required samples and set off for Ouray and the assay office.[16]

For Walsh, secrecy and disguise were now the order of the day. Andy Richardson could be trusted, yet Tom did not tell his friend the truth about the unimpressive milky quartz until later. He did have to include Ouray assayer Harry Strout in his small circle of knowledge, but by one account Tom had a clever method of distracting the man. Strout found that Richardson's samples from the galena zinc streak returned $8 a ton in gold, while Walsh's samples from the common-looking rock ran as high as $3,000 a ton. To the man's astonishment at the richness of the ore and the probability that it had been found nearby, Tom merely replied, "[C]onfound those children, they've gone and mixed up a lot of Cripple Creek specimens with some recently obtained in the district and this is the result." He also took some samples to Leadville for assay, far away from the eyes and ears of Ouray.

Evalyn tells us she was the only other person her father trusted with the information. He was still not feeling well, and the family needed to know his story. Carrie was away tending to her sick mother, and eight-year-old Vinson might have trouble keeping the secret. Tom called his ten-year-old daughter into a room and closed the door. He reminded her of a trip the two had taken to the mountains and the promise of riches he thought they held. His latest trip had proven him correct. He showed her the unimpressive milky quartz and wet it with his tongue to distinguish its tiny threads and circles of gold. When she was ready to jump for joy, he reminded her that they were sharing a very important secret. "Daughter," he whispered, "I've struck it rich."[17]

THE FABULOUS CAMP BIRD MINE

CHAPTER SIX

A MINE NAMED FOR A GRAY JAY

Tom Walsh had found the Gertrude's long-held secret. In reality, what he had found had evolved over an eternity (see Appendix B for a description of Camp Bird Mine geology). The central feature of the area is a major geologic structure created by volcanic activity during the mid-Tertiary period, 28 to 32 million years ago. Massive caldera-forming volcanic eruptions poured out huge volumes of pyroclastic material in what are now called the San Juan Mountains. One of these eruptions formed the Silverton caldera as a collapse feature during an extremely violent episode. During this collapse, several large transverse faults broke out from the caldera in distinctive curving patterns. Mineral-laden hot water freely circulated through the faults, depositing lead, zinc, and copper minerals. In the fault now known as the Camp Bird vein, those waters deposited gold and lots of it. Gold was not deposited continuously along the vein but was concentrated at or near junctions with cross-veins, in what are called ore shoots.

The gold ore of the Camp Bird vein was concentrated in four main shoots, named the Discovery, Bluebird, Gertrude, and Hematite. A few smaller shoots were also found along the vein. The highest-grade gold deposits usually consisted of small, irregularly shaped grains dispersed throughout a quartz matrix. The Camp Bird is a gold vein in what is largely silver country. Distinct gold-bearing hydrothermal solutions filled the Camp Bird vein in a separate mineralizing event. Gold is so valuable that it is sought even though it occurs in mere ounces within a ton of rock. These bonanza ores mined by Walsh averaged 1.64 ounces of gold per ton, with some ore running as high as 200 ounces per ton (giving that richest ore an incredible value of $4,131.60 per ton using the average 1900 price of $20.658 per troy ounce). Geologist Tom Rosemeyer, writing in 1990, described the Camp Bird ore as gold occurring in its native state, having a deep butter-yellow color, and alloyed with 5 to 20 percent silver. He found that "the majority of the gold is not readily visible to the naked eye, occurring as fine flecks and narrow dark bands in the quartz," a description not unlike Walsh's original findings.

It was not unusual to discover such valuable ore deposits still hidden after years of prospecting. The great Cripple Creek deposits were found beneath lands believed useful only for ranching. A persistent cowboy and part-time prospector named Bob Womack discovered Cripple Creek gold but realized very little of the coming bonanza. Tom Walsh did not have to persevere quite as long as Womack, yet he did hold on to his find until he reaped a fortune.[1]

Tom had already claimed a sizable portion of Imogene Basin. Now, he needed to move quickly and quietly. During the remainder of 1896 he acquired nearly all the remaining claims and staked most of the basin's unclaimed ground. While it is a common belief that he purchased nearly the entire basin for around $8,000, at least one commentator has put the figure closer to $25,000. Yet another source has him paying $60,000 for the Una claim alone. Deeds of record in Ouray County show a total consideration (payment) of $52,850 for Walsh's 1896–1910 purchase of mining claims in the Imogene Basin. However, not all deeds recite consideration, and deeds sometimes state the wrong consideration. The conservative Walsh had a practice of never paying more than the value of the ore in sight. In this case, he probably did not even pay that much.

Whatever the exact figure, it was a bargain at any price when compared with what happened next. The discovery remained a secret until the fall of 1896. When it was finally made public, Tom Walsh owned just about everything in the basin, and many experienced miners shook their heads in disbelief.

In the words of renowned mining engineer T. A. Rickard, who inspected the property, "Moral: Never fail to test the ore of a drift that is penetrating into new ground, and never assume that ore is poor because it *looks* like ore you know to be poor." In the words of former owner William Weston, "The man who sells for a big price in cash a colt that years after becomes a derby winner, and who then regrets he sold it, has a mean streak in his composition. He ought to be glad that the other fellow made a good thing out of it." Not everyone who had given up on the Imogene was as charitable as Weston.[2]

In the winter of 1896–1897, Tom Walsh and Andy Richardson directed the work that would turn a small adit into a paying mine. Eight miners helped Walsh and Richardson extend the drift east and west along the rich gold vein. Tom and Andy felt the mine needed a new name. Overlooking the usual sources, those invoking such glorious matters as victory, wealth, heroic or mythical figures, or women's names, Walsh chose the name of a common and somewhat meddlesome resident of the area: a noisy jay (actually the gray jay, *Perisoreus canadensis*, or camp bird) known for stealing food from campsites. According to one story, a flock of them had devoured Tom's lunch when he returned from his discovery. Under the circumstances, he considered the jays a good omen, and the mine became the Camp Bird. Other sources paint a less colorful story, one noting that Camp Bird was an existing claim staked by Richardson, the name perhaps used by Walsh to distract attention from the Gertrude. Furthermore, the Camp Bird claim was probably the site of the ore slide that had first tipped Tom off to the existence of gold. Of course, it is possible that all three stories are true. However, Camp Bird was not an uncommon name for a mine or claim in Colorado, possibly because the birds were very common. No fewer than sixteen Camp Birds could be found within the state in the late nineteenth century, many of them predating Tom's bonanza. The earliest was located in 1880, in Park County.[3]

The mine duly named, work on the most famous of the Camp Birds proceeded rapidly. The first two cars of ore were shipped in October 1896. Three cars followed in November, six in December, five in January 1897, seven in February, and progressively increasing numbers of cars thereafter. The small, ten-stamp U.S. Depository Mill, one mile away, processed the first ores. From the original adit, now called the Gertrude level, the miners took out an overhead stope 120 feet long by 129 feet high and a raise to the surface about 200 feet above. Another adit at about the same elevation, called the Blue Bird level, reached the Camp Bird vein in July.

By August 1897, the outside world began to realize that Walsh had found a treasure. On August 14 *The Engineering and Mining Journal* admitted that, until two weeks before, it had found nothing extraordinary to tell its readers about the rather remote mine. Now, however, it could report that the mine had produced more than $800,000 in gold and silver since the previous fall, with production gradually increasing. The mine boasted a pay streak four to five feet in width. The milled ore was packed to the nearest railway station at Ironton by a train of fifty burros. The reporter summed up the Camp Bird Mine as one of the most valuable opened in the San Juans in recent years. While not mentioned by the *Journal*'s reporter, to get to Ironton the sure-footed burros needed to traverse a path over the 12,500-foot Richmond Pass. From the small town in the Red Mountain Mining District, a rail line built by Otto Mears could carry the ore south to smelters. While Walsh's own smelter in Silverton may have been the initial destination, it closed sometime in 1897. The smelter's part-owner and manager obviously had a bigger goal in mind. The ores could also have been sent to the Omaha and Grant smelter in Durango. It is probable, however, that the mine soon began to send its production on the longer but all-downhill route to Ouray, for shipment to Pueblo smelters.[4]

In September 1897 the workers began to drive a new adit called the 2-level, located 220 feet lower than the Gertrude at 11,500 feet. Walsh planned a more modern mill using twenty stamps to crush and process seventy tons of rock per day. He located the mill site two miles below the mine, at the junction of Canyon and Imogene creeks. A small settlement that soon developed at the site took the name Potosi, after a 13,700-foot peak to the northwest. All the while, Walsh's workers kept surveying and locating additional claims. On November 12, 1897, Ouray's *Silverite-Plaindealer* announced, "Thomas F. Walsh has placed the Camp Bird on good condition for winter work. . . . The shipments of gold ore continue to come down with no diminution in quantity or quality. Between 80 and 100 men are on the payrolls and it is the consensus of opinion among the workmen that they could receive no better treatment in any other mine in the state." Part of that treatment was the building of a temporary boarding-house about halfway between the mine and Ouray, near the future location of the mill. The building also housed a telephone connection to the mine's Ouray office. Work on the new mill commenced December 14.

In the early stages of the mine's development, Tom kept Andy Richardson as his mine manager. Andy possessed a wealth of experience in the Imogene Basin, and Tom appreciated his loyalty. However, as Camp Bird grew, it needed an experienced manager, and Andy had worked mostly as a prospector. Late in 1897 Walsh replaced Richardson with John Benson. Benson's work with Walsh dated back to Cripple Creek, where he managed the Deer Horn Mine for Tom. Later, he ran Tom's successful Black Hawk Mine in Rico. The two men had probably known each other in Leadville even before that time. They also shared

Ireland as a homeland. Benson received high praise for his management of the Camp Bird. Andy Richardson continued to serve as the mine superintendent.[5]

A NEW MILL AND A LONG AERIAL TRAMWAY

During the week of February 11, 1898, the 2-level adit reached the Camp Bird vein 750 feet into the mountain. A month later a raise from the 2-level reached the Gertrude level. At about the same time, the new stamp mill, completed in mid-February, was reported working perfectly in all respects. Interestingly, part of the successful mill's machinery came from a source that in the not-too-distant past had brought Walsh only sorrow. He had purchased what was left of his failed Kokomo smelter and incorporated its better parts into his new mill. The stamps weighed 800–850 pounds each and dropped 6 inches to crush the ore. They repeated this action 90–100 times per minute, an amount that varied depending on the setting for maximum gold recovery. Water from the roaring creeks supplied its power for the five ice-free months of the year, with a 110-horsepower Reynolds-Corliss engine operating the remainder of the time.

It was a simple mill to construct, for the ore was free milling and did not require a chemical treatment to separate the gold from waste rock. The Camp Bird ore contained free gold particles embedded in quartz. Thus the mill needed only Blake crushers, pulverizing stamps, and machinery for amalgamating and concentrating to make the final separation. The process works like a gold pan. Gold, being denser than the other minerals, will naturally sink to the bottom of the pan. To separate free gold from crushed waste rock, the mill utilized thirty 6-foot Frue vanners. This machine used a slightly inclined rubber belt to carry the materials, which were washed with water while being shaken sideways. As the wastes drifted away with the water, special mercury-coated copper plates caught the dense gold, which mixed with the mercury to form amalgam. The 16-foot-long by 53-inch-wide plates captured an estimated 75 percent of all free gold passing over the vanners. Manager John Benson felt his mill was losing too much gold value. A reporter for the *Denver Republican* credited Benson with placing a mercury-filled well below each plate to catch all free gold escaping the plates. The amalgam was then heated in a retort to drive off the mercury as a vapor, leaving the gold and silver as a metallic blob known as a "sponge." Benson may have invented the mercury-filled wells, but amalgamation was a well-known method for catching gold.[6]

The mill also employed a new type of machinery called the Wilfley table. Invented by Tom's former business partner in Kokomo and Cripple Creek, these slanted, vibrating tables were able to separate a concentrated mixture of valuable minerals from waste rock. This concentrate was carried by the table's vibrations down the slanted surface and spilled into a trough that ran along the table's edge. Walsh and Benson placed six Wilfley tables (which had a greater capacity than the Frue vanners) in an auxiliary mill. The entire mill operated continuously for the rest of 1898 and for some time afterward. It processed fifty tons of ore per day, producing both a gold-silver retorted sponge and a gold-silver-copper-lead concentrate.

In September 1898 the workers began driving another major adit, the 3-level, at 11,200 feet. An approach of heavy timbers supported its mouth for a distance of about 300 feet to protect against snow slides. A short Houston tram connected the higher adits with the 3-level. It was a form of single-wire rope Hallidie tram, named after the inventor of the San Francisco cable car system. However, something faster than a burro or mule was needed to carry the mine's ever-increasing output down the 9,000-foot route, with a 1,350-foot vertical drop, from the mouth of the 3-level tunnel to the mill. Walsh settled on a Bleichert aerial tramway to do the job. He hired tram builder E. H. Taylor, who quickly put sixty-eight carpenters to work on the job. Construction began September 15, 1898.

The construction of this immense tramway, together with the Camp Bird's contribution to a large increase in Ouray County gold production, caught the attention of the Denver press. One reporter was impressed with the hard work and ingenuity of Taylor and his crew. Walsh had demanded that Taylor complete the work in ninety days, before the worst snows closed the roads for the winter. The two men soon agreed that the time might be shortened if Walsh supplied all the men and materials while Taylor provided the super-vision. Plans called for a main tramway and a system of subtrams radiating from the main line in all directions, which would keep the mill running day and night. Sites for the tram's towers were carefully surveyed, the ground was cleared to bare rock, and substantial masonry piers and snow splits to divert avalanches from structures were erected. The project was completed without a mishap in a record forty-eight days. The new tram's buckets held 700 pounds of ore, with the capacity to haul 12 tons per hour. Eventually, it would carry 100 to 140 tons of ore per day. Like the mill, it ran flawlessly for a long time. The press reported that its only maintenance cost was grease, with the original traction wire rope still in operation after more than a year. This attested to the accuracy of design and construction, for such ropes normally had an operating life of only four to five months.

By the end of 1898, the Camp Bird mill was producing about $150 worth of concentrate per ton of ore. Animal power was still the mode of transportation from the mill to Ouray's rail connection. Two mule pack trains a day carried the concentrate down the steep Canyon Creek Road, another route Otto Mears had carved into the side of a canyon wall at a grade too steep for a railroad. From Ouray, rail lines carried the Camp Bird's riches to the smelters at Pueblo.[7]

THE GREATEST GOLD MINE IN THE WORLD

The year 1899 saw further adit construction, especially as the 3-level pushed toward the vein. Higher up, another adit at the Hancock level tapped lead and silver values in a vein that intersected the Camp Bird near the Gertrude level. The elevation of this new level fell between the Gertrude and 2-levels, revealing large quantities of low-grade ores. Walsh and Benson liked its potential and began plans for a new experimental lead mill. However, their biggest project for the year was construction of a permanent boardinghouse, completed in October at a cost of $40,000. The three-story structure was located near the portal of the 3-level; it featured steam heat and electric lights and could house 400 guests. It achieved fame as one of the greatest accommodations ever built for mine workers and is further described in Chapter 7. By the end of 1899 the mine and the mill employed about 225 men.

The December 3, 1899, edition of the *Denver Republican* carried a full-page article entitled "Story of the Wonderful Camp Bird Mine." Calling the mine a "[g]olden monument to the shrewdness and enterprise of Thomas F. Walsh," the article provided a thorough description of its history and current operations. The Camp Bird now boasted just under $3 million in total production, with 4,400 feet of adits at the three levels exposing the vein and more than 6 miles of the vein actually traced. All gold production had been taken from the 120-by-129-foot stope in the Gertrude level, a 2,300-by-40-foot stope in the 2-level, and the drifts along the remainder of the exposed Camp Bird vein. Since the miners had removed little more than one-eighth of the total vein, the mine's future potential looked great. Walsh's shrewdness was reflected in the care he took to identify and assay both his original discovery and every few feet of all newly exposed vein structure. The ore discovered by these methods, according to the *Republican*, "stands alone among the ores of Colorado as yet discovered. It is a pure white quartz, streaked with seams of black telluride ore. There is no indication of the values contained in either material, and yet the white quartz frequently carries from six to eight ounces in free gold, while the streaks of telluride sometimes run as high as 200 ounces." The ore body in the mine was 3 to 14 feet wide, with 75 percent of its values yielding to amalgamation. Walsh also held to a firm policy of development rather than production, requiring that several years of future production be blocked out before any increase in output. His staff was efficient and experienced, reflecting his hiring and management skills. Singled out for praise in their work were Benson, Richardson, mill superintendent W. H. Coates, and electrician A. H. Fiery, all of whom were paid top wages. The reporter concluded, "[W]hen the extent of the underground development is taken into consideration, the assertion that it is the greatest gold mine in the world is fully warranted."[8]

The workers extended the 3-level adit, eventually cutting the Camp Bird vein in the spring of 1900. From portal to vein, this level now stretched 2,300 feet. By November, miners had developed 1,500 feet of drifts along the vein on either side of its intersection with the adit. Eventually, this level became the source of all mining for Walsh. Production was increasing so rapidly that new stamps had to be added to the mill each year. By 1900, sixty stamps raised its capacity to 200 tons per day. A March report noted that the previous year's operations had required $250,000 for machinery alone and 1.7 million feet of lumber for construction and mine timbering, with further large outlays predicted for the current year. Also in March 1900, the experimental lead mill commenced operation. Another experiment was in the use of cyanide to further extract gold from the large volume of tailings produced by the Potosi mill. Despite the free-milling nature of the gold, inevitably, some of it had escaped all the concentration and amalgamation processes to pass into the mill tailings. San Francisco metallurgist Frank L. Bosquin's tests proved that the cyanide process could capture 80 percent of the gold in the tailings, producing an output of $3 per ton at an expense of 75 cents per ton. A 150-ton cyanide mill was completed in August 1900, but by November it was insufficient to treat the required volume. Benson doubled its capacity. The Camp Bird had reached just about its greatest surface extent, with 103 lode mining claims and twelve mill sites covering a total of 941 acres.[9]

Noted geologist Charles W. Henderson appraised the Camp Bird in July 1900. He reported that from its inception in 1896 through that date, the mine had produced a value of recovered metallic contents (gold, silver, lead, copper) of $2,535,512, with a profit to Walsh of $1.65 million. In the same month, T. A. Rickard reported the same production values as Henderson in a report prepared for prospective London purchasers, responding to rumors that the mine was for sale. Rickard appraised the mine's 1900 value at $6 million, with an estimated $6,118,800 in reserve. He found the mine's valuable ore averaging five feet in width along the vein, which would bring $48 per ton in gold value. However, as will be seen in Chapter 13, one other expert disputed Rickard's values.

John Benson dismissed reporters' questions about any sale, stating that he just needed to go about developing the mine. While rumors circulated for nearly two years, Walsh and Benson continued with business as usual. The mine produced more and more gold, requiring the ever-improving technology of the time. In 1901 they increased the number of stamps at the mill to eighty while doubling the cyanide plant's capacity. The Camp Bird plants now received electric power from the Vance Junction station west of Telluride, requiring transmission for twenty miles over Imogene Pass. Periodic reports told of discoveries of rich new veins of ore, likely just extensions of the long Camp Bird vein. One such report in February 1902 also told of extra mounted guards assigned to Camp Bird stage shipments bound for Ouray, said to be totaling $5,000 to $10,000 daily. Actually, extra guards had been a reality since an 1899 robbery. Benson agreed that many new development expenditures had been made in the last year but stated that no new additions of great value would be made during the rest of 1902. The sale of the Camp Bird came within three months.

In a later appraisal, Henderson found that from the time of his July 1900 report through April 1902, the mine had recovered additional metal valued at $1.5 million, with Walsh's individual profit placed at $750,000. No wonder Evalyn later called the operation a "gold engine." For its final two years in her father's ownership, she reported daily profits at $5,000, virtually guaranteeing that the Walsh family grew richer every day. When compared with Henderson's figures, Evalyn's daily income statement is an exaggeration in the long term. However, as the press had already noted, there were days when the rich mine's output exceeded even Evalyn's estimates.[10]

A RAGS-TO-RICHES MYTH

A common myth holds that Tom Walsh, destitute and down on his luck, found a very rich deposit of gold ore and proceeded rapidly to build a world-class mine that paid for itself. As a practical matter, this would have been nearly impossible. The ore could not have been dug from the ground, processed, and sold on the market quickly enough to pay for the extensive capital improvements placed on the Camp Bird. True, those mainstays of western mining development, eastern bankers and investors, were noticeably absent. Walsh had firmly stated his philosophy of never going into the mining stock business or engaging in "flotations of property on a stock basis." Even Walsh's longtime business partner David Wegg was not involved in the Camp Bird. Wegg knew about the Camp Bird and Walsh's success. Apparently, he was firm in his decision to retire from mining in the area, for the two men remained friends.

Yet despite the dark tone of some of his 1895 and early 1896 letters (which might have been overly pessimistic), Walsh had apparently run into a bit of luck before finding his rich mine. Reporters at the time largely credit his Black Hawk Mine at Rico. Taking over a gold mine that had been losing money, he soon found a large shoot of sulphide ore for which a Durango smelter was willing to pay a premium. The mere fact that the ore was sent to Durango, much more accessible by rail than Silverton, is one more indication that Walsh was in the mining business as well as the smelter business. According to one source, he "cleaned up a neat little fortune." Even his earliest Ouray properties, such as the Black Girl and American Nettie, and the San Bernardo Mine near Telluride, brought him small profits. The early development of the Camp Bird required Tom to reach into his own pocket, and the money was certainly there. By one estimate, before he received any return on the property, he had paid nearly $100,000 for labor, supplies, acquisition of adjoining properties, water and timber rights, experimentation in milling, and other steps to perfect his plans. He is said to also have paid hundreds of dollars for assays. If the need arose, he had excellent credit with Colorado's bankers from his long dealings with them. In fact, his only loan to develop the Camp Bird came from his old friend David Moffat, then president of the First National Bank of Denver.

Three years after the discovery of the Camp Bird, a Denver reporter referred to the stories of poverty before riches as "mere fairy tales." Today, there seems to be no hard evidence, such as mine production or bank records, that might firmly establish how or where Walsh held the financial reserves to develop the Camp Bird. One can imagine the shrewd Walsh keeping a nest egg for a rainy day and feeling "poor" if required to tap into it for everyday living expenses. Nevertheless, the conclusion seems abundantly clear: Tom Walsh knew how to survive the Silver Crash and then profit handsomely from it, searching spent silver mines for a golden lining.[11]

WALSH ON LABOR

CHAPTER SEVEN

CARING FOR A DIVERSE WORKFORCE

The Camp Bird Mine and mills employed up to 500 laborers during Tom Walsh's tenure. The lack of records from the mine during this time prevents us from seeing the workers in the day-to-day world of time, payroll, and production schedules. However, the 1900 U.S. census, taken at about the halfway point of Walsh's ownership, provides a onetime glimpse of their lives from a different perspective.

The census's Imogene Precinct was essentially the same area as the Camp Bird and Walsh's smaller mine, the Hidden Treasure. Any residents of the precinct not directly employed by Walsh probably still made a living from his mines. The census taker entered 270 names for the precinct (which should be reduced to 269, since Henry Charlsen is listed twice). Of those, 230 were laborers, and 130 of that group listed their occupation as miner. The miners' ethnic backgrounds differed greatly from those of surrounding mines. The dominant group of miners in the area called themselves Tyroleans, listed in the census as claiming either Italy or Austria as a birthplace. These rather recent immigrants must have felt at home in an area that greatly resembled their native Alps. The workforce of the nearby Revenue and Virginius mines in the Sneffels Precinct was heavily Tyrolean. By contrast, the Camp Bird hired a more ethnically diverse group. Exactly half of the miners, 65, had been born in the United States. Walsh and Benson must have shown some preference for their homeland, as the Irish comprised the largest foreign-born group at 19 (with many U.S.-born miners also listing Irish ancestry). Next in line were Canadians, followed by Germans, English, Danes, Swedes, Tyroleans, Finns, and one Norwegian (Charlsen). The era was noted for its bias against newly arrived Italians, which may have carried over to Tyroleans as well. However, the Camp Bird management probably did not harbor this prejudice so much as it did the desire to obtain, and the ability to pay for, the services of experienced miners. The average age of Camp Bird miners was 34.1 years. The largely Tyrolean force of the Sneffels Precinct averaged 29.8 years.

The rest of the laborers carried out a variety of jobs. The mine and its supporting cast employed 31 day laborers, 15 carpenters, 8 blacksmiths, 5 waiters (hotel and boardinghouse), 2 guards, and 2 cooks and a baker. Other jobs included millwright, vanner tender, battery tender, teamster, bookkeeper, electrician, night watchman, electrical motorman, dynamo tender, and drayman. What might be termed supervisory and professional positions included superintendents, foremen, engineers, hotel and boardinghouse managers, assayers, and amalgamators. This group was ethnically similar to the miners, but with an even greater percentage born in the United States. Five employees were age sixty or older, with Canadian-born miner Christopher Ward the "dean" of the group at seventy-three. Another miner, Henry Byrnes, was the youngest at seventeen. Only two women worked at the Camp Bird: boardinghouse keeper Mary Burus and Carrie Chandler, a cook. Mary's husband, Marcus, toiled as a carpenter, making them the only married couple in the workforce. Carrie lived with her uncle, Daniel Chandler, and brother Robert, both miners. All employees were white. The census records for the Imogene Precinct do not show the names of any workers who commuted from Ouray, and that group included Walsh, Benson, Richardson, and perhaps several others who dared to tackle the steep daily route up and down Canyon Creek Road in return for superior comforts at home. Most of these workers, no doubt, held better-paying jobs.

Entire families did live at the Camp Bird, nineteen in fact. Nearly all of these families consisted of a working husband, wife, and small children. They lived in the small houses of the Potosi settlement near the mill. The husbands' occupations cut across a variety of the positions at the mine and mill. The family of drayman Charles Scales was the largest of the group, for his wife and four children lived with him. Two of the Scales children and five others were "at school," probably in Ouray. The majority of the Camp Bird laborers were single men, 161 in all. Twelve of these were widowers, and 8 were divorced. Twenty-seven men stated that they were living away from their families. While those families could have lived as close as Ouray, in the transient world of mining they might also have been a nation or even a world away.[1]

Whatever the demographics of his mining venture, it presented a test as to whether Tom's newfound wealth in any way changed his outlook on those less fortunate. Evalyn recalled that her father and John Benson had seen labor-related violence in other camps and agreed that there should be no problems with their workers at the Camp Bird. In 1894 Walsh expressed his concerns in a letter to David Wegg, bemoaning, "As I write our country is almost in the throes of anarchy. The Pullman strike has stopped everything, caused riots and bloodshed, especially in Chicago, with millions [of dollars] of property destroyed. I don't know what we are coming to. You should rejoice at being both out of office and out of the country."[2]

Walsh poured much of his early Camp Bird profits into surface improvements, including a self-contained community with shops, warehouses, and its greatest showpiece—the famous three-story boardinghouse. Knowing that at over 11,000 feet miners frequently became snowbound, their boss brought them all the comforts of home, rated as on a par with the best hotels in the area. The Camp Bird miners slept in rooms designed for two, equipped with marble-topped basins and porcelain tubs in the lavatories, not to mention hot and cold running water. The mine itself was early to electrify, and the boardinghouse had electric lights as well as steam heat. Miners ate off china plates in spacious dining rooms served by modern kitchens. Camp Bird milk bottles later became collectors' items. The miners had time for leisure. In an era when twelve-hour shifts were common in mines, Walsh restricted his to eight hours. The two shifts a day commenced at 7:00 A.M. and at 7:00 P.M. The recreation and smoking rooms held pool tables, subscriptions to seventeen newspapers and magazines, and comfortable chairs for reading. Walsh also made certain that the Union Hall in Ouray received the same leading periodicals as his boardinghouse. On the second story was the company store, featuring all kinds of clothing and supplies and also paper and pencils for writing letters home. For all this, room and board cost one dollar a day, a standard rate throughout the area even for housing much less accommodating.

By contrast, a 1901 edition of *The Miners' Magazine*, the voice of the Western Federation of Miners (WFM), described the average mine bunkhouse of the time. The miners' clothing, still wet from work, hung on nails as close as possible to the few available heaters. Some wet clothes doubled as pillows on filthy bunks. Floors covered in candle grease and tobacco juice and seldom scrubbed were the norm. In winter, cold air and snow blew in through cracks in the walls that shrunk during the summer season.[3]

When miners worked the Camp Bird, they found the latest in compressed air drills and electric locomotives to haul the ore to the surface. Foul, dust-filled air was a frequent health problem in mines, but the Camp Bird's air was rated exceedingly good, with natural ventilation supplemented by air from the drills. Also, the four-hour breaks between shifts allowed the dust to settle. Camp Bird payroll records during Walsh's ownership have not survived. One source has noted that wages for the eight-hour shift ran as high as $4.50 per day for miners and engineers, while blacksmiths earned $4. Another stated that while the machine men driving the tunnels earned a base rate of $3 per day, that amount could be advanced in proportion to the number of feet driven in a month. Two hundred feet of rock work in a month entitled the men to $7 per day. There were few months in which this goal was not met.[4]

AN ISLAND IN A STORMY SEA OF STRIKES

By taking care of its laborers, the Camp Bird avoided strikes. The mine did have employees who were union members, but as Walsh later reported, he was always able to reach compromises with their leaders. Such was seldom the case for other mines of the times, in the San Juans or elsewhere in the West. A strike occurred near the Camp Bird in 1896. On December 3, workers walked off their jobs at the Revenue and Virginius mines, demanding eight-hour shifts and expressing grievances against supervisors. The mine manager was Hubbard Reed. Years before, Reed and his brother had driven the adit for the Gertrude and Una claims and then acquired the Una. Earlier in the year, he had sold the Una to Walsh when the latter purchased most of the Imogene Basin. The Una, like the Gertrude, proved to contain a sizable portion of the Camp Bird vein. Now Reed, with a good record as a manager, faced his first strike. Matters were soon settled after threats of violence, and normal conditions returned by February 1897. However, this was only a small part of increasing labor agitation throughout the West. For Hubbard Reed, it was a bitter pill when Tom

Walsh found the mineral wealth that had eluded Reed for so many years and then to see Walsh provide benefits to workers that Reed's struggling mines could not match. Hubbard Reed soon left the area.

Walsh had already witnessed some of the earliest labor-related violence to hit the Colorado mining industry near his holdings in Cripple Creek and Leadville. The 1894 strike in Cripple Creek was an early effort by the newly formed Western Federation of Miners (the infamous WFM or even "Western Federation of Murderers" to mine owners). It succeeded, largely because of support from Colorado's one-term Populist governor, Davis "Bloody Bridles" Waite. Waite received his nickname from an inflammatory speech in which he proclaimed that, against the strong hand of money power, his Populist allies should fight until the blood flowed up to the horses' bridles. The main goals of the strike were $3 per day in pay and the eight-hour day. Even Winfield Scott Stratton, who remembered his roots and supported the workingman, was hit. However, he was also among the first to enter into negotiations with labor and agree to the $3, eight-hour day.

In 1896, the newly formed Cloud City Mining Union, an affiliate of the WFM, struck Leadville's mines. The workers again sought the $3 day, a figure already paid by some mines. Among the staunchest holdouts for keeping the $2.50 day was John Campion, lord of the booming Little Jonny Mine and an old friend of Tom Walsh's from his Leadville days. Violence flared not long after the strike began. This time the state militia arrived at the behest of the pro–mine owner governor, Albert McIntyre, Waite's successor. After a prolonged strike lasting well into 1897, the owners prevailed. Campion and his allies simply had more money, time, and staying power. They commissioned spies to infiltrate labor ranks and exploited differences among the miners, many of them ethnic related. The return to the status quo meant many miners lost their jobs. The entire community suffered, for many of the mines that had closed during the strike had flooded and remained closed. Campion left the field shortly thereafter, destined to make a second fortune in sugar beets on the Colorado plains.

In 1899 Democratic governor Charles S. Thomas and the Colorado legislature passed a law requiring an eight-hour maximum workday for miners, smelter workers, and other occupational groups. However, the Colorado Supreme Court declared the law unconstitutional in 1902. The law's supporters then tried a constitutional amendment, which passed in 1903. However, the legislature turned the enabling laws into a watered-down version of the amendment, with loopholes whereby mine and smelter owners could still require ten- to twelve-hour workdays. With little help from the state, labor leaders such as William "Big Bill" Haywood of the WFM continued to promote strikes around the state. In 1901–1902, Telluride was the scene of labor violence. On July 3, 1901, a band of 250 armed union men attacked the big Smuggler-Union Mine, killing three non-union workers. The following year a mine manager was assassinated in his living room. The wages complained about fell into the $3–$3.50 range; daily shifts were usually at least twelve hours. These and other incidents around Colorado and the West culminated in the Cripple Creek violence of 1903–1904.[5]

Throughout the period, the Camp Bird Mine sat like an island in a stormy sea. It suffered no strikes during Tom Walsh's tenure or for some time thereafter. International mining engineer John Hays Hammond tells in his autobiography of one undated incident at the Camp Bird. Hammond frequented the mine, first as a representative of potential buyers and later as its general manager. One day he heard a rumor that a delegation from the International Workers of the World was headed for the Camp Bird. Hammond accused this group (better known as the IWW or the "Wobblies") of responsibility for the 1903–1904 Cripple Creek violence. Actually, the IWW did not come into being until 1905, and its predecessor, the WFM, was implicated in the Cripple Creek problems, which eventually led to its demise. Whatever the source of his troubles, Hammond immediately took action, calling a meeting of the miners, mill hands, foremen, and clerks. He asked if they had any grievances against management. The reply was negative; the workers said they liked the mine's owner and manager and even the food. The Camp Bird men told Hammond they would take care of the situation and quickly organized a delegation to meet the IWW in the canyon below the mine. There, with menacing gestures, as Hammond related it, they ordered the agitators to leave. Whether this occurred before or after Walsh sold the mine, his legacy was such that during a turbulent period in 1903 the Camp Bird mill men, including union members, still voted down a strike. Walsh's buyers continued many of his labor practices, including paying above-average wages and offering workers reasonable hours.

Statements by individual workers regarding their treatment also provided reasons for labor to cooperate with Walsh. One veteran miner working there at the time called the mine "one of the best managed.... [T]he manager and owner of the Camp Bird mines are greatly liked by their vast army of employees for their considerate treatment, which is largely responsible for the constantly increasing earnings of the wonderful mine."[6] Walsh had also continued to operate the nearby Hidden Treasure Mine, whose lower-grade ore kept it from reaching the Camp Bird's status. The mine's foreman from 1896 to 1902, Harry T. Cook, found Walsh in the habit of rewarding loyal employees. Cook recalled, "At the close of our business relations he presented me with $4,000 to show his appreciation for my services and he gave four other faithful workers like amounts." An 1899 article in a Ouray newspaper describing Walsh's leadership style found that "he has about him trusted employees. He does not have to suspicion [sic] them or place checks upon them to know a trustworthy man. His knowledge of man is as complete as his command of details. He has never been a 'boss' in the sense of asserting his superiority. He is always with all men a gentleman. He is obeyed, not because of his position, but because the ruling power is stamped on his jeans. Success has not turned his head but has added to his care to see that he shall be more successful." Tom Walsh, as we will see, held steadfast to his beliefs about the treatment of workingmen. His miners had a new champion to replace David Day, one in a better position to help them.[7]

IDEAS UNLIKE THOSE OF MANY OF HIS PEERS

Few other western miners of the time had a champion like Walsh. His attitude toward his miners placed him in a distinct minority among his peers. Even his friends and contemporaries held far different views on labor. David Moffat, owner of mining and smelting properties throughout Colorado, had never worked as a miner. This was one reason for his fury when union miners struck his Leadville and Cripple Creek properties. Moffat, his partners, and fellow owners in the districts held firm on wages and called in pro-owner sheriff's deputies and state militia to quell strikes, often violently. A letter written by Moffat's business partner Eben Smith summed up the attitude of many Colorado owners toward labor organizers, many of whom came from Tom Walsh's homeland. Smith told an associate to plan on closing down his Leadville mines "unless lightning strikes and kills off all the Irish."[8]

Spencer Penrose and his partner Charles Tutt enjoyed one of the West's greatest mining fortunes. Their families later donated a substantial portion of that fortune to charity. The partners' C.O.D. Mine became one of Cripple Creek's first big revenue producers. After selling it for a large profit to a French concern, Penrose and Tutt turned to milling the rich Cripple Creek ores. Once again their operations led the district. The fruits of their continued Colorado success soon led to profitable Utah copper ventures. Their labor practices, however, led to bitter clashes with miners and unions. In Cripple Creek, Penrose and Tutt joined Moffat in supporting the strikebreaking Colorado state militia, which put down the 1903–1904 strike with questionable strong-arm tactics. In Utah their labor record was even worse. Workers at Penrose and Tutt's Utah copper operation endured low wages and miserable working conditions. Many were fired for supporting union activities.

The famous Guggenheim family made a fortune from Colorado mining and smelting. Their philanthropy eventually became their trademark, especially in the world of art. However, it is debatable how much philanthropy was extended to their laborers. Simon Guggenheim, a future U.S. senator, did work long hours in 1899 to negotiate with smelter workers in Pueblo and avert a strike that crippled the industry elsewhere. However, his actions were atypical of the family's general attitudes toward their workers. Simon's father and the family patriarch, Meyer, rose from poverty in a European ghetto to wealth in America. He credited his own hard work for his success, with few handouts from others, and therefore had trouble understanding labor's demands for shorter hours, higher wages, and better working conditions. He evicted Leadville miners from their shacks so he could build a tailings pile. Meyer's sons usually followed their father's labor practices. The family's smelting empire was a rare part of the industry to survive the Silver Crash, but much of that good fortune could be attributed to their moving plants to Mexico and benefiting from the cheap labor there. The Guggenheims' employees often took part in the strikes of the late nineteenth and early twentieth centuries. When this happened, the family brought in strikebreakers, usually recent immigrants who would work for cheap wages and did not realize that they could be subjected to violence.[9]

In his book *The Bonanza Kings*, author Richard Peterson compares the results achieved by Walsh and other prominent western mine owners in their labor dealings. While the general attitude of U.S. capitalists of the time was one of standing up to labor in a tough and uncompromising manner, Peterson found Walsh to be among a small group of capitalists who proved that cooperation and accommodation with labor could bring profits without accompanying strikes and violence. Denver smelter owner Dennis Sheedy was another member of this group. Sheedy learned a lesson from a late 1880s strike. From that point forward he followed a policy of kindness, with an office door open to his laborers. He also paid for leave and medical assistance for injured workers, a rarity for the time. South Dakota's Homestake Mine built the great fortunes of owners George Hearst, Lloyd Tevis, and James B. Haggin. If the Smoky Jones legend was true and Walsh had become their partner, he probably would have endorsed many of their labor policies. They included a wage of $3.50 per day, an eight-hour workday, and a company hospital dating back to the mine's early days in 1879. Hearst's wife, Phoebe, gave the town of Lead a library and a free kindergarten. The result was a peaceful relationship between labor and management that lasted for decades, broken only once by a 1909 lockout.

Tom Walsh supported this conciliatory style of management in his most famous statement on the subject of labor:

As employers, treat your men with humanity and justice. Provide them with clean, comfortable quarters, wholesome food, and keep medicine at hand for their use. Money spent for their comfort is well-spent, for besides the good results in work, you get their appreciation and loyalty, which is of incalculable value.

Strikes can nearly always be avoided by having a heart-to-heart talk with your men, by fairly and squarely presenting the state of the case from their standpoint as well as your own. In dealing with them try to get at the best side of their nature. To use a mining phrase, you will be prospecting in human hearts and may discover beauties of character little suspected.[10]

Other mine owners of the time probably found Walsh a bit naive in making such a statement. Indeed, in our era, with the hindsight of 100 more years of labor-management strife, the advice still seems idealistic. Still, Walsh demonstrated its worth. His statement reflects personal warmth, yet he could be firm at the right moment. Peterson also found that he had the right work background. His earlier time as a miner was one asset. Here Walsh joined the ranks of former miners such as Hearst, Stratton, John Mackay of Nevada, and Marcus Daly of Montana. They were responsive to their workers even after they had earned millions. Another plus was local residence, for absentee owners were often targeted by strikes. John Mackay lived near his Comstock holdings and spent more time below ground than above, even after he had found his bonanza. Dennis Sheedy stayed nearby in Denver, for he placed a high value on communication with his employees. Even though he later moved his family away from Ouray, Walsh frequented the Camp Bird and remained a major part of community life, first as a benevolent mine owner and soon as a philanthropist.[11]

LABOR ON WALSH

Perhaps the best indication of organized labor's attitude toward Tom Walsh is what it did not say about him. *The Miners' Magazine* of the WFM in Denver represented the small union mine worker, treating mine owners as a bitter enemy. It even attacked owners and national leaders who offered support to labor. The magazine accused Marcus Daly of buying his workers' votes. If nothing else, John MacKay was guilty of being rich while many of his workers remained poor. Republican president Theodore Roosevelt could do no right. William Randolph Hearst earned a WFM rating of "way below zero" after the 1909 lockout of Deadwood union laborers. The magazine accused Simon Guggenheim of murder because of his remote connection to a 1904 incident in Denver. Although he continued Walsh's labor practices at the Camp Bird while serving as its general manager, John Hays Hammond had "perjured his black soul" by lying on the witness stand and sending Idaho union members to the penitentiary.

When reporting on labor conditions in the San Juans, *The Miners' Magazine* usually omitted Tom Walsh and the Camp Bird. The magazine paid close attention to a December 1900 strike at the Ouray smelter, supporting workers who wanted $3 a day, not $2.50. When WFM leaders toured the San Juan region in September 1900, they approved the organization of Red Mountain workers by the local Ouray union. An April 1902 report on the state of Local No. 15 in Ouray found it in good shape and growing in members. The Camp Bird was not mentioned on either occasion. The biggest problem reported in 1902 was the presence of Ouray's Chinese citizens. John Kennedy, a prominent member of the Ouray local, praised union formation at an Arizona mine in a September 1900 letter to the magazine's editor. Kennedy worked at the Camp Bird, where his letter was postmarked, yet neither he nor the editor suggested that his mine should also be unionized.

On three occasions *The Miners' Magazine* actually spoke of Walsh in a positive light. In January 1901 it reported Walsh's statement that he intended to keep the Camp Bird. The magazine found this to be good news for the miners employed by him. Later in the same year, Ouray Local No. 15 planned a Labor Day picnic. Thomas F. Walsh had accepted an invitation to address the gathering, joining, among others, WFM official John M. O'Neill (editor of the magazine). The Camp Bird and Bachelor mines agreed to close for the day, with the expressed hope that "other mines in the area will be as liberal." When the April 1902 edition of the magazine reviewed articles in other publications, it noted with favor that the leading contribution to the February issue of the *American Monthly Review of Reviews* was from the pen of Thomas F. Walsh, making an appeal for national irrigation.

In short, if Tom Walsh had only a truce with organized labor, that fact placed him far ahead of almost any other western mine owner.[12]

WHAT TO DO WITH MILLIONS OF DOLLARS

CHAPTER EIGHT

MR. AND MRS. THOMAS F. WALSH
INVITE YOU TO BE THEIR GUEST

Walsh remembered others in the area besides his employees. Ouray's miners had established their own hospital in 1887, ably assisted by David Day and the *Solid Muldoon*, who aroused (some say shamed) the townspeople into addressing the need. The Sisters of Mercy took over the job of administering to the sick and injured. The small hospital lost numerous contributions after the 1893 Silver Crash, and in 1895 the Sisters announced they would soon close if no more money were available. Relatives of one sister took over responsibility for patient care while the others tried to raise funds. By 1899, they were unable to pay their $3,500 loan from the local bank. Tom Walsh, a rather lapsed Catholic, came to their aid and paid off the mortgage. His only terms were that his loan would never come due as long as the Sisters ran the hospital. Later, acting

as U.S. commissioner to the Paris Exhibition of 1900, he donated $1,000—
one-third of his salary—to finish paying for the hospital's new heating apparatus. Walsh donated the remainder of the salary to charities in Denver and
Washington, D.C.

Each year at Christmas, the Reverend Charles Ferrari, pastor of Ouray's
Catholic Church, could expect to receive a check from Tom Walsh, in an
amount he was forbidden to disclose to the public. He was to distribute the
money in equal amounts to all four of the town's churches. Tom gave a cart
and a Shetland pony to a young girl who was crippled for life. Evalyn tells of a
young man in tattered clothing, riding without a ticket and about to be thrown
off a train, who soon found he had a ticket and money for better clothes, all
courtesy of her father. The recipient later wrote Tom that the generous act had
turned his life around. When possible, Walsh played the role of anonymous
benefactor. Ouray's sheriff later admitted that the Camp Bird's owner had been
providing him with money to care for the town's poor. One Camp Bird miner
told a reporter that his boss had "directed his manager, Mr. Benson, to see that
no poverty or destitution exists in Ouray or its vicinity. When discovered it
must be quietly and instantly relieved." At a time when big businessmen such
as Andrew Carnegie were establishing the social custom of philanthropy, Tom
Walsh followed suit, probably more so than the average millionaire. According
to one later tribute, "[H]e did not hold back from showing the world the
unwritten obligations of wealth."[1]

Ouray needed a public library as well. The man who saw to it that miners
were well-read now did the same for the rest of the town. He established the
Walsh Library upstairs from City Hall in 1901. It eventually held 11,000
volumes, making it one of the most valuable collections in the West. The books
included the works of Drs. Sigmund Freud and Carl Jung and every copy of the
Congressional Record. Tom also provided a bell for the building's tower. Sadly,
the bell was the only part of the structure to survive a 1950 fire, although a new
City Hall and library were built within three years.

"If you receive a card to this effect: 'Mr. and Mrs. Thomas F. Walsh
invite you to be their guest,' no matter what the occasion or in what part of
the world, let nothing less severe than a case of appendicitis or sudden death
prevent your acceptance." That was the advice to the public from an old friend
of Tom's, General Frank Hall. Later a noted Colorado historian and politician,
Hall was then writing for *The Denver Post*. He had known Walsh since their
days together in Central City. Hall joined an exclusive group of citizens from
eastern Colorado on a special train to Ouray provided by Walsh. The dignitaries included Governor and Mrs. James B. Orman and the mayors of Denver

and Colorado Springs. The occasion was the banquet to dedicate the library, held on July 24, 1901. It proved to be one of the greatest events in the town's history. The banquet was held in the large hall of the building housing the library. Guests sat at tables adorned with wildflowers, served by well-trained waiters from the area's principal hotels and entertained by an orchestra. Hall and his fellow guests sparingly consumed high-quality wine out of respect for a host who was "averse to any indulgence in drink beyond the limit of refined moderation. His preference would be to have no wines upon his tables." After a full-course dinner, speeches ran long into the evening, praising the special gift from Mr. and Mrs. Walsh.

The grand tour continued the following day with carriage rides to the Camp Bird, where the guests were impressed by the state of the mining technology and the miners' living accommodations. They found manager John Benson training technical students from the United States and foreign lands on the practical business of mining. A second dinner, nearly on a par with the previous night's extravaganza, awaited the guests at the boardinghouse dining room. The waiters and orchestra had preceded the guests up the mountain.

As to the mine's ownership, General Hall found that "Mr. Walsh has no partners except his wife." The general described Carrie as "a very pretty, well-educated, thoroughly refined and attractive woman; rather tall, somewhat slender, lithe and graceful, a glorious mate for her husband." Pressed by Hall as to whether they might ever sell the Camp Bird, Tom replied:

> No, I have given that [idea] up. I believe it will be worth many millions more than it is now ten or twelve years hence through the plans we are proceeding upon and I am content to watch and supervise their execution. Fortune has been very good to me since you and I parted at Central City years ago. When my boy, now 14 years old, shall have completed his education in the schools, he will master every detail of my business. During his present vacation he is at the mills familiarizing himself with all the departments. Later on he will take up the mining branch. He has an ardent love for it, and it will be cultivated.[2]

MOVE TO WASHINGTON

The Walsh family loved the small city of Ouray and the tributes of its citizenry. Nonetheless, gold money continued to pour in, and their newfound financial independence meant they could live anywhere they chose. By late 1897 a move was nearly certain. In October of that year, the family left on a train trip. Evalyn later remembered that the Thompsons accompanied them, but she had forgotten the reason for the excursion. In her book she paints a picture of terror, of being thrown from her sleeping compartment into the blackness of entanglement in her bedding and train cushions. Her father rescued her along with the rest of the party, seriously injuring his hands while breaking glass to escape their overturned railcar. Once outside, they witnessed the roar of flames from the burning train and heard the screams of the wounded and the bellowing of cattle. Their westbound passenger train had collided head-on with an eastbound cattle train. Evalyn tells of holding a dying man's head in her lap. She places the death toll at least at thirteen but believes it was probably higher since flames consumed the entire train.

Stories in contemporary newspapers bear out little of Evalyn's sad tale. By these accounts, the Denver and Rio Grande Railroad passenger train left the tracks early on the morning of October 3, 1897, near the small town of Cotopaxi in Colorado's Arkansas River Canyon. The train was in fact eastbound, and it derailed as a result of a defective axle on one car. It did not hit another train, and there was no fire. Two people died. Tom Walsh received only minor injuries while helping the others escape and gave one of many accounts to Denver newspapers. He praised the car's porter for his quick actions in preventing a fire and further disaster and also for recovering jewels belonging to Carrie. Otherwise, he faulted the railroad for not better securing its cushions, which nearly led to Evalyn's suffocation. *The Denver Republican* identified Walsh as affiliated with the Silverton smelter "and a well known mining man of the San Juan."[3]

One additional fact about the wreck seems more than a coincidence. Only two days before, Tom's next-oldest brother, Patrick, had passed away in Florence, Colorado. Patrick frequently helped Tom with his mining efforts, and the two families were close. Nonetheless, Evalyn seems to have forgotten that connection to the accident. Years later, after she had published her book, Evalyn received a letter from Patrick's daughter Minnie, mourning her father Patrick, who died "when he was forty-seven years old, as a result of over exposure, mining thru snow, and a cold that he never got over, in the making of the West."[4] Had the unfortunate train continued on its course from Cotopaxi, it would have taken the Walsh family to Florence in a few hours. The forgotten reason for the trip was Patrick's funeral. For John Thompson, this might have been one more chance to impress Tom Walsh. However, since Patrick had assisted Tom in his Ouray mining ventures as recently as 1895, Thompson probably knew Tom's brother well.

Whatever the circumstances, Evalyn seems correct in her statement that the train wreck was one more reason to leave the remote Ouray. Mountain train travel was dangerous, as were other means of getting around in the rugged terrain. Only shortly after they returned to Ouray following the accident, Tom's normally sedate horse spooked on a trip back from the Camp Bird, nearly plunging both of them into a chasm. Carrie's health problems resulting from the high altitude were increasing, and she wanted to leave. The family made a quick decision to leave Ouray before winter set in. Their destination was far away. They rented a suite of rooms at the Cochran Hotel in Washington, D.C., for the winter of 1897–1898. It soon became their home.[5]

ENTERING THE MOST
EXCLUSIVE RANKS OF POLITE SOCIETY

For the next few years, the Walshes spent their summers in Ouray. Washington, however, was where Tom wanted to spend more and more of his time. He had been a man of modest means until recently, with little education and no important family or business ties, yet he quickly established relationships with national leaders. Governor Charles Thomas felt the reason for such a phenomenal rise in his friend's status was simple. Tom Walsh, now with his financial status more than secure, wanted to use his money to enter the most exclusive ranks of polite society. A well-informed friend (probably Charles Thomas himself) told Walsh that the only way to gratify that desire was to "move to Washington and there devote himself to the entertainment of Cabinets [sic], diplomats, Congressmen, and casual visitors of distinction."[6]

In so doing, Walsh was not alone among western millionaires. According to another observer of the time, the flamboyant social critic Lucius Beebe, the nation's capital "held more appeal in those days for newly solvent westerners than rock-ribbed and impersonal New York. Where the Vanderbilts and Belmonts were impervious to *arrivistes*, a senator who had been assisted into office could always be counted on to help the socially ambitious on their way up the ladder." In his book *The Big Spenders*, Beebe often resorts to sensationalism in tales of the social climbs, accompanied by social foibles and falls, of the newly rich. However, Beebe's description of the socially ambitious Walshes is accurate, at least during their early Washington years. He found them neither wild nor vulgar but rather prudent and cautious. He concludes, "They knew that money existed to buy nice things and they had the money."[7]

Evalyn well remembered an early dinner party given by her parents at the Cochran Hotel soon after their arrival. The special guest was the daughter of a senator, one of their many new friends. Carrie was nervous and shy wearing her first evening gown. Tom, on the other hand, was the life of the party, friendly to all. Evalyn described the family's first winter as one of making many new friends and learning a lot. A prominent publisher, John R. McLean, his wife, Emily, and their son, Edward, were among those new friends. The McLeans, owners of the *Washington Post* and *Cincinnati Enquirer*, represented one generation more of entrenched wealth and considerable political power. John McLean is said to have wielded that power by keeping secret dossiers on the private lives of important public figures. At their first meeting, Evalyn describes the son, known as "Neddie," as her age, eleven, and "gawky." Lucius Beebe found the younger McLean "spoiled as a mackerel three hours in the sun." According to both Evalyn and Beebe, Neddie's mother paid her son's young companions to let him win at games. Despite her first impressions, many more meetings were in store for Evalyn and Neddie.

At first, Tom and Carrie's dream of entrance into the highest levels of Washington society moved at its usual cautious pace. Camp Bird revenues now totaled nearly $50,000 each month, yet the senior Walshes felt it prudent to return most of this sum to further development of the mine. The family creed remained "Can we afford it?" The children were to receive fine educations yet not be spoiled. Their parents sent each child to one of the city's best private schools, Vinson to Friends Select School for Boys and Evalyn to Mount Vernon Seminary. Annie MacDonald, the family's longtime servant, had become Evalyn's friend and confidante and was now her escort to school. Each morning the two arrived by streetcar or on foot, to the derisive stares of Evalyn's more affluent classmates. Evalyn noticed that her father was granting her mother's every wish, including buying her an expensive set of furs, and wondered if she could achieve the same result. One morning while he concentrated on shaving, she presented her request. Could he afford to hire a horse and carriage for her travel to school, at least some of the time? Tom astonished her by laughing heartily, then replying that yes, he could rent her a horse and carriage. Not long afterward he called her to the street in front of the hotel, where sat a blue Victoria carriage with the top down, pulled by two magnificent prancing sorrels answering to the commands of a deep-voiced coachman complete with silk hat and gloves. His name was Terrill, and his job was to drive Evalyn to school in style every day. The following morning she was deliberately late so she could arrive to the "oohs" and "ahs" of the other girls lined up to enter. For Evalyn, a watershed event had just occurred. The Walshes of Washington were now truly rich.

In December 1898 they purchased their first Washington home, at the corner of LeRoy Place and Phelps Place. The former owners were the renowned traveler and lecturer Conrad Jenness Miller and his wife, Anna. Located in one of the city's fashionable carriage neighborhoods, the three-story brick mansion came complete with cultured furnishings. Evalyn found it magical to walk from the hotel straight into a new home where she found "no ugliness either outside of it or in it." Such magic, she noted, could be worked for $58,129.91 in cash.[8]

A CANDIDATE FOR HIGHER OFFICE

Many in Colorado still considered Walsh a resident of their state, one whose wealth and prominence might prove to be an asset in Washington. His name soon came to the forefront in upcoming congressional and senatorial elections. His party of choice was Republican, another break with the tradition of Irish immigrants. Tom supported his party with his substantial pocketbook and in return received serious consideration for the 1899 congressional race in the district that included Ouray. By November, however, the party had picked another contender. Walsh felt he could do more for the state's development by staying where he was, as owner of the Camp Bird Mine. His Republican kingmakers had lost their enthusiasm as well. In June of that year, Tom spoke in support of the mandatory eight-hour workday, as proposed by Democratic governor Charles Thomas.

In 1902 Walsh's name was put forward once again, this time to challenge Colorado senator Henry Teller. Once a dedicated Republican, Teller had left the party because of its nonsupport of silver coinage, a vital Colorado issue. He was now a Democrat. A delegation of Colorado Republicans came to Washington to petition Walsh for the race, only to receive an indifferent reception. Pressed on the issue, he replied that even if assured of election as senator (then chosen by the state legislature), he did not want to change his plans for the future, which included no political ambitions. They did include being happy and content in his home circle, free of the trouble and cares of political life. The widely respected Teller eventually won the 1902 contest, and the degree of animosity it generated, in the Colorado legislature and elsewhere, might have given Walsh one more reason to shun politics.

In the 1904 election, the *Ouray Herald* suggested to its readers that no Walsh-for-senator rumors should be taken seriously. Walsh had been even more emphatic to the Denver press, stating to both the *Post* and the *Daily News* on June 26, 1904, "I have not given the political situation any thought. I am not a candidate for any office. I love Colorado and her people and am always ready to spend my money in boosting the state. All I want in return is the good will of the people."

When it came to appointed positions, however, Walsh was much more responsive. His many donations and his social prestige were enough to bring his name to national party leaders' attention. One such leader was the president of the United States, William McKinley. Early in 1899 Tom and Carrie received the first of many invitations to White House receptions. Later in the year Tom served on the Finance Committee of Washington's National Peace Jubilee, marking the end of the Spanish-American War. Evalyn attributed that membership to his having "made a contribution."[9]

A PROMINENT MEMBER OF NATIONAL SOCIETY

CHAPTER NINE

THE GREATEST AMERICAN IN PARIS

Soon, President McKinley had an important need for Walsh's services overseas. Early in 1900 a presidential commission arrived, appointing him a U.S. commissioner to the International Exposition to be held in Paris later in the year. At this critical point in history, the president was asking Walsh to show his adopted nation to the Old World he had left more than thirty years before.[1]

The French city had hosted many impressive fairs, both national and international, but none could top the grand Exposition of 1900. Its total attendance figure, more than 50 million visitors in just seven months, surpassed all previous international fairs and would not be broken for more than sixty years (by the New York World's Fair in 1964, a two-year fair). Earlier fairs had displayed mechanical and architectural wonders, such as the Eiffel Tower in 1889, but they were only that, wonders. Now at the start of a new century, these wonders were being transformed into usable forces, machinery to master those forces, and products for public consumption. Electric lights now brightened entire cities, not just laboratories. In the words of the fair's historian, Richard D. Mandell, writing a half-century later, "In a march of material progress that shocked some observers, new machines rendered outmoded and, as if by magic, transformed into junk those that were the ultimates in efficiency just a few years earlier."[2] Of the fair's major items on exhibit, only wireless transmission and radioactivity were brand new. Mandell also found something that would never be duplicated: "It was the last time anyone tried to include *all* of man's activity in one display. The pace of technical and artistic innovation since then has made inconceivable any plan for assembling the evidence of man's creativity in one exhibit, however immense."[3]

For Walsh and his fellow commissioners, the challenge was to demonstrate the advancement of U.S. culture, especially to Europeans. They faced stiff competition, but in the end their young country earned the respect of the entire world. The United States also spent the most money of any nation on its exhibits (a good part of which went for oceanic transport, a cost the Europeans did not have to bear). Yankee spirit and ingenuity brought forth pavilions full of the latest developments in agriculture, printing, publishing, forestry, transportation, and all forms of heavy industry. On the Fourth of July the United States presented a Lafayette monument as a gift to the French court. John Philip Sousa's marching band gave three rousing concerts each day.

Some other nations showed industrial might to meet the U.S. challenge, but still others simply featured their culture. Sweden's pavilion resembled an ancient Norse church, Turkey's a mosque. Greece and Serbia presented fine art galleries, destined for long-term use back home. Japan, noted for its art in past shows, brought more of the same but added tubular boilers and armaments. Finland was still a grand duchy of the czarist empire, but it displayed its independent spirit in a pavilion considered the architectural jewel of the Exposition. The Russians had little reason for jealousy. The French made sure that the czar, their military ally, had plenty of space. One use of that space was to display a huge model of the entire Trans-Siberian Railroad.

In the end, the United States took honors for mechanical ingenuity, the Japanese for taste, and the Germans for nearly everything else. As their French hosts cast a wary eye, German ingenuity claimed the show, with giant mechanical cranes, spotlights, bottled liquid air, and models of luxury liners. Dynamos were the show's greatest phenomenon, and Germany displayed the largest in the world. It generated 5,000 horsepower, yet required only two men for operation. The French may have feared the industrial and military competition, but U.S. historian Henry Adams feared something far worse. Then in his sixties, Adams had witnessed much of nineteenth-century progress during his ongoing "education." He summed up the meaning of the Exposition in a chapter of his book entitled "The Virgin and the Dynamo." To this point in history, he reflected, admiration of great works of art, often with holy themes, had dominated human intellectual thought. This fair, like its predecessors, had an incredible collection of art. However, public attention was inescapably drawn to the dynamos, and Adams was part of that attention. As he ominously foretold in the third person, "To Adams the dynamo became a symbol of infinity. As he grew accustomed to the great gallery of machines, he began to feel the forty-foot dynamos as a moral force, much as the early Christians felt the cross. . . . It is a new century, and what we used to call electricity is its God. I can already see that the fellow who gets to 1930 will wish he hadn't."[4]

On the Champs de Mars, not far from the dynamos, lay the U.S.-built Palace of Mines and Metallurgy. Here, Walsh and fellow contributors from his industry presented an exhibit worthy of their country's artistic and industrial might, in an equally grand building. A bronze and marble facade extended along the entire front of the exhibit, with the sculpted heads of Rocky Mountain sheep, American eagles, and the seals of the various states and territories and Indian nations. Inside were views of a wide variety of mining-related activities, including mines themselves, mills, iron and coal docks, sluices, and tramways. The more than 3,000 ore specimens from 600 profitable mines included iron, copper, tin, building stones, clays, gems, semiprecious stones, ores and nonmetallic minerals, coals, and cokes. For all this, the commissioners could thank Special Agent Victor Heikes, who had personally inspected every prominent mining camp in the Rocky Mountain region. Walsh's Camp Bird Mine exhibit included specimens and a description of mine development and activity, complete with a statement that the mine produced $5,000 in gold a day. Tom encouraged his fellow Colorado mine owners to contribute as well. Next door, his friend John Campion exhibited leaf and crystallized gold from his Leadville mine. This was just part of the extensive Campion collection that later formed the core of what is now the Mineral Hall of the Denver Museum of Nature and Science. Colorado as a whole presented 156 exhibits of all varieties.[5]

As impressive as it was, the Camp Bird exhibit might not have brought much acclaim to its creator, considering the sheer immensity of the fair. Tom and Carrie Walsh did receive a great deal of attention, however, for they had imported something far more eye-catching than a mine display. The family and its entourage took over the entire second floor of the Elysee Palace Hotel, where Walsh hosted dinner parties for up to 400 persons at a time. Legendary soprano Mary Garden, who had just made her Paris debut, entertained at one event.

However, the couple's best was saved for a June 25 Seine cruise. Tom and Carrie rented two riverboats for 200 guests, mostly national and state commissioners and prominent members of the Colorado delegation. The guests enjoyed an elegant luncheon, followed by dancing to an orchestra, as the boats drifted along the scenic river. The correspondent for *The Denver Times* found Tom and Carrie the most popular Americans in Paris. They were probably the first representatives of Ouray, Colorado, even if only part-time residents, to receive such accolades. Regarding its favorite son, the *Ouray Herald* proudly proclaimed: "He discovered that the French people had to be shown and he is showing them. The purple of royalty bows to the yellow gold of Tom Walsh. He believes that a genuine Coloradan can capture as much as the kingly monarch. Tall, rawboned, blue-eyed, good natured, the type of man behind the pick, he has practically become the greatest American in Paris." While less grand, similar articles appeared in both U.S. and European newspapers.[6]

Her parents relegated fourteen-year-old Evalyn to a Paris convent, where she was to improve her French and her personal conduct. Annie MacDonald went with her, but the two soon became disenchanted with the sober and strict environment. After a daring escape, they re-presented themselves at the Elysee Palace. Her father believed Evalyn's tale of cruelty by the nuns, but the parents then assigned a stern French governess as her next companion. Evalyn convinced the woman that rides on the Exposition's hot air balloon and Ferris wheel were essential to her Paris education. The governess became ill after they were stranded for hours on the latter contraption. Evalyn's remaining observations are of Paris street life and the many new and very rich friends her family made.

At the conclusion of the Exposition, the Walsh family sailed for New York. The press was curious about the Irishman-turned-westerner who had dazzled the world in Paris. A reporter for New York's *The World* found that his subject presented a study in contrasts, of dignity with a touch of lingering humility:

> Mr. Walsh represents the true Tipperary type and even today has a fascinating trace of the Tipperary brogue. But even from his appearance alone almost any Irishman would guess that he was a "Tip." Mr. Walsh is about 6 ft. tall and weighs 195 pounds. His full mustache is reddish although his hair is brown. His eyes are his most striking feature. They are blue and seem to pierce through and through a man. He was dressed in a sack suit of tweed which looked as though he had worn it for some time without pressing and which might have cost when new about $25.[7]

PROMOTER OF THE WEST

Back home, Walsh wanted to show western Colorado to his friend, the president. In early 1901, learning that the McKinleys would pass through the state on a June railroad excursion, Walsh invited them to be his guests in Glenwood Springs. Sounding like an enthusiastic local booster, Tom touted the resort town's many attributes in a March 27 letter to George Cortelyou, McKinley's secretary. They included "an ideal elevation, a ride of an hour or so over the good roads of the nearby mountains, a plunge in the pool, good music and some fresh mountain trout, and above all absolute rest amidst beautiful scenery."[8] The excited Denver press picked up the tone, predicting an elaborate reception in Glenwood Springs, since the Walsh hospitality had become unequaled in Washington. Gold souvenirs and fine china were to be the order of the day, with every room in the Colorado Hotel specially redecorated.

Sadly, the extravaganza was called off in May because of Mrs. McKinley's illness, although Walsh made one last unsuccessful attempt at convincing the presidential party that the bracing air and mineral baths might cure what ailed the First Lady. It was to no avail, so Tom thanked Secretary Cortelyou for his hard work by sending him Glenwood Springs souvenirs, including a card case made of Colorado gold and silver adorned with the state flower, the columbine.

The Coloradans did not give up easily, however. Word of a new Walsh plan soon reached the press, a summer-long house party for Washington society leaders in Ouray. Probably an exaggeration from the start, the idea was soon replaced by the July 1901 celebration of the opening of the Walsh Library. Tom Walsh had failed in his first attempt to entertain a president in the state he loved. Later, he would succeed. In the meantime, his reputation as a charming and graceful host, perhaps even an extravagant one, was making its mark on the society he wanted to impress. The pattern was set for him to be friend and confidante of three consecutive presidents and other prominent citizens of the nation's capital. In 1902, when Tom joined the exclusive Metropolitan Club of Washington, his sponsor was Secretary of State John Hay. Considered by historians to be one of the greatest secretaries in U.S. history, Hay could trace his role in Washington back to his days as personal secretary to Abraham Lincoln. Hay's wife, Clara, later recommended Evalyn to the exclusive Dobbs Ferry Girls School.[9]

More high-level appointments awaited the renowned host and promoter. In 1903, Colorado governor James Peabody appointed Walsh to the Colorado World's Fair Commission, a body of seven prominent citizens assigned to use $100,000 in appropriated state funds to display Colorado's resources the following year in St. Louis. Another appointee was Mrs. Leonel Ross Anthony, better known to *Denver Post* readers by her pen name, Polly Pry. Despite Polly's tendency to scrutinize and criticize the affairs of the rich and famous, she and Walsh no doubt got along well. The previous year Tom had granted Polly an interview at the all-male Denver Club. Accustomed to find Colorado's *nouveau riche* living in misery over their wealth, she found the opposite in Walsh. This millionaire was down-to-earth and accommodating but also happy and self-assured: "The calm serenity of his look, the air of bonhomie with which he shakes hands, the twinkle of his Irish eyes and the sincerity of his voice, proclaim the man who would make the best of any situation on earth."[10] She was astounded that such a man also hosted $20,000 dinners.

Walsh did have to employ tact and even humility in some of the new situations his prominence presented. In 1902 Henry Teller, the senator Tom had refused to challenge, selected Evalyn to christen the new battleship *Colorado*. The choice aroused criticism from *The Denver Post* and some Colorado citizens, who felt Cora Peabody, the governor's daughter, deserved the honor more than a millionaire's daughter. Teller remained firm, but as the controversy heated to a point Tom may have found ridiculous, he "cheerfully, willingly, and of my own volition" withdrew Evalyn's name. Earlier in 1902, Walsh had donated Camp Bird gold for the casting of the sponsor's badge at the launch of the cruiser *Denver*. He probably felt he had received sufficient acclaim for his role in establishing Colorado's connection to the growing U.S. Navy.[11]

THE PRESIDENT'S MINING ADVISER

In September 1901 the assassination of President William McKinley shocked the nation. It came a year after Tom Walsh and other Americans had displayed their national pride at the Paris Exposition and only a few months after Walsh had planned the Glenwood Springs reception in the president's honor. Vice President Theodore Roosevelt assumed the duties of the nation's highest office at age forty-two, the youngest man ever to hold the job (then and now). The new president and Tom Walsh were friends. They may have met as early as September 1900 when Colorado senator Edward O. Wolcott feted vice presidential candidate Roosevelt at Wolhurst, the senator's estate near Denver. Many prominent Colorado Republicans were present at the occasion. Walsh had been a guest at Wolhurst for such events and liked the estate so much that he later bought it. Now, following the nation's tragedy, he offered his friend condolences and encouragement that "[t]he outpouring of sincere love for our martyred President and the great trust and confidence reposed in our new President fills the patriot with throbs of joy and makes him feel proud of being an American citizen."[12]

Walsh was not Roosevelt's premier political representative in Colorado, as is sometimes suggested. That honor fell to Philip B. Stewart, a rich and influential citizen of Colorado Springs who was also a hunting partner of Roosevelt's (something to which the animal-loving Walsh would never aspire). Stewart's main job was to build a political base and dispense federal patronage, the type of political work Walsh did not find attractive. Nonetheless, the new president could count on Walsh for advice and make use of his rising influence. One of Roosevelt's great concerns was labor strife, a growing problem early in his administration. While organized labor such as the Western Federation of Miners (WFM) might disparage the rich Republican in the White House, Roosevelt could claim credit for settling a major mining labor dispute in 1902. He successfully brought labor and management to the table to stop a crippling and violent Pennsylvania coal strike, the first time a U.S. president had confronted and resolved such a problem. His willingness to accommodate the requests of United Mine Workers president John Mitchell shocked some conservatives.

Tom Walsh knew something about dealing with mine laborers, and in 1904 Roosevelt sought his help in Colorado. Strikes at mines, mills, and smelters shook Cripple Creek, Telluride, Trinidad, and other mining areas with unprecedented violence. On June 6, 1904, an anarchist dynamited the railroad station at Independence, a small mining town near Cripple Creek, killing thirteen men and wounding many more. Most of the victims were nonunion laborers. Many local residents and nearly all mine owners blamed the WFM. The previous year the miners' union had aggressively recruited members in the local mines, then called them all out on strike and intimidated both owners and nonunion workers. Republican governor James Peabody had called in the state militia in 1903, at the behest of the Cripple Creek District Mine Owners' and Operators' Association. In time, the owners' group and the militia were charged with their share of intimidation, leading some to believe they might actually have carried out the bombing at the station. Now faced with an even larger tragedy, Peabody once again ordered the militia and its allies in law enforcement to intervene. They moved swiftly, rounding up WFM members, throwing them on railcars, and deporting them to the Kansas line where they were left to fend for themselves. The building housing a pro-union newspaper in Victor, near Cripple Creek, was destroyed.

Theodore Roosevelt received requests and accusations from both sides. Typical of these was a letter from a Denver attorney named John Murphy, beseeching the president to rein in the militia and enclosing tragic clippings from Colorado newspapers. One tale told the sad fate of W. H. Morgan, a Cripple Creek mine owner and union sympathizer. Morgan had swallowed poison after receiving threats from the militia. Roosevelt believed Peabody had overreacted, creating the impression he was motivated by the opinions of mine owners rather than by a desire for law and order. Should he intervene, as he had in Pennsylvania?[13]

Against this backdrop of confusing and heartrending reports, Roosevelt turned to the cool and knowledgeable Tom Walsh for an answer. The president had just appointed Walsh as a delegate to the 1904 American Mining Congress. By Evalyn's account, Roosevelt now asked her father to use his influence to settle the disturbed conditions in the mines. She remembered that the presidential demand forced cancellation of a 1904 trip to Europe and sent the family to an unimpressive part of Colorado, which she described as the "littlest hole I ever got into in my life." Beyond this, she could remember little of her father's role in the matter. Where exactly the family traveled is unknown, but it is unlikely that Walsh would have taken his family to a strife-torn area.

Tom reported his views to the Denver press on June 26, 1904 (including his affirmation of noncandidacy for the U.S. Senate). He and his family were staying with friends at Denver's posh Brown Palace Hotel (which hardly matches Evalyn's description of their Colorado destination). Walsh addressed a hotel crowd that included reporters and some of his former employees. He stressed the need for law and order. He felt that radicals in control of the labor movement should be replaced by more conservative leaders, such as those guiding the Brotherhood of Locomotive Engineers. Walsh could speak from experience, for "[w]hen I was in Ouray I had occasional trouble with my men, but I always appealed to the wiser and conservative members of the union and always managed to compromise matters." As for the governor's decision to call out the militia, "The masses of people in the East seem to uphold Governor Peabody. They feel that the acts of the military have at times been somewhat severe, but they also do not lose sight of the fact that had the military not interfered there probably would have been lots of hanging by vigilante committees." When asked what the president's role would be, Walsh replied that he was satisfied that Roosevelt had not committed himself on the subject. "The President," he assured the crowd, "is a conservative and shrewd man and will not venture any opinions or expressions until he has carefully examined . . . both sides. . . . The things for which President Roosevelt is criticized are the very ones for which he ought to receive commendation. He showed his regard for the welfare of the people in the Pennsylvania strike in taking a hand in the matter; also by throttling unlawful combinations of capital."

Walsh found it impossible for Roosevelt to take a role in the proceedings in this state, where he felt the troubles were different from those in the Pennsylvania crisis: "In Colorado the state government has taken the matter in hand, and is thoroughly able to cope with the situation. Any interference on his part in this state would be unwarranted. In Pennsylvania the state machinery took no hand in the proceedings and President Roosevelt stepped in and settled the strike."[14]

Later, in a July 3 letter to Roosevelt, Walsh gave a similar report, concluding that "the labor troubles will soon disappear. The Western Federation of Miners are greatly if not almost wholly to blame for the terrible crimes that have been committed. The militia, whilst they may have been harsh in their actions, have certainly prevented wholesale lynchings in Cripple Creek." The remainder of Walsh's letter concerns Roosevelt's 1904 election campaign, in which Tom had been quite active. He states that he will next travel to Indianapolis as part of a delegation to notify Indiana senator Thomas Fairbanks of his nomination as vice president. Roosevelt, seeking election as president for the first time, was concerned that labor problems might cost him the Colorado vote. He remembered that in 1900, as McKinley's running mate, their staunch rhetoric in favor of the gold standard had cost them the vote of this pro-silver state.

In the end, Roosevelt took Walsh's advice and refrained from any intervention in Colorado's difficulties. Even after Colorado's two senators, Henry Teller and Thomas M. Patterson (both Democrats), petitioned the president for assistance, he found no reason for federal intervention. Instead he left matters to his old Rough Rider friend, Colorado adjutant general and militia commander Sherman Bell, whose heavy-handed tactics against labor supporters resulted in a costly victory for mine owners.

Roosevelt did order an investigation by his commissioner of labor, Carroll D. Wright. Wright's official report of the disturbance, finding fault with both sides, reached the president's desk in January 1905. However, the strike had ended in midsummer 1904, as predicted by Walsh, with the mines reopening to largely nonunion labor. Theodore Roosevelt and his running mate, Thomas Fairbanks, won an overwhelming victory in the 1904 election, carrying Colorado and most other states. Roosevelt continued to receive low marks from the WFM, however. Tom Walsh had severely criticized the organization, yet he received the same treatment the union had nearly always given him: silence.[15]

A SPOKESMAN FOR PROGRESSIVE IDEAS

The president and the mining millionaire shared many beliefs about democracy and the treatment of working Americans. In his speeches, Roosevelt extolled the need for equal justice and equality, without distinction based on wealth and privilege. To modern historians he did not completely carry out the true meaning of those statements, especially in the area of racial discrimination. Nonetheless, these were unusual statements for a U.S. president up to that time, followed by unusual action. Theodore Roosevelt also became famous for his attack on business combinations, seen as attempts by the rich to succeed at the expense of the poor. Walsh publicly espoused similar ideas, making him an unusual millionaire for the time. While his friend the president won the votes of appreciative citizens, Walsh did not use his rhetoric to climb the elected political ladder.

Walsh did succeed, however, as an early advocate of Roosevelt's conservation policies, especially in the area of irrigation. With the president's blessing, given in a May 4, 1903, speech in Denver, Tom became a founder and the first president of the National Irrigation Association. He did not have to look far from his old home in Ouray to see the need. To the north, the Uncompahgre River flowed through a fertile but largely undeveloped area around the towns of Montrose and Delta. Early settlers found enough water in the valley bottoms for raising cattle and growing orchards but could not bring water to higher lands that also held the potential to be productive. Pleas to bring irrigation to this and similar areas of the West reached the ears of Walsh and of Roosevelt.

The National Irrigation Association worked closely with the president, cabinet officials, and Congress to secure passage of the 1902 National Irrigation Act, also known as the Newlands Act (named after its sponsoring senator, even though the name might also signify the law's purpose). The new law provided for a reclamation fund, built from assessments on the proceeds of sale of public lands in sixteen western states, together with all the mechanisms to start extensive irrigation projects. It also created the Reclamation Bureau within the Department of the Interior to carry out the purposes of the act.

The new bureau's pilot project was irrigation of the Uncompahgre Valley, where many believed arable lands could be increased from 30,000 acres to 175,000 acres through water diversion. The project got under way in 1905, as engineers drilled a 5.8-mile tunnel from the Black Canyon of the Gunnison River under the Vernal Mesa and into the open lands east of Montrose. Since the east tunnel portal on the Gunnison actually lay higher than the lands to be irrigated, the downward-sloping tunnel would supply a large quantity of water to lands located too high for earlier irrigation efforts. An extensive system of canals further expanded the irrigation network. By 1909, new water through the tunnel reached the Uncompahgre Valley. The project was not completed without cost overruns and other problems, yet in the end it made vast new acreage productive and set a model for other western land reclamation.[16]

Walsh felt one major benefit of irrigation was its aid to ordinary citizens who wanted land for a new life away from crowded cities. On October 6, 1902, he delivered his presidential address, "The Humanitarian Aspect of National Irrigation," to the National Irrigation Association Convention in Colorado Springs. Walsh lauded the roles of President Roosevelt, Secretary of the Interior E. A. Hitchcock, Secretary of Agriculture James Wilson, and friends in Congress for obtaining passage of the National Irrigation Act. The act had created the addition of "a new empire as important as that drained by the Mississippi River and its tributaries." This was not what was foremost in Walsh's mind at the moment, however. Rather, it was providing for those persons with "the pressure of poverty upon them, and the haunting fear of future want." They could be found in many places but especially "in great cities, where the very forces which have created our present prosperity as a nation have also operated to make a certain fringe of half-employed and semi-prosperous." For them, the new law would bring "the dream of home and independence which will come to many a struggling family with the announcement that one more fair valley of Arid America has been thrown open to settlement."[17]

Walsh continued to be active in the association for several years. After it merged with the Trans-Mississippi Congress, he served as the 1908–1909 president of the larger organization. Its goal was also development of the West. Tom also worked on another aspect of that development, the Good Roads Movement. He addressed the group's November 1900 convention in Chicago and remained a vital part of the push for better routes to and through the West. In 1906 he brought the Good Roads Conference to Denver. Theodore Roosevelt sent a congratulatory telegram to Walsh and his fellow conferees, praising their work in an area he strongly supported. At the conference a bill was drawn up for creation of the Colorado State Highway Commission and for a system of state roads planned and constructed under the commission's guidance. The measure did not pass the Colorado legislature that year, but the good road advocates persisted. On May 5, 1909, the State Highway Commission became a reality.

Tom Walsh had become comfortable in his role as the guiding light for organizations promoting the good of the West and many other causes as well. He loved being the chairman who could preside at conventions, deliver keynote addresses, and lend his influential name to causes. Of course, he had few rivals in the world of entertainment for convention-goers. He seems to have held less love for the more political aspects, such as lobbying, leaving these tasks to others. Little communication has survived in which Walsh directly contacted legislators seeking their support. His influence was more "behind the scenes," and his name appears only twice in the Congressional Record during the years 1900–1910. In 1903 he was appointed a member of the Memorial Association of the District of Columbia. On May 21, 1908, his letter favoring establishment of the U.S. Bureau of Mines and Mining, and referring to the importance of such rare minerals as vanadium and radium, was read into the House Record.

On one occasion, however, Walsh did make a different sort of goodwill gesture toward the members of the U.S. Senate. In a letter dated March 5, 1908, Charles G. Burnett, the secretary of the Senate, heartily thanked Tom for his gift of a case of whiskey, adding, "I can only get square by telling the senators what a fine fellow you are and what a privilege I consider it to call you my friend." No legislation pertaining to causes supported by Walsh was before the Senate at the time. However, Tom Walsh could count a number of senators, as well as Burnett, as his personal friends.[18]

Thomas F. Walsh, 1850–1910. Courtesy, Colorado Historical Society.

Carrie Bell Reed Walsh, 1859–1932. Courtesy, Colorado Historical Society.

Tom Walsh with his son, Vinson, and daughter, Evalyn. Courtesy, Western History Department, Denver Public Library.

Early view of downtown Leadville, Colorado, showing Tom Walsh's Grand Hotel. Courtesy, Western History Department, Denver Public Library.

Attorney Charles Spaulding Thomas, future Colorado governor and U.S. senator, rented an office from Walsh in the Grand Hotel building. The two men became lifelong friends, and Thomas frequently represented Walsh in business deals and litigation. Courtesy, Colorado Historical Society.

Andy Richardson discovered Ouray County's Imogene Basin, naming it for his wife. Believing it held only silver values, he showed the area to his friend Tom Walsh, who "struck it rich" in gold. Richardson continued to help Walsh with the early development of the Camp Bird Mine. Courtesy, Ouray County Historical Society and the Collection of Doris H. Gregory.

A historic and spectacular view of Ouray, Colorado, seen from a nearby mountain. Courtesy, Colorado Historical Society.

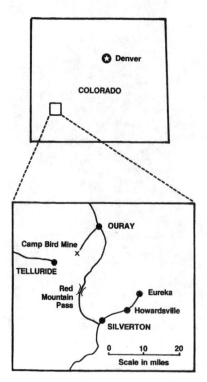

Location of the Camp Bird Mine in southwestern Colorado and in relation to local towns and landmarks. Courtesy, Tom Rosemeyer.

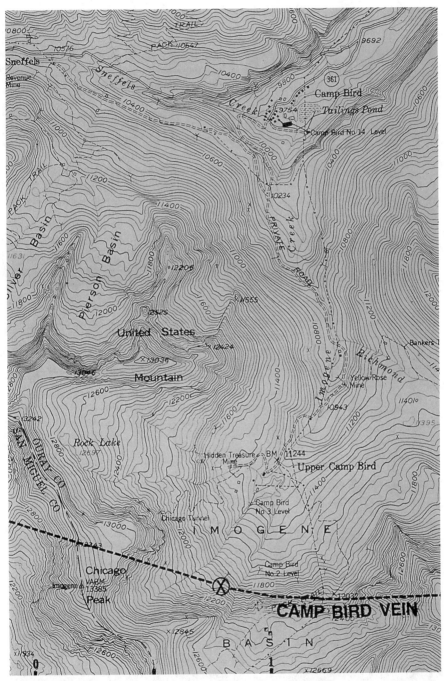

Topographical map showing the Camp Bird Mine, its surroundings, and the location of the Camp Bird vein and Tom Walsh's discovery of rich gold ore in the Gertrude claim. Courtesy, Tom Rosemeyer.

The 3-level of the Camp Bird Mine at 11,200 feet, showing mine workings and the famed Walsh boardinghouse on the right. Courtesy, Colorado Historical Society.

The dining room of the boardinghouse. Its food was rated on a par with the finest local hotels. Courtesy, Western History Department, Denver Public Library.

The miners' club room in the boardinghouse, a rarity among the normally sparse living accommodations in western mines of the time. Courtesy, Ouray County Historical Society and the Collections of Arthur Erickson and Doris H. Gregory.

The Camp Bird Mine's Bleichert aerial tramway hauled ore down the mountain and miners in both directions. Courtesy, Colorado Historical Society.

Tom Walsh in his office at the Camp Bird Mine. Courtesy, Ouray County Historical Society and the Collection of Ruth and Marvin Gregory.

The Camp Bird mills, in a photograph taken a few years after Walsh sold the mine in 1902. The lines of the tramway can be seen descending from the mountain to the right. Courtesy, Ouray County Historical Society.

Walsh used the proceeds of his rich gold mine to construct the sixty-room "Walsh Palace" at 2020 Massachusetts Avenue in Washington, D.C. Finished in 1903, it became the scene of some of the city's most lavish entertaining. Courtesy, Colorado Historical Society.

The grand staircase of the Walsh Palace, said to resemble that of an ocean liner. Courtesy, Colorado Historical Society.

The first-floor main drawing room at 2020 Massachusetts Avenue. Courtesy, Colorado Historical Society.

In the summer of 1905 the Walsh family sublet Beaulieu, a Newport, Rhode Island, "cottage," from Cornelius Vanderbilt. Their idyllic summer ended in tragedy when their son, Vinson, was killed and their daughter, Evalyn, seriously injured in an automobile accident. Courtesy, Colorado Historical Society.

Grief over their son's death brought the Walsh family back to Colorado, where they purchased the thirty-two-room Wolhurst mansion in Littleton, with its 534-acre grounds, from the estate of former Colorado U.S. senator Edward O. Wolcott. Courtesy, Littleton Historical Museum Collection.

Tom Walsh loved animals, serving as president of the Colorado Humane Society. This sign at Wolhurst, and a similar one at the Camp Bird Mine, expressed his feelings. Courtesy, Littleton Historical Museum Collection.

This Estate was Renamed "CLONMEL" by the President of the United States WILLIAM HOWARD TAFT on the occasion of his visit to MR. and MRS. THOMAS F. WALSH September 22nd 1909

President William Howard Taft assisted Tom Walsh in rechristening his Littleton estate "Clonmel" at a gala event in September 1909. Courtesy, Western History Department, Denver Public Library.

President Taft and Carrie Walsh stroll the grounds of the newly christened Clonmel estate. Courtesy, Western History Department, Denver Public Library.

Tom Walsh addresses the Pikes Peak Centennial Celebration in Colorado Springs in 1906. His speech, calling for a federal income tax and a department of savings banks to aid the poor, was deemed a plan for "modified socialism" by The Denver Post. *It may have cost Walsh a seat in the U.S. Senate, although his general lack of interest in politics was a larger reason. Courtesy, Colorado Historical Society.*

Simon Guggenheim, the Pueblo, Colorado, "smelter king" and Tom Walsh's friend, succeeded in winning the 1906 Senate race after expending large sums from his personal fortune. Courtesy, Colorado Historical Society.

Walsh formed a long-term friendship with the controversial King Leopold II of Belgium, also acting as his mining adviser. Walsh attempted to defend his royal friend against charges that the king led a promiscuous lifestyle and permitted atrocities in the Congo. From the July 1902 edition of the American Monthly Review of Reviews.

David Frakes Day received international acclaim as the flamboyantly outspoken editor of Ouray's Solid Muldoon. *Later, as editor of the* Durango Democrat, *Day castigated Walsh for his friendship with King Leopold II. Courtesy, Colorado Historical Society.*

THE PRICE OF AFFLUENCE

CHAPTER TEN

KEEPING BLACKMAILERS AT BAY

Wealth and prominence carry a darker side as well. All too soon, Tom Walsh found that lawyers and courtrooms were as big a part of his life as testimonial dinners, impressive appointments, and mention for political office. Rivals and their legal counsel came forward, claiming rights to the rich Camp Bird properties and unpaid commissions, while others sought a variety of damages. Walsh fought these efforts and sometimes won, but he usually settled out of court. To his dismay, more of his fortune was passing to his lawyers than he wished.

In one celebrated case, a New York attorney named Detlef Hanson claimed that while living in Ouray, Walsh had engaged in an affair with his client, a woman named Violet Watson. His complaint accused Tom of promising the young woman marriage and wealth. Watson had spent one summer in Ouray, and she could have met Walsh. Little else was proven as to any liaison between the two. However, attorney Hanson was known for bringing such lawsuits against rich and prominent persons and doggedly pursuing them until the defendant tired and offered settlement money. The state of New York deemed his persistent efforts to get money from Walsh so frivolous that Hanson was disbarred. Walsh and his lawyers settled with Violet Watson in an undisclosed agreement. Undaunted, Hanson sought to regain his license to practice law and even sued his own client for betraying him by accepting the settlement with Walsh without his knowledge. The same suit accused Tom and his lawyers of conspiracy to rid Hanson of his livelihood. Suits by Hanson continued even after Walsh's death, all of them unsuccessful.[1]

"Blackmailers!" screamed a 1901 edition of a newspaper friendly to Walsh, the Ouray *Plaindealer.* Still, some Ouray townspeople were willing to risk shame to make a buck off the wealthy and popular Tom Walsh. That same year a local group organized a company known as the Camp Bird Extension. It staked mining claims in portions of the Imogene Basin that Walsh had either missed or felt were not worth acquiring. Camp Bird Extension's president, James H. Robin, was an old antagonist dating back to Tom's earliest days in Silverton, and its fiscal agent was none other than John Thompson. The company allegedly drilled a tunnel toward the Camp Bird vein, offering reports of its progress to the mining press. One November 1903 report actually disclosed a rich strike of gold-bearing quartz. However, little more, at least in the way of mining developments, was heard from the Camp Bird Extension. Its main purpose seems to have been to create a nuisance for the larger Camp Bird Mine.

Under the federal Mining Law of 1872, the owner of a lode mining claim might pursue "apex" rights. If a vein reached the surface or had its highest point, known as its apex, on the claim, the owner could follow that vein down underground past the side lines of the claim. Therefore, even though valuable ore deposits might be found directly under one claim, the holder of a nearby claim could still be declared the owner of those deposits upon proof that they were part of a vein structure that "apexed" on his or her property. Apex lawsuits were a favorite of western mining lawyers. Obviously, proof of a continuous vein that apexed elsewhere could be difficult to obtain. It might be necessary to hire trained geologists to testify as expert witnesses on the location and direction of the vein structure (real or as geologically projected). In places such as the Imogene Basin, where ores occurred in shoots rather than continuously, a continuous vein would have been especially hard to prove. Nevertheless, claim owners often settled apex suits rather than go to the time and expense of hiring lawyers and experts and conducting trials. Therefore, the owner of a claim having little or no value might, through persistence, obtain a cash settlement or outright purchase of the claim from a rich neighbor wishing to dispose of the lawsuit. That is what the Camp Bird Extension hoped to accomplish.

In this case Walsh refused to settle, deciding instead to fight in the District Court for Ouray County. In a series of suits and countersuits, neither Walsh nor the Camp Bird Extension emerged a clear winner. The court's 1908 rulings found Walsh to be the owner of some of the claims in dispute and the Camp Bird Extension the owner of others. The suits had little impact on the success of the Camp Bird Mine, but the Camp Bird Extension Mining Company disappeared soon after the verdicts were handed down. Its founder, James H. Robin, committed suicide over his company's failure. As often happened, the only real winners were probably the lawyers. In this and other cases, Walsh continued to fight suits involving title to Camp Bird property after he had actually sold that property, out of both agreement with the buyers and his own sense of moral obligation.[2]

A Maine corporation, the Cosmopolitan Mining Company, claimed it had not received proper notice of the sheriff's sale that resulted in Walsh's purchase of the Gertrude, Hidden Treasure, and other claims. The Cosmopolitan, a company that was never successful at anything other than initiating litigation, had acquired the interest of the bankrupt Allied Mines Company. Cosmopolitan had performed a small amount of tunnel work but was in bad economic condition in 1896 when the Ouray County sheriff seized all of its property, including the mining claims, for nonpayment of a debt to a freight-hauling company. Service of the notice of the suit was presented to John M. Jardine, onetime mayor of Ouray and now the alleged agent for Cosmopolitan.

For some time following the sheriff's sale of the claims, deemed of little value at that time, no attempt had been made to amend or set aside the sale. After it became public knowledge that Camp Bird's success was based largely on the Gertrude's wealth, Cosmopolitan came back to life. In a 1900 suit filed in the Federal District Court for Colorado, Cosmopolitan's principals claimed that Jardine was not in fact their company's agent and that therefore the sheriff's sale was invalid, entitling them to be declared the owners of the claims. Such ownership would mean that Walsh must buy back the claims at their present value and give Cosmopolitan all earnings to date, a proposition worth more than $1 million. After numerous filings, hearings, and postponements, the matter came to trial in June 1902, with Charles S. Thomas representing Walsh. Judge Marshall of the U.S. Circuit Court for the District of Colorado ruled that Jardine was in fact the company's agent and directed a verdict in favor of Walsh, who was also awarded his court costs. Nonetheless, Cosmopolitan appealed to the U.S. Supreme Court in 1903. In 1904 the highest court in the land dismissed Cosmopolitan's suit for want of jurisdiction. Walsh was finally victorious, but at great costs of time and money.[3]

BETRAYAL BY AN OLD FRIEND

For Tom, no lawsuit was likely more heartbreaking than one brought by his old friend John Thompson. Their many discussions and trips to the mountains had occurred when Tom was a smelter manager and mining promoter of no great standing. His work with Thompson produced no tangible results, probably because, as Tom discovered early on, Thompson knew little about mining. The two families remained on cordial terms as late as 1900, when they traveled to Europe together. Walsh even loaned Thompson money on various occasions, none of which was repaid. Nonetheless, jealousy of his friend's success was foremost in Thompson's mind, and he devised a scheme to lay his hands on some of the Camp Bird's profits. He first tried blackmail. Writing to Walsh in late 1900 and early 1901, Thompson intimated that he possessed certain personal letters that could be damaging to Walsh's reputation. The nature of the letters and what it might take to make them go away are matters Thompson omitted from print. However, in personal meetings and other communication, it became obvious that his old friend, like attorney Hanson, was claiming that Walsh had engaged in an affair with a young woman in Ouray. John Thompson was, of course, only acting as his protective friend in this matter.

Whatever the asking price for the friendship, Walsh rebuffed the offer and contacted his attorney. Charles Thomas found that a Mrs. Noble and her daughter, Hazel Pughsley, were involved. He sent investigators to Ouray and to Duluth, Minnesota, where the family was from. The Ouray investigations soon bore fruit. Walsh could not remember ever having met the two women. However, as Thomas discovered, a former domestic in the Noble household had an interesting story to tell. As the attorney told his client, "Mrs. Nobel [sic] was prone to speak of you to Hazel on all possible occasions. She urged Hazel to make herself as agreeable to you as possible and to spare no pains in that direction. She invited you to dinner two or three times and on each time dressed Hazel herself or superintended her dressing in order that she might be made as attractive as possible. That Hazel was particularly instructed about wearing low neck dresses on these occasions, with as much of a bosom exposure as was consistent with social requirements. That on each occasion you failed to appear, in consequence of which the old lady was very angry and Hazel very much disappointed." Thomas's investigation also turned up proof that the two women had tried to blackmail at least one other man in Ouray.[4]

Thompson's scheme had backfired, so he turned to the justice system for help. In June 1903 his attorney served his summons and complaint on Walsh and filed it with the Supreme Court for New York County, where the Thompsons now lived. The complaint alleged that plaintiff Thompson and defendant Walsh had been working as partners since 1894, in different parts of Colorado. Then, in 1896, Walsh had invited the plaintiff to Ouray County where the two would prospect in certain areas and share anything of value that was found. Interestingly, while the complaint mentions operations in the Imogene Basin, the only two claims alleged to have been examined according to the agreement were the Oro Cache and the Chicago. The larger Camp Bird property is not mentioned. Walsh, Thompson further alleged, had dismissed these two claims as holding little mineral value (which in point of fact was the truth). A disappointed Thompson then moved to New York, where late in 1900 Walsh informed him that the Oro Cache had in fact proven very valuable. Thompson sought damages for the value of his share of the partnership and for the fraud perpetrated upon him.

An enraged Walsh sent the complaint to his New York attorney, Julian T. Davies Sr., telling him in the cover letter:

> I am sending you a summons of a small piece of attempt at blackmail, made by a creature whom my family and myself had done innumerable services for. The allegations he makes can be contradicted by the hundreds, and if necessary, by the thousands. The case does not involve any interests of value whatever, and, as I said, can be readily disproved. There is another side to it, however: This man Thompson has been so ungrateful, has proven himself such a notorious scoundrel, that I am very anxious to land him in the penitentiary if I can. I am sending you with this, a hurriedly drawn memorandum of my experiences with him, and also my answers to the allegations he has made.

Tom's answers to the complaint denied most of Thompson's claims. He declared nearly all of the alleged prior dealings to be false. With regard to the Oro Cache claim, its samples showed no value, and "Walsh gave up the idea of purchasing that prospect at that time, and it was only until some months afterwards that he bought it, and a great number of other claims, regardless of their value, but to protect himself against blackmailers." As for the fraud allegation, "Walsh never practiced an atom of fraud in his life and he never will."

Julian Davies succeeded in having the case transferred to the U.S. Circuit Court of Appeals and then filed a demurrer, asking that it be dismissed on grounds such as wanting in equity, failure to state contract terms in definite and certain terms, no interest shown in the subject matter, and inadequate consideration.

Especially damning was Thompson's claim that, despite continuing as a resident of Ouray until 1900 and having frequent contact with Walsh, he did not hear of the Camp Bird Mine until the New York contact in late 1900. By October 1903 Davies had good news for his client. Judge Wallace in the United States Circuit Court of Appeals had not only sustained the demurrer to the entire bill and dismissed it on the spot with costs but also went so far as to say that he did not think Thompson and his counsel would ever be able to draw a good bill of complaint.[5]

Thompson and his attorneys did not give up easily. They filed a new case in the same court in December 1903. The new, amended complaint was more carefully drawn. The alleged sharing agreement between the two men now included most of Ouray County, and Thompson had contributed large sums of money to the venture. While Thompson still claimed no knowledge of Walsh's success until late 1900, the extent of that success now included the entire Camp Bird property, not just two claims. All this was included in the partnership the plaintiff had been denied, and he prayed he might receive his share of the property and the profits and proceeds from sales it had produced.

The case dragged on in the court for more than two years. Tom and his attorneys mustered the support of a large number of his colleagues, past and present, who knew anything of his dealings with and without Thompson. Former partner David Wegg abruptly dismissed a request for assistance by Thompson's attorneys and threw his considerable support and influence behind his old friend. As a result of deception by Thompson, Andy Richardson inadvertently made statements that might have backed the former's position. However, upon discovering what had happened, he quickly corrected his statement in favor of Walsh. Even Mrs. Noble and Hazel came forward, claiming that they too had been victims of Thompson's. In seventy-eight pages of transcripted testimony, Walsh and his witnesses succeeded in contradicting most of Thompson's claims. The alleged letter from Walsh to Thompson detailing their agreement had somehow disappeared. Several witnesses attacked Thompson's lack of knowledge of the Camp Bird, and Thompson admitted that he had read newspapers lauding its success. Thompson's involvement in the Camp Bird Extension was a further contradiction, for he had assisted that company by placing New York ads that touted the company's plan to cut the Camp Bird vein.[6]

Finally, on August 15, 1905, the court entered judgment in favor of Walsh, awarding him his attorney's fees and costs. Thompson immediately appealed. By November 1905, Tom's legal expenses in the suit exceeded $25,000. Tom was under intense personal strain as well. On February 26, 1906, Attorney Davies argued all afternoon on his motion to dismiss Thompson's appeal. In a March 9 hearing, as Davies explained to Walsh, he intended to "examine Thompson in supplementary proceedings, and endeavor to discover, first, whether he has any property which can be applied to the payment of the judgment; and, second, where his funds for the prosecution of his action against you came from." Thompson failed to appear, his default noted by the referee.

Nonetheless, Thompson and his lawyers had shown incredible tenacity and could be counted on to present at least one more delay tactic, however frivolous. Walsh had the right to expect that the court would award him every cent of his extensive attorney's fees and court costs on account of that frivolity. Still, on March 23, the attorneys for the parties agreed to a settlement. The suit was dismissed the following day, the actual terms of settlement undisclosed. However, appended to the back of a letter from Davies to Walsh is the notation, "Deed conveying tax title to be executed to Mrs. Thomas F. Walsh, Last Quarter Mine at Cripple Creek." That property had been the only project the two men ever developed alone, with no other parties involved, and they had placed title in their wives' names. Walsh had left the Last Quarter in the care of Thompson, who failed to pay real estate taxes but later redeemed the property in his wife's name only. For all their time, legal expense, and frustration, the one thing the Walshes had to show was a mining claim, half of which they already rightfully owned. However, it may have represented a large part of the Thompsons' worldly belongings. Tom Walsh was rid of John Thompson once and for all. He may well have heeded the advice given by more than a few lawyers that a bad settlement usually beats a good trial.[7]

THE WALSH PALACE

CHAPTER ELEVEN

EXPECTATION FOR CONSPICUOUS CONSUMPTION

As Tom Walsh managed his successful mine and dealt with his attorneys, he and his family climbed ever higher in the society they wanted to impress. Soon the magical house at the corner of LeRoy and Phelps was not enough. In April 1901, Tom purchased 26,000 square feet of land on Massachusetts Avenue, N.W., a newly fashionable D.C. neighborhood. Soon thereafter, he commissioned Danish-born New York architect Henry Andersen to build his dream. Andersen had received acclaim in the nation's largest city for designing a variety of works, including many residences, apartment houses, and churches. Among his works were the Don Carlos Apartments, 76th Street and Madison Avenue; Acadia Apartments, 115th Street at 7th and St. Nicholas; Sans Souci Apartments, 30–32 West 124th Street; and the Lutheran Church of the Covenant—all in New York City. Now he set forth designing what an adoring Colorado press termed

"The Walsh Palace." Andersen's building permit, filed October 16, 1901, estimated the cost at $300,000. It would eventually reach $835,000.

Proud that Colorado would "contribute to Washington one more residence of the highest type," *The Denver Times* proudly presented the initial plans to its readers in its October 18, 1901, edition. Walsh's Massachusetts Avenue palace would have a frontage of 80 feet and a depth of 100 feet, with sixty rooms. Four stories high, in French Renaissance style, the exterior construction would be of granite and light brick. Entering the first floor, guests would find a main hall 20 feet wide, with a reception room to the right and drawing rooms and a library to the left, all of which together could form one salon 100 feet in length. A large dining room occupied the rear of the first floor. All floors above the first were to be served by an electric elevator. The family would occupy the second floor, with a breakfast room and sitting rooms in addition to spacious bedrooms and baths (whose tubs a later source described as small swimming pools). The third floor would be devoted to entertaining guests, with eight guest chambers and accompanying sitting rooms. The same floor also contained an amusement room, with a stage attached "designed especially for Master Walsh and his friends." It also housed the rooms of a housekeeper and servants. The fourth floor would also serve to entertain guests, containing a handsome ballroom with a lobby 30 feet square, retiring rooms for guests, and sewing rooms. The basement would hold private offices, billiard rooms, wine rooms, electrical apparatus, and space for other uses. The mansard roof of iron and tile surrounded a skylight over a court that extended down to the second floor. For woodwork, the first floor's principal rooms contained mahogany, with Flemish oak in the dining room and a variety of wood elsewhere.[1]

Architect Andersen and the builders carried out the plans largely as predicted by the *Times*. However, as evidenced by the significant rise in costs, some important changes and additions were made. Most notable was a distinctive entryway and central hall rising from the first floor to a stained-glass, domed skylight with a Y-shaped central staircase reminiscent of an ocean liner. The second and third floors overlooked the central hall, with impressive galleries. Eight Roman brick chimneys served eight fireplaces, with a roof garden as well. Vinson's theater was moved from the third to the fourth floor, where Evalyn remembered it sharing space with the ballroom. For musical entertainment, Tom ordered an immense baroque pipe organ. He retained a well-known church organist to serenade diners, even when they only consisted of Carrie and himself. In addition to Renaissance style, the architecture of the finished structure combined baroque and rococo details within an "art-nouveau parti." Ninety years later, two critics of Washington architecture found the total effect "bulbous and vulgarly overblown, rather than gracefully curvilinear." They also noted windows too widely spaced and not graduated in size for the palace architecture. The best feature, the critics felt, was the "copper-clad conservatory on the east façade, with its spectacular stained-glass windows."[2]

The interior of the great house needed furnishings. Tom and Carrie hired the prior owner of their former residence, Mrs. Anna Jenness Miller, to scout around for the best available Persian rugs, French paintings, furniture, and other finery. Miller set up an artist's studio as her New York office just to satisfy the Walshes' demands and even shopped abroad for paintings and bric-a-brac. One of her bills to Tom totaled $550,000, including tapestries from Paris, two Steinway pianos, carpets and rugs worth $23,000, $5,500 for marble, and $8,500 for silverware. The library was so well stocked that the book-loving Carrie feared she might be able to read only about one-tenth of the collection. At a final cost of $2.1 million, incurred over several years, the work was finally done. "How the money went!" exclaimed Evalyn.[3] In reality, her family mirrored the rest of the moneyed class. Economist and social critic Thorstein Veblen later found that a wealthy man like Walsh, "to be accepted into high society . . . had to advertise the existence and extent of his wealth, that is, he had to satisfy the elitist expectation for conspicuous consumption."[4]

SOME FAMOUS NEIGHBORS

The conspicuous consumption of high society was well reflected in the Walshes' new neighborhood. Typical of the local splendor was fashionable Dupont Circle, a block and a half east of 2020 Massachusetts. Here newspaperwoman Eleanor (Cissy) Patterson and her family threw lavish parties in their mansion, earning Cissy a place among the "Three Graces of Washington." The other two graces were Alice Lee Roosevelt (daughter of the president) and Countess Marguerite Cassini (daughter of the Russian ambassador). All three partook of the Walsh family social scene as well. In time, the slightly younger Evalyn became a sort of junior partner to the graces, awed by the casual way they smoked cigarettes and powdered their faces.

Just east on the same block as the Walsh Palace sat the Blaine Mansion at 2000 Massachusetts. Its builder, James G. Blaine, had helped found the Republican Party and then served as House speaker, senator, secretary of state, and unsuccessful presidential candidate. Following his death, the family sold the mansion to inventor George Westinghouse in 1901. Westinghouse, who had revolutionized rail travel with his air brake, soon turned to the new and thriving field of electricity. His generators electrified much of the United States and Europe, and his companies eventually employed 50,000 people. Like Walsh, he enjoyed lavish entertaining. At one party Mrs. Westinghouse is said to have slipped a crisp $100 bill into each napkin of the 100 guests.

A few blocks away, on Sixteenth Street, stood the large red sandstone home of Tipperary landlord William Scully. For a man who had appeared to be a sort of villain in his and Walsh's native country only a few decades before, Scully now held the respect of the U.S. press as the owner of vast tracts of rich land in Illinois, Nebraska, Kansas, and Missouri. His treatment of his tenants was much more benevolent than his past record in Ireland, but Scully preferred to spend most of his time in London. His wife, Angela, and their children enjoyed Washington's social life, getting to know the Walshes well. Any thought of the disparity in their husbands' Irish origins must have been put aside when the families got together. Reporters noted with favor that the Scullys' social star was rising, since Angela Scully frequently assisted Carrie Walsh with her famous Washington entertaining.

Ironically, just before the Walsh Palace arose on the strength of Colorado mining money, a grand residence nearby that had been built and sustained by Nevada and Montana mining money was torn down. William Morris Stewart was a Nevada attorney who rose to prominence in lawsuits over the rich Comstock silver lode. He became the new state's first U.S. senator and a driving force behind enactment of the Mining Law of 1872, which governed the way Tom Walsh and many others prospected for minerals on public lands. In the 1870s Stewart constructed his fabulous, pentagonal, turreted Stewart Castle at 1913 Massachusetts Avenue. It was considered one of the city's earliest grand residences. By some estimates its cost broke Stewart financially, for he soon returned to Nevada to again practice law and rebuild his wealth. The Stewarts nonetheless kept their Washington castle, and when William returned as a senator in the 1890s, his wife, Annie, used it for elegant enter-taining. Then in 1899 they sold the castle to William Andrews Clark. Made fabulously wealthy by Butte, Montana, copper as well as banking and rail-roads, Clark had arrived as his state's senator, only to lose his seat on charges of corruption. He was subsequently reelected but in the meantime had decided not to keep his new mansion. Clark was so rich he could find a large house expendable, and he ordered the castle demolished. At first he planned to build his own new house on the site. After a disagreement over the plans, he built a New York mansion instead. The site remained vacant until erection of a bank in the 1920s.[5]

ENTERTAINING THE ELITE IN A LEGENDARY MANSION

The Walsh family moved into their palace in the fall of 1903. Evalyn would have only grudgingly accepted the word *nouveau* to describe anything to do with the family or their residence at the time. To her, they were "in." Passing cab drivers showed their riders the home of the "Colorado Monte Cristo," one more sight in a special part of the city. 2020 Massachusetts (or just "2020" to the family) became the setting for some of the city's most talked-about social events. One of the first took place on December 8, 1903. The social reporter for Washington's *Evening Star* found it "one of the most sumptuous affairs ever given in the Capital. . . . The dinner table was adorned with yellow orchids of a very beautiful variety, their coloring being the keynote to the superb decoration of the board, where a service of gold made from glittering nuggets taken from the Camp Bird Mine was used for the first time. A recital on the organ in the music room was an accompaniment to dinner." The guest list included Admiral Dewey, Senator and Mrs. Bisland Wetmore, Senator and Mrs. Mark Hanna of Ohio, Senator and Mrs. Chauncey Depew of New York, and Belgian minister and baroness Moncheur.

The honored guest a few weeks later, on December 29, was Miss Alice Roosevelt. At age seventeen, Evalyn was deemed too young to attend the event, which also marked the first time the large Louis XIV salon on the first floor was put to use. The dancing began at eleven in the top-floor ballroom, which Evalyn remembered for "its walls all yellow with brocade, with yellow hangings and yellow fabrics covering all the benches and chairs around the room." She also recalled, "It was one o'clock when the cotillion began, led by Major Charles McCawley of the Marine Corps, and Alice. Sixty couples passed the tables where favours had been piled: gold pencils for men, lace and tortoiseshell fans for the ladies. . . . I got a fan, anyway."[6]

A New Year's Eve party, described later in the *New York Times*, seems to have reached the upper limit for entertaining on a truly grand scale: 325 guests consumed 480 quarts of champagne, 288 fifths of Scotch, 48 quarts of cocktails, 40 gallons of beer, and 35 bottles of miscellaneous liquors. Once again, liquor seems to have been provided to keep the guests happy. Evalyn remembered that her mother never drank, while the light-drinking Tom found that whiskey upset his stomach.

On at least one occasion, Tom called upon an old acquaintance from his mining days to entertain at 2020. He learned that his fellow Deadwood posse member, Captain Jack Crawford, was now well-known on the Chautauqua circuit. In mid-January 1907, the poet-scout presented his Black Hills poetry and stories to ninety guests. Their ranks included ten U.S. senators, twenty congressmen, Vice President Fairbanks, and Mrs. Marshall Field. Walsh later sent Crawford a congratulatory note, assuring him that "Washington is ringing with your praises."[7]

One of the three graces, Countess Marguerite Cassini, placed the Walshes' social life in a different light. As she remembered in her 1956 autobiography:

> Many people smiled behind their backs at Mr. Walsh's social blunders (while continuing to accept his invitations) and Mrs. Walsh was never amused when he talked about the old days when he was only a miner, but I always thought there was something very sweet in his frankness. So many people wanted you to forget their beginnings! In that tremendous mansion of his he had built the ballroom on the highest floor and put in an elevator to reach it. But since they would ask four hundred people and the elevator held only four at a time, it always took an hour and a half for everyone to get up there.[8]

Vinson's attraction to the theater also caught the public's attention. Well before the move to 2020, Tom was supporting his son's interests, with a playhouse over the stables at the LeRoy and Phelps house. Here, in February 1903, *The Denver Times* reported that Vinson and his friends were fitted up with "a real stage, real scenery, a drop curtain, footlights, trapdoors in the stage, wings, dressing rooms and everything that goes to make up a theatre." A real theater produced real plays, and the *Times* reported that the next performance was "Captain Racket," tickets $1 each: "Last year, to belong to Kermit Roosevelt's Rough Riders was the thing for the boys here in Washington. . . . This year, however, the theatre gang holds the center of the stage." Tom paid for an instructor, Charlemagne Koehler, "who really has performed with Booth and Barret." Now, with an even better theater at 2020, Vinson the magician emerged, performing Houdini-like escapes. "You should have heard the loud clapping of Tom Walsh's hands whenever Vinson did a card trick or lifted a live and squirming rabbit from a hat," his sister Evalyn recalled. Her father "loved that boy beyond my powers of expression."[9]

Legends developed about the great Walsh Palace. One held that somewhere in the house Tom had hidden a huge Camp Bird gold nugget. After various rumors surfaced as to its existence and location, a Seton Hall professor with a keen interest in mining lore reported in 1953 that he had found a twelve-by-fifteen-inch slab of gold ore in the facing supporting the house's piazza. To avert a new gold rush, he quickly notified the public that it was of sufficiently low grade to yield about $100 and that Mr. Walsh no doubt intended it to be symbolic.

Another legend held that an entire floor was reserved for one special visitor. The initial plans and details of the house seem to rule this out, yet a large space on the third floor was designated for guest accommodations. In the end, Vinson's theater was moved to the fourth floor, leaving most of the third floor available. The Walsh Palace was definitely intended to impress the highest level of society, and its owners had a certain guest in mind. That guest was a king.[10]

A KING FOR A FRIEND

CHAPTER TWELVE

A PERSONAL EMPIRE IN AFRICA

Walsh first met the king in 1900, at the time of the Paris Exposition. Belgian industrialist Charles Naegelmackers, president of the International Sleeping Car Company, was one of many new European friends Walsh made at the fair. In June Naegelmackers invited the U.S. mining millionaire to a business meeting in Ostend. He hoped an infusion of Walsh money might assist his ailing company. As his country's monarch was a major investor in the company, Naegelmackers felt King Leopold II's presence would influence Walsh's decision. No agreement was reached at the first meeting, but the Belgians prevailed upon Walsh to return in three months. In the meantime, King Leopold attended at least one of Walsh's parties in Paris, and a strong friendship began to develop. At the second Belgium meeting, in September 1900, the capitalist and the king once again pressured Tom to invest. He replied frankly that he was not interested in the 3 to 4 percent annual return promised by the sleeping car company. Why should he be when mining brought him 10 to 12 percent and sometimes even 20 percent returns each year? Leopold, the owner of vast and largely undeveloped African mineral properties, was impressed. The conversation immediately shifted to mining, as Leopold sought to enlist Tom as his mining partner. Naegelmackers supported the move, with sleeping cars forgotten for the time being. Walsh again deferred, requesting a few weeks to consider the offer.

By the end of October the Denver press had made up his mind for him. "Walsh Now a King's Partner," proclaimed *The Denver Times*, announcing an agreement between the two men and adding to the growing myth that the king had entrusted millions of his dollars to Tom's care. The paper accurately saw the achievement of high social distinction as one more advantage for Walsh. Arriving at Denver's Brown Palace Hotel in November, Tom sought to diffuse the excitement. Yes, he was leery of the king's attention at first, suspecting the early offer of friendship was made merely for financial reasons. Now he denied any major involvement and any carte blanche permission for him to use the king's money. Fruitful discussions had taken place, he found Leopold a charming companion, and he would be an interested party in the king's affairs. Yes, he had been asked to invest his money as well as his expertise, but he left it unclear how either would be accomplished. In the end, Walsh never did disclose any precise terms to the press.[1]

In fact, the business relationship and personal friendship between the millionaire and the Belgian king would last throughout both men's lives. However, in Leopold II, Tom Walsh could not have found a friend more different from himself. It was a difference far more profound than the disparity of the two men's origins. In 1830 the Belgians had finally achieved independence after centuries of rule by other European powers. They had overthrown their Dutch overlords and now felt they needed a king of their own. Their choice was a German price, who became Leopold I. During a reign of more than thirty years, he founded the Belgian dynasty and won the loyalty of his new subjects.

Leopold I died in 1865, succeeded by a son who was initially shy, unimpressive, and much less popular than his regal father. Realizing this, the newly crowned Leopold II quickly sought to change his image and to make his own name and reputation. In an era of empire building by European powers, why not seek to claim overseas colonies? The Belgian people showed little interest, so Leopold set out on his own. Obtaining an audience with explorer Henry Stanley, he learned of a rich yet little-known area in west-central Africa not claimed by other colonial powers. Under the guise of a benevolent society that wanted to abolish slavery (as practiced by Arabs, not Europeans), Leopold first obtained commercial concessions over the vast watershed of the Congo River. Military control soon followed.

Ivory was the king's first commercial target, but it was soon eclipsed by rubber, a commodity of growing worldwide importance. To finance his African operations, Leopold coerced his reluctant countrymen to loan him millions. They complied, but because they had not assisted him from the start, the Congo became Leopold's personal colony, not Belgium's. When he sought official recognition from world leaders, the jealous Europeans were reluctant to come to the table. Undaunted, Leopold courted a new sponsor. After being lavishly entertained by the king's New World connections, U.S. president Chester A. Arthur gave his recognition. Europe's powers soon had no alternative but to fall in line. In 1885, Leopold finally received the world's acceptance of his "humanitarian" plan for the Congo.

When Leopold II first met Tom Walsh in 1900, he was well on his way to becoming one of the world's richest men as a result of the Congo's immense supply of rubber. Now the king saw the region's minerals as a second wealth builder, with the need to court mining men like Walsh so he could develop them. At the same time, the world was seriously questioning Leopold's altruistic motives. Leopold the philanthropist and humanitarian welcomed missionaries not just from Belgium but also from Sweden, Britain, the United States, and other lands. Generally, their presence supported the claim that the people of the Congo enjoyed the king's protection against Arab slave traders, as well as his concern for their spiritual lives. Missionaries could usually be expected to stay out of local politics. However, several of them looked around, asked questions, and witnessed the unspeakable. Together with other observers such as foreign envoys, businessmen, and humanitarians, they exposed the Congo as anything but Leopold's benevolent effort. For future writer Joseph Conrad, sent on a commercial mission, conditions he found abhorrent provided the background for his classic work, *Heart of Darkness*.[2] Any of a number of Leopold's lieutenants could be the prototype for his tyrannical Kurtz. No one did more work than British journalist and reformer E. D. Morel, who made the Congo's conditions the subject of a lifetime crusade. Morel got his start while stationed by a shipping company in Antwerp, Belgium. From its docks he could see that while many valuable commodities arrived from the Congo, only guns were sent back.[3]

The observers found a network of rubber-based slave camps with human-rights abuses on a massive scale. Hostages were taken and frequently abused to secure rubber output. Hands and heads were cut off as punishment for disobedience or poor production. Female hostages were raped or forced into prostitution.

When a village or district fell behind its rubber quota, Leopold's soldiers often responded by murdering everyone they could find. Killing squads were required to account for every cartridge used, with a victim's severed hand as evidence. In 1896 a German newspaper reported, without a challenge from Congo authorities, that 1,308 hands had been turned over to one particularly notorious official in a single day. Another state officer carelessly reported to a U.S. missionary that his corporal had accounted for the use of 6,000 cartridges but that the death toll would be higher because children were often killed with the butts of guns. Since the precious rubber grew on vines, the prescribed harvest method was to tap the vine. To meet harsh quotas and avoid persecution, however, some villagers resorted to cutting off the vine, which killed the plant. If such a practice were discovered, the entire village faced extermination.[4]

Not just entire villages but also traditional ways of life were destroyed so the Belgian king could enjoy his rubber profits. Villagers learned to flee into the jungle when soldiers arrived, leaving their homes to be plundered. Lacking food and shelter, many died of starvation and exposure. U.S. Presbyterian missionary William Morrison estimated in 1899 that at least 50,000 persons were hiding in the forests near the post he served, while the women and children left behind usually fled to his mission for protection. At about the same time, an English explorer found a devastated Congo area of 3,000 square miles in which every village had been burned, leaving skeletons everywhere. Disease became another mass killer of the Congolese, in time claiming more lives than bullets. Lack of food and shelter was one cause, but a larger factor was the spread of diseases imported by whites, such as smallpox and sleeping sickness. Many laborers were conscripted into harsh duties, such as long-haul porterage, and were left in a weakened condition that fostered sickness.

When the Congolese revolted against such rule, as they frequently did, they were put down bloodily. Revolts by some tribes lasted as long as twenty years, inflicting heavy casualties on Leopold's men. In the end, however, the whites' superior firepower won out (in what they termed "pacification" expeditions). Belgians also exploited the traditional ethnic hostilities of the many local groups. Modern estimates put the death toll among Congolese from all causes at well into the millions during Leopold's reign, 1878–1908. The king's legacy of cultural and economic instability has arguably continued to this day.[5]

In his role as the king's adviser and would-be investor, Tom Walsh never set foot in Africa, and neither did Leopold. It is nonetheless preposterous to claim, as did his supporters (including Walsh), that Leopold was unaware of the excesses of his forces in the Congo. In 1908, he decided to sell his colony to his country. The terms of sale called for payments to the king in millions of francs, never mind that he had not repaid the millions the Belgians had loaned him earlier. Once the deal was complete, the king treated Brussels to what might be termed the greatest bonfire in the country's history. The conflagration continued for eight days, as every record of the king's activities in the Congo was burned in the furnaces of the royal palace. When one of his military aides asked Leopold about the source of all the smoke and soot, the king replied, "I will give them my Congo, but they have no right to know what I did there."[6]

All of Leopold's records of his dealings with Walsh may have joined the rest of his archives in their destruction. We know little of what transpired in their meetings, all of which took place in Europe. We do know that Tom's period as an adviser coincided with Leopold's main thrust to develop the Congo's mineral resources and that the king bestowed high praise on his new friend from the United States. On one occasion, at a magnificent luncheon in Brussels, Leopold instructed his mining experts to listen to Walsh, who had much to teach them. In 1903, when asked who were the leading U.S. businessmen and financiers he knew and admired, Leopold responded with the names Thomas F. Walsh, J. Pierpont Morgan, and James J. Hill.

Did the well-read Walsh hear of the protests against his friend's conduct? Leopold, once shy and insecure, had developed at least some charm in his later years and had even more charming friends and agents on his side, especially in the United States. His foremost ally in the country was the powerful Senator Nelson Aldrich of Rhode Island, father-in-law of John D. Rockefeller Jr. and grandfather of future vice president Nelson Aldrich Rockefeller. Aldrich, his son-in-law, and such prominent U.S. citizens as Bernard Baruch and the Guggenheim family all received major Congo concession rights. One of Aldrich's jobs was to keep reform-minded candidates from being appointed to the position of U.S. consul general to the Congo, and he successfully blocked every one. The king could count on the cardinal of Baltimore for religious backing, together with a pro-Leopold Vatican. Among the duties of the king's U.S. friends was making certain that men like Walsh received and believed only sanitized versions of the Congo story.[7]

Nonetheless, U.S. readers had been seeing accounts of brutality by Leopold's Congo administration dating back at least to 1890. In that year a black U.S. lawyer, journalist, minister, and historian named George Washington Williams met Leopold and then traveled to the Congo. Williams published his findings in a letter to Leopold. While addressing "Your Majesty," Williams proceeded as tactfully as possible to place blame for abhorrent conditions dating as far back as the Stanley expedition and in closing to inform the king that his government was engaged in the slave trade. Williams followed up a few months later with another report to U.S. president Benjamin Harrison. Soon his subject was picked up by the *New York Herald* and other U.S. and foreign papers, including some in Belgium. Williams died of tuberculosis in 1891, but others in his country carried on his message.[8]

Tom Walsh was always loyal to a friend, especially a very important one. Early in 1902 he attempted to both praise and defend Leopold in the U.S. press. The Walsh Papers contain Tom's nineteen-page handwritten draft on the subject (with additional pages probably missing). He presents the monarch as a loyal friend and a benevolent, almost father-like leader of his people. Walsh portrays Belgium as the home of contented and prosperous citizens, benefiting from the king's generous land-distribution system that should serve as a model for all of Europe (especially Ireland, with its notorious absentee landowners). He makes only one reference to the Congo, as the source of the raw materials that bettered the Belgians' existence.

Walsh sent the draft to a friend, William E. Curtis, a widely respected international journalist. Curtis's response casts doubt on its worthiness for publication. He questions Walsh's statement about the affection Queen Victoria had held for her distant cousin the king. Curtis, to the contrary, felt the British queen disliked Leopold. He further criticizes Walsh for not directly discussing the king's alleged scandals (in fact, Walsh does not discuss them at all). Curtis recommends sending the document to *Harpers' Weekly*, possibly because it had run a pro-Leopold article by an English supporter as recently as 1900. Here Tom's article must have died, for it does not appear in any 1902 edition of *Harpers' Weekly* or any other major U.S. publication.

By this time, opposition to Leopold in the U.S. press was on the rise. Typical was a far different account than the one previously given of the lot of the Belgian people. In its August 1902 edition, *The Miners' Magazine* of Denver found that "Belgium is said to be the richest productive country in Europe, yet nearly all the children of the laboring classes, except sucklings, are forced to work in the mines or factories in order that Leopold, the gayest libertine monarch on earth, may revel in the mad whirl of bestial sensuality."[9]

TO BE A KING'S PARTNER

As pressure from the king intensified, Walsh had to decide if he should add Congo investment and possible direct involvement to his adviser's role. He admitted to a suspicious Carrie that he had seen engineers' reports showing Congo gold and copper potential that would dwarf the Camp Bird. While the reports Walsh viewed have not survived, his statement about the Congo's mining future was correct. In 1900 Leopold established a company to explore and develop the copper-rich Katanga province. Ore discoveries the next year led to construction of a railroad, followed by the first smelter in 1911. The most extensive mining operations occurred after Leopold had sold the land and subsequently died. However, their conduct carried all too familiar themes. Five thousand Katanga laborers died between 1911 and 1918. The workers were forcibly recruited, led away roped together, and disciplined with a whip, just as in the days of the rubber system. As before, they brought their colonial masters impressive profits. In copper alone, production that started in 1911 reached 100,000 tons' annual production by 1928. By 1985 the nation was producing 460,000 tons of copper per year, 7 percent of the world's total. Diamond and gold mining also became fairly profitable.[10]

Evalyn tells of a memorable business trip to the king's chateau in the French Pyrenees. It was September 1902, and she was sixteen. Her childhood observation of Leopold was of a large man with incredibly stiff posture. Ever curious, she managed to bump into him when their carriage swung around a turn, discovering that his upright demeanor was caused by a bulletproof vest. The king talked with her father for three days. Tom once confided in Evalyn, in a rage, "The way they handle things down there in the Congo—I wouldn't touch it." At the end of the conference Leopold and Tom shook hands as fellow businessmen might. Evalyn felt she and her father knew something the king did not yet suspect, that Tom's mind was now firmly set against further involvement in the Congo. He did, however, hope the two men could remain friends, and a business deal of another kind might someday be in the cards. Leopold's final promise was to visit America for the 1904 St. Louis Exhibition, where Evalyn suspected he wanted to observe Americans making money and make sure more of it flowed across the ocean to his African domain. The king did not keep the promise. After departing, Tom's final comment to his daughter was, "I'll keep my money home where I can see it. Of course, I don't mind little flyers."[11]

What might have been Walsh's Congo bonanza passed instead to another Irish American millionaire, Thomas Fortune Ryan, in partnership with King Leopold and the Guggenheim family. Their ventures, starting in 1906, found some gold and millions of dollars' worth of diamonds. Walsh could have added the Congo to the Black Hills in the category of missed opportunities. However, the Congo tale seems not to have survived as a family story of a blunder turned into a learning experience. Otherwise, Tom had his way, for his friendship with the king continued. The fact that he honored Leopold by setting aside a floor of his mansion for him demonstrates that he held the king in the highest regard.

However, the honored guest who never set foot in Africa also never set foot in his reserved quarters at 2020 Massachusetts Avenue.

Tom's business role never grew past that of adviser. This role included giving advice on copper deposits in the Congo and on the king's gold mines in Korea and Manchuria. Tom made casual inspections of ore samples from those regions, which greatly impressed Leopold. He also passed on to the king his belief that the Congo held one of the world's greatest and richest copper deposits, in which he was proven correct. On at least one occasion Walsh sent mining experts, including John Benson, to Africa. However, as he later steadfastly asserted, his duties never advanced beyond this level, and he engaged in no mining ventures with the monarch. Contrary to some rumors at the time, Leopold did not become an investor or partner in the Camp Bird. As General Hall correctly reported after the 1901 gala, only Carrie could be considered a partner in the mine. When it was sold, Tom Walsh alone received the proceeds.[12]

SELLING THE CAMP BIRD MINE

CHAPTER THIRTEEN

ADVICE OF A FAMOUS ENGINEER

Despite his July 1901 statement to General Frank Hall denying any intent to sell, Tom had already opened the door to possible buyers of the Camp Bird. Most of the speculation centered on John Hays Hammond. During a colorful career, mining engineer Hammond had bought, established, and sold famous mines, made friendships with world leaders, and sometimes dodged bullets. While working as an engineer near Johannesburg, South Africa, he was convicted of attempting to overthrow the Boer government of Transvaal. Hammond, who later admitted to some complicity in the revolt, received a death sentence from the Boers. A visit to his jail cell by the touring Mark Twain lifted his spirits somewhat. Then he was granted a last-minute reprieve as a goodwill gesture (which included a stiff fine but did not prevent the Boer War between, on the one side, Transvaal and the Orange Free State, and, on the other, the British).

Hammond's relationship with Walsh began around 1900, soon after the former's brush with death in Africa. It is unclear if Hammond entered their business dealings as an independent mining consultant or as an agent for a potential buyer. At the same time, he represented a British syndicate, the Venture Corporation of London, in its purchase of Winfield Scott Stratton's rich Independence Mine at Cripple Creek. In his autobiography Hammond gives a simple (and somewhat self-serving) account of winning Walsh's trust. The Venture Corporation wanted to expand beyond the Independence in Colorado. T. A. Rickard, Hammond's bitter rival, had prepared a very favorable report on the Camp Bird for the British investors. Rickard and his associates valued the net ore in sight at $6 million and recommended that their client purchase the mine for that amount. Venture Corporation asked Hammond for a second opinion, and he concluded that the value was less than $3 million. Venture Corporation took his advice and turned down the deal.[1]

The following year, Hammond met Walsh in Glenwood Springs, Colorado. Walsh wanted to know why he had come up with the lower value. Walsh, Hammond discovered, was motivated by more than financial gain. "I've already made several millions out of the mine," Tom told him, "but I don't want to be tied up any longer. I've been in these mountains for many years. My children are growing up. I want them to have an education and some social life, and I'd like to play around in politics myself. There's nobody I can trust to manage the mine properly. My manager, John Benson, can't stand the high altitude any longer, and I don't want to train a new man."[2]

Hammond gives no dates for his contacts with Walsh. In the end, he tells us the two men agreed on Hammond's new offer of $3 million in cash, along with stock and royalties from future production. At the closing, Hammond found that Walsh had the integrity to honor a verbal part of the original agreement, even though it was incorrectly stated to Walsh's benefit in the written contract. Walsh instructed his attorney, Charles Thomas, to delete language that would have given Walsh more than the agreed-upon power to dictate his percentage of future ore payments. Later, he refrained from sending accountants to check on mine operations, stating that as long as Hammond was the mine's consulting engineer, he needed no one else to protect his interests. Walsh, Hammond concluded, was honest himself and gave others credit for possessing the same quality.

Evalyn and her mother felt Tom was hypnotized by John Hays Hammond. Carrie was very averse to any sale, arguing on one occasion, "What can you buy that's half so safe as a six-mile vein of gold right through your own land?" Evalyn agreed with Hammond's account that Tom wanted freedom from the continual struggle of owning and developing a large mine. The Hammonds and Walshes did develop a close friendship, and young Jack Hammond became a playmate of Evalyn and Vinson's. The two families spent time together in Colorado and summered near each other on the Massachusetts coast in 1903. Later, the Hammond family lived not far from the Walshes in Washington.[3]

Denver newspapers closely followed the many rumors of the sale of the Camp Bird, already regarded as one of Colorado's premier mines. Their accounts paint a roller-coaster ride of on-again, off-again deals, with prices and terms often out of line with Hammond's simpler story. The July 29, 1900, edition of *The Denver Times* led off the speculation, announcing, "The Camp Bird Reported Sold." Negotiations with Venture Corporation were complete; the total price was undisclosed but was said to run in the millions. Rickard, the buyer's representative, was refusing to discuss anything. Within two weeks the Denver *Mining Reporter* warned that the rumors were not credible, yet the *Times* persisted. Finally, in late September, in its first mention of Hammond's presence, the *Times* admitted the sale might be off or at least delayed while Hammond recovered from an illness. His recovery must have been rapid, for three days later, on September 30, the banner headline read, "Camp Bird Mine Sold for $6,500,000." The price would be paid in cash by December 1, and the Venture investors were said to include one notable U.S. businessman, J. Pierpont Morgan. According to another rumor, Morgan and his cronies then intended to turn around and sell the mine for twice what they had just paid Walsh. Variations of the sale story continued for nearly two months, until a firm November 6 denial by Rickard and another by Walsh in December seemed to lay the matter to rest. While the Venture Corporation deal was off, at least one rumor arose of a sale to another British millionaire. Then all was largely quiet until early 1902.[4]

On April 21, 1902, experts representing Venture were again reported to be examining the mine, with a closing imminent. This time the rumor was correct. The deal closed on May 6, 1902, although the following day the true price was still not available, with a Ouray editor predicting Walsh would receive $11 million. The paper correctly identified the buyer as a newly formed company, Camp Bird, Ltd., whose principals included the Britons of the Venture Corporation and some U.S. citizens. The best estimates, then and now, hold that Walsh received a total of about $6 million for his fabulous mine, in the form of cash, stock, and royalties on future production. The deed of record in Ouray County shows consideration of $3.125 million, representing just the cash payment at the closing. In the words of a *Denver Times* reporter in the May 13, 1902, edition, "The true sum . . . will probably never be known unless

Mr. Walsh cares to satisfy public curiosity." In point of fact, the value of his stock and the royalties he would receive were based on the probability that the Camp Bird could continue to produce as it had during the Walsh era, something Walsh knew better than anyone. John Hays Hammond agreed, and in a May 29, 1902, report to *The Denver Times* the great engineer admitted that he had to raise both his valuation and his predictions for the mine. He now found ore in sight with a gross value of $5 million. Hammond concluded, "In my opinion the prospective value of the property is very great."[5]

INVESTING A FORTUNE

His Camp Bird money in hand, Walsh paid Charles Thomas $30,000 for his legal fees in negotiating and closing the sale. At the same time he wrote a check to John Benson for $200,000, consideration not disclosed. Benson owned no equity in the company, and this sum vastly exceeded the salaries of the very best mine managers at the time. A bonus for years of hard work and loyalty is the best explanation.

Despite his wealth and newfound freedom, Tom did not abandon mining. The extent of his mining revenues or losses in the era after Camp Bird is unknown, but his continued pursuit was not for the purpose of adding to his wealth. Rather, he held a lifelong love of the mining profession. He definitely found no new Camp Birds. In 1904 Walsh joined America's last major gold rush, to Goldfield, Nevada, but discovered more rattlesnakes than gold and suffered a bad case of food poisoning. A promising tunnel proved to be a breeding ground for the reptiles, abruptly ending further exploration. John Benson, who accompanied him, later told the tale of how he and Walsh narrowly escaped with their lives after eating tainted food in the camp. The two men probably did not make a cent for all their efforts. Walsh, however, showed his public-spirited side. In October 1904 he petitioned his friend, President Roosevelt, to grant a post office to Columbia, Esmeralda County, Nevada.

In 1906 Tom learned of gold potential near Hartsel, Colorado, about ninety miles southwest of Denver. He told a Ouray reporter that the Hartsel gold camp might prove to be another bonanza, but it needed further examination. Unfortunately, Tom's journey to make that examination ended in a train wreck. Tom received only minor injuries but was badly shaken. He soon dropped the matter, and nothing further came of the Hartsel "gold rush," for Walsh or anyone else. A history of the area makes no mention that Hartsel was ever a gold camp.[6]

Soon, Walsh had less and less time to devote to active exploration. However, to the end of his life, mining promoters pursued his wealth. Tom remained open-minded, frequently listened, and sometimes invested. The Walsh Papers disclose many offers from colleagues old and new. Felix Leavick sought to involve his old friend in many ventures, in Mexico, British Columbia, Washington State, Wyoming, and Jamestown and Cripple Creek in Colorado. Andy Richardson felt he should look into the uranium and vanadium potential of Ouray County. David Wegg thought the two men should renew their old partnership and explore Arizona copper properties. Others directed his attention to the farthest reaches of the hemisphere, from the Klondike to Costa Rica, Panama, Bolivia, and Uruguay.

His closest friends and advisers seem to have felt it was their duty to shield Walsh from the more outlandish schemes. While Tom took a great interest in the many proposals of a California promoter, William Dunham, John Benson developed a strong dislike and distrust for the man. He warned Tom about Dunham, on one occasion calling him one of the most dishonest and deceitful fellows he had ever met. The words fell on deaf ears. Tom invested with Dunham, and the actual results are not known. In fact, his financial papers disclose little in the way of either income or expense from these mining ventures. He no doubt ignored or rejected a number of them. However, Tom's usual caution combined with shrewdness never left him. He maintained his Camp Bird wealth, and any losses on individual mining deals seem to have been written off as foreseeable consequences of playing the game he loved.[7]

Walsh also joined in Washington, D.C.'s real estate business, just as he had in Denver nearly twenty years before. If he could not build more world-class mines, at least he could build new office buildings. Early in his Washington stay, Tom returned to another old business, purchasing the city's Oxford Hotel. By 1906 downtown Washington held the Colorado and Ouray buildings, Thomas F. Walsh proprietor. However, the mining developer who professed to love his double-digit returns on investment should have found capital real estate a bit boring. If 1904 can be considered a typical year, the return on the Colorado Building was a mere 4 percent on the cost of the lot and 6.73 percent on the cost of the building. In reality, the real estate investments were one more manifestation of a long-held Walsh trait, dating back to when his carpentry work took precedence over mining. As usual, Walsh sought to establish a bedrock of financial stability and only then ventured into more speculative fields. Indeed, even before the Camp Bird sale, the Walsh family invested much of its rapidly accumulating wealth in safe and low-yielding bonds.[8]

Walsh also tried his hand at his original profession in Colorado: railroading. The first time he did so was to help both the Camp Bird and the citizens of southwestern Colorado. The Denver and Rio Grande Western Railroad had a virtual monopoly on hauling ores out of the San Juan region. At the time, eastern interests such as the Gould family controlled the railroad and ignored the concerns of western mine operators and other users of the line. Walsh was indignant when the railroad refused to give him uniform rates on Camp Bird ore. Others who needed to transport lower-grade ores found the prevailing rates of eleven to fourteen dollars per ton prohibitive.

The September 6, 1901, edition of Ouray's *Plaindealer* carried the welcome news that competition was on the way. Tom Walsh, together with John Benson, their local attorneys, and other leading citizens, announced the formation of the Pueblo, Gunnison & Ouray line. Incorporation papers had been filed with the secretary of state, and the annual meeting was set for November 3 at the railroad's home office in Ouray. The railroad was to start at the smelting center in Pueblo, then head west into the mountains in a shorter line than the existing road, in "almost an air line" as the *Plaindealer* described it. It would cross Custer, Saguache, southern Gunnison, and probably northern Hinsdale counties before reaching Ouray. The proposed line was standard gauge all the way, whereas the Rio Grande required a shift to narrow gauge near Salida. Rates were to be low, with the confident prediction that the Rio Grande would practically have to haul ore free of charge to compete. Remote mining districts would finally receive rail. Best of all, the line would extend west to Salt Lake City and connect with a line to the Pacific owned by the man who nearly became Tom's Washington neighbor, Senator William Andrews Clark of Montana.

Ignored in all the optimism was the plain fact that to accomplish this feat along the nearly 300-mile proposed path, the line needed to cross three major mountain ranges. The Rio Grande route might be longer, but it traveled the less snowbound valleys and lower passes. Most likely, the promoters never laid one rail or tie of the "Walsh Road." On July 31, 1902, after the sale of the Camp Bird, its demise became official. *The Denver Times* accused Walsh of no longer caring about railroad rates now that he had his fortune. Tom was probably guilty as charged, but he was also guilty of exercising good business judgment in discontinuing an unrealistic venture.[9]

Walsh made one other railroad investment out of Colorado pride and loyalty rather than sound business judgment. His friend David Moffat wanted to carry out his longtime dream of giving the city of Denver a direct rail connection to the Pacific. Construction of the Denver Northwestern and Pacific Railroad, usually called the Moffat Road, began in 1902. The line climbed the Front Range west of the city in a long series of switchbacks until cresting the Continental Divide at the 11,600-foot Rollins Pass. It then dropped by the same fashion into the valleys of the Fraser and Grand (later Colorado) rivers on the west side before embarking on a planned course north and then west to Salt Lake City. The Moffat Road never reached the Utah city, stopping at Steamboat Springs, Colorado, in 1908. The line did succeed in opening up northwestern Colorado and later reached another forty miles west to the town of Craig and its coal mines. However, the high cost of snow clearance and weather delays in the twisting mountain route meant the railroad always lost money. It also met with strong opposition from major eastern railroad interests such as the Goulds and Harrimans, who denied it access to Denver's Union Station and placed other roadblocks in its way. These tycoons of the Union Pacific and Rio Grande did not want a through route from Denver to compete with their own transcontinental lines.

The most infamous action by the eastern interests was to block the railroad's progress in Gore Canyon of the Grand River near Kremmling, Colorado. While involvement of the Harriman interests and others has not been proven, circumstantial evidence shows that they backed a shadowy company called the New Century Light and Power Company. This concern bought up land in advance of the Moffat Road surveyors and proposed to dam and flood the canyon. When Moffat's attorneys questioned their bona fide purpose, the company relinquished its rights in favor of the U.S. Reclamation Service. The government agency proposed an irrigation project, which quickly gained support from such faraway groups as the Los Angeles Chamber of Commerce (a precursor to the extensive diversion of Colorado River water to California later in the century). Even as engineers' tests proved that the canyon was not a good dam site, the case dragged on in the Department of the Interior. Eventually, it caught the interest of Theodore Roosevelt, who sent a confidential investigator to the canyon. The president called for hearings in Washington and heard the Moffat side testify that there was collusion between the Reclamation Service and rival railways. It is unproven but probable that Tom Walsh used his personal influence with Roosevelt, for the president finally ruled for the railroad in 1905, calling it a benefit to the West. Moffat, Walsh, and their supporters had won, but at the cost of very expensive delays.

Moffat had invested much of his sizable fortune in his dream, and he lost nearly all of it before his death in 1911, while he was making one final, unsuccessful trip to New York to try to enlist backing from the same wealthy easterners who had supported his projects of an earlier era. Some say David Moffat died by his own hand, although this is highly unlikely, given the promoter's indomitable spirit. A broken heart provides a better explanation. Walsh and a number of prominent Denver citizens also lost money on the Moffat Road. Tom's investment of at least $150,000 was later declared valueless. Through it all, he seems to have felt the support of a friend and a cause was more important than other business considerations. In the end, the Moffat Road supporters proved to be visionaries. Other Denver citizens carried out David Moffat's dream, taking his line to a Pacific connection many years after the deaths of Walsh and the railroad's founder. The seven-mile-long Moffat Tunnel under the Continental Divide opened in 1928, bypassing the snowy Rollins Pass route. Construction of the Dotsero Cut-off in western Colorado later connected the old Moffat Road with the Denver and Rio Grande Western Railroad line from Pueblo to Salt Lake City. By 1934 it was possible to travel by rail directly west from Denver to Salt Lake City and then on to the West Coast.[10]

DEATH, AND A RETURN TO COLORADO

CHAPTER FOURTEEN

VINSON

Life in Washington included a mansion with twenty-three servants and considerably more rooms. For Evalyn and Vinson it meant a childhood they could not have imagined only a few short years before in Ouray. Their wishes were their father's commands. Automobiles soon replaced theater as the center of Vinson's life. He became a seasoned driver and a terror on the streets of Washington in his Pope Toledo (sometimes pursued by police on bicycles). John Hays Hammond recalled that during his family's 1903 summer stay near the Walsh family on the Massachusetts coast, the parents organized an automobile club. The fathers paid their sons' dues and then quickly passed a by-law imposing fines and removal of license for any member reported speeding. The rule did not stop Hammond from encouraging his son Jack to engage Vinson in a high-speed race when the latter had the audacity to pass them on the road. No fines were imposed, and the by-law was soon forgotten.[1]

That same year, Vinson enrolled at the Washington School, along with his cousin, Monroe Lee. Monroe's mother, Carrie's sister Lucy, had died in a 1901 carriage accident near the family's Kansas City home, and now her son spent much of his time with the Walsh family. In a December 1903 letter to Walsh, the school's headmaster reported both boys' grades. Monroe scored all As and Bs, Vinson Bs and Cs. Headmaster Louis Hooper added, "Vinson is handicapped by his absence; out of forty-seven school days since the beginning of the year, he has been absent twenty-one and tardy three times. The boy is bright enough and can learn his lessons quickly, but naturally when he is absent nearly half of the time the results must of necessity be poor." Evalyn credited the absences to another of Vinson's passions: hockey. The following year he enrolled in the Hill School at Pottstown, Pennsylvania. His schoolwork improved, but the Pope Toledo came to school as well, for a company representative wrote directly to Vinson about the machine's care and condition.[2]

To land a position on the school newspaper at Hill, Vinson needed to bring in the most advertising dollars of all the student-candidates. His father was happy to contact a number of New York business owners who owed him favors. His December 2, 1904, letter to clothier C. F. Wetzel probably mirrored the others:

> My son is very anxious to get on the editorial staff of the "Dial", the school journal of the Hill School at Pottstown, Pa. (Dr. Meig's School) and in order to get on he must secure a certain number of paying advertisements. He has *honored* me (Heaven help me) by appointing me one of his canvassers for securing ads. In writing me of my appointment, he condescends to name a few of the great advantages a full page ad. in the Hill School official paper will bring,—the undivided patronage of the 275 pupils of the school; the patronage of the great town of Pottstown, who all read the "Dial" with religious fervor; the patronage of the doting parents of the aforesaid 275 hopefuls; and last but not least, the great American public, whose decerning [sic] judgment will cause them to give their patronage to those who advertise in this high-class, well edited, spicy, rare, meritorious journal. Joking aside I would be pleased if you can take a page from the boy; if you can do so, fill out the enclosed blank ($30. for a page) and mail it to Vinson at Pottstown; in fact in any event return the blank.[3]

Wetzel came through with a one-page ad, and Evalyn tells us all the others did the same, to Tom's delight. His son easily won the spot on the paper. Vinson soon ordered a $115 dinner suit from Wetzel, proving the patronage theory correct. The previous summer his father had been very proud when Vinson shot a bear in Colorado, although Tom was generally opposed to killing animals. The father's show of love and affection for the son had not diminished since the day Vinson pulled a rabbit from his hat in his private theater. Tom Walsh's children could do no wrong.[4]

Tom, Carrie, and Evalyn took one of many European trips in January 1905. Vinson stayed behind at school, while Evalyn attributes her inclusion to her parents' wish to keep her an ocean away from Ned McLean and a possible marriage proposal. Arriving in Rome, they met Pope Pius X, recalled by Evalyn as an ordinary-appearing man amid the pomp and ceremony of the Vatican. She came away mystified that Tom, admittedly the only member of the family to have ever been a Roman Catholic (but by now a Mason), was the only one to receive the pope's blessing. Tom was overjoyed. Evalyn, who joined the Catholic Church later in life, found her father "tethered to the Church by bonds fixed on him in his childhood."

The remainder of the trip was decidedly secular. Evalyn became romantically involved with an Italian prince named Altieri (while yet another prince waited in the wings). Marriage rumors were flying, but as Evalyn confided to a family friend, she wanted a red Mercedes even more than a prince. Vinson became her defender, admonishing Carrie in a letter: "I am afraid from your letters that you have been blinded by the thought of a title and are thinking about the high position it would give you rather than [about] sister's happiness." Finally, fearing payment of a larger dowry and a life of unhappiness for his daughter, Tom chose to spend $18,000 for the car. Evalyn had guessed his response in advance, for she immediately told him which Paris friend would make the purchase and how the car could be shipped to Venice.[5]

Summer 1905 found the Walsh family in Newport, Rhode Island. Journalist Cleveland Amory later described the splendor of the island resort, in its glory from 1890 to 1914. The Astors and the Vanderbilts, the Belmonts and the Van Alens, the Goelets and the Oelrichs were firmly in the saddle. "But if Newport was New York in the center," Amory clarified, "and Boston, Philadelphia and Baltimore on the edges, the welcome mat was also out for the Pembroke Joneses from the rice fields of North Carolina, the E. J. Berwinds from the coal fields of Pennsylvania, the tinplate Leedses from Indiana and the coke-operating Paul J. Raineys from Ohio."[6]

The Walsh family more closely resembled the names at the bottom of the list, yet in their drive for upward mobility they succeeded in renting from and even socializing with those at the top. "Beaulieu" was a brick and brownstone residence (or "cottage," in the resort terminology of the time), located on fashionable Bellevue Avenue. Evalyn traces its 1862 origin to Peruvian wealth, followed by William Waldorf Astor's acquisition. The property was alleged to be "hoodooed." It was subsequently rented to Cornelius Vanderbilt, who in turn sublet it to Walsh. Tom, Evalyn recalled, wanted a big place in which to entertain. She found Newport society "kind." The family could have witnessed the splendor of Newport firsthand, for Bellevue Avenue was the site of the daily, 3 P.M. "coaching parade," which, Amory recalled, was "a spectacle never equaled at any other resort. Vanderbilt coachmen wore maroon coats, Astor blue. As the rubber wheels of the coaches whirred silently around behind the rhythmic clop-clopping of the horses' hooves, all Newport paused to stare."[7]

Then one day in August everything came to an end. On the 19th the family chauffeur drove Evalyn and Vinson in her Mercedes to a luncheon at the prestigious Clambake Club, an association limited to 100 of Newport's most esteemed residents. The senior Walshes did not attend the party, given by Mrs. Clement Moore. On their return, Vinson demanded to drive, providing a lift to such socialites as Eloise Kernochan, Herbert Pell Jr., and Harry Oelrichs. The young motorist drove swiftly past other automobiles and climbed the grade behind the beach, then started down Honeyman's Hill. "We were going fast," Evalyn remembered, "when I heard something like a pistol shot and the Mercedes began to sway and pitch. A rear tire had blown out. One of us screamed, and in that second we struck the flooring of a bridge that carried the road over a creek. I heard the chilling sound of splintering wood, and then our car bounced through the rail and threw me into a dreadful darkness."

Evalyn found herself pinned under the car in the creek, with a severely broken leg and other injuries. She called for her brother and was told his injuries were minor. Other friends who had arrived on the scene helped her into an ambulance. Where was her brother? She demanded to see the car's steering column, often the cause of a driver's death, but saw it was intact. She did notice that a large bridge timber jutted into the car. In fact, Vinson was dying at about that very time. Throughout her trip to the hospital and for some time afterward, she was told her brother had survived, yet he never appeared. Later, reading a note of condolence carelessly left at her bedside, she finally learned the truth. The day of Vinson's funeral, Tom and Carrie had arrived at her bedside in normal attire, changing into formal dress for the service after leaving the room.[8]

Tom wrote Theodore Roosevelt on September 5, 1905, from Newport, in response to the president's expressions of sympathy:

> My dear Friend, Mr. President, I want you and Mrs. Roosevelt to know that
> Vinson's death was caused by an unavoidable accident and not by reckless

running. A front tire burst—four feet from a bridge. The dear boy stuck to his wheel like a hero when he could have saved himself by jumping, shut off the electricity and fluid and undoubtedly saved his sister and the lives of others of the party. Knowing what an interest Mrs. Roosevelt and you took in Vinson, and how he loved you both, I felt it my duty in justice to the dear boy's memory to let you know the facts. My daughter's limb is doing well but her mind constantly dwells upon her brother so much so that we are moving her from here to Garden City, Long Island Wednesday night to get her away from the place where she and her brother spent so many happy hours together. Thanking you dear President for your sympathetic telegram and asking Almighty God to save and preserve you and yours from any such affliction as has come to us and taken away for the time being at least all interest in life. Sincerely yours, Thomas F. Walsh.[9]

The house in Newport was closed, and the family moved temporarily to a hotel in Garden City. Here, on October 20, Tom penned a letter to Tim Kennedy of Worcester, Massachusetts, another Tipperary native who had married Tom's cousin Joanna. Tom wanted all his cousins to know "that Evalyn is gaining daily and that she will come out of this ordeal barring future accidents without a mark, and whilst our hearts are crushed with a grief that never will leave them yet we feel that we have so much to be thankful for in the miraculous escape of our daughter." The family would next journey, perhaps even relocate, to California or Colorado, "anywhere to get away from things that remind us of our dear boy. . . . [Messages] come to us from every country and nationality, from hovels and palaces, from princes and kings, and what was dearest to us, from the poor and the humble."[10]

The family did return to Washington but to the Shoreham Hotel rather than 2020 Massachusetts. Evalyn had been taking morphine for pain and now needed more of it. She never completely recovered from her injuries and developed an addiction to the drug as well. One consolation was the attention she received from her young friend Ned McLean. The heir to the publishing fortune was now a more mature eighteen. When it looked as though her leg might have to be amputated, Ned rushed to his influential father. John R. McLean knew a renowned doctor at Johns Hopkins Medical Center who recommended a new and risky surgery for Evalyn. The surgeon, Dr. John Finney, gave her only a 50 percent chance of surviving. The family left the decision to Evalyn. She agreed to the surgery and begged to have it done in her room at 2020 Massachusetts. Her spacious bathroom became the operating room.

By January 26, 1906, Tom reported to Tim Kennedy that "Evalyn is doing well since the operation, no fever. In the operation the surgeons cut into the break, found the bones were never set, trimmed the edges, brought them together and fastened them with a silver plate." The hopeful father expected a complete recovery for his brave daughter. Evalyn actually required seven months to recover to the point where her life resembled its previous level of activity.[11]

Something very vital had been removed from Tom's life when he lost his son, and it never returned. His dreams for Vinson's future had changed along with the boy's many whims, from heir to the Camp Bird to actor to newspaper editor to sportsman. All such aspirations were far beyond anything Tom could have imagined when he was his son's age. One friend noticed that a languidness had begun to replace Tom's former boyishness and lighthearted nature. Evalyn tells of finding him disconsolate at her bedside early in her recovery. He told her he would return every ounce of gold from the Camp Bird back to the earth if it meant he could have Vinson, and her health, back again.

For a short while, Tom plunged into Washington social life to hide his grief. At the same time, he was still embroiled in the lawsuit with John Thompson. His mental state was probably one more reason he reluctantly agreed to a settlement with Thompson. Then, he abruptly turned his attention to a return to Colorado. He felt the family needed a change of scenery, and a magnificent estate he admired was for sale. It was Wolhurst, where Walsh, Theodore Roosevelt, and many others of prominence had been entertained over the years. Tom sent his brother-in-law Arthur Lafferty, a Denver businessman, on a January 1906 investigation of the property.[12]

WOLHURST BECOMES CLONMEL

Walsh's former host, Edward Oliver Wolcott, was a new U.S. senator from Colorado in 1890 when he purchased a ramshackle ranch property three miles south of Littleton. Later described by Colorado author Caroline Bancroft as a "dashing blond giant and bachelor Beau Brummel of Denver, brilliant, moody and eloquent," Wolcott wanted to impress his bride-to-be. He commissioned Denver architect T. D. Boal to construct a great rambling residence among the grove of large cottonwood trees on the property. Wolcott named the estate Wolhurst, a combination of his last name and a term for a grove of trees or woods. Here the senator and his wife, the former Frances Metcalfe Bass, entertained lavishly. However, in 1900, the year of vice presidential candidate Roosevelt's visit, the Wolcotts' marriage was annulled. From then on the senator only used his Colorado estate for political entertaining when visiting the state, preferring to spend his time on the East Coast and abroad. He lost his bid for reelection to the Senate in 1903. Wolcott died in Monte Carlo on March 1, 1905. He willed his Littleton estate to his brother Henry, who had little need for the property. By early 1906 it was available.[13]

Attorney C. A. Chisholm of the Wolcott family's Denver law firm sent Walsh a detailed description of the splendors of Wolhurst's 534 acres. The main dwelling house at Wolhurst was a three-story brick mansion with thirty-two rooms, including a forty-eight-foot by thirty-foot living room, a slightly smaller sun parlor, and spacious lounging and billiard rooms. Lighting was electric, with artesian water heated "by hot water giving first class service." The property also boasted a small bungalow with attached greenhouse, a stable and coach barn, a farm barn with stalls for sixteen horses and eight cows, a sizable paddock, and two separate farmhouses. As to further amenities, "The dwelling house stands in spacious grounds sloping down to a lake of about 16 acres. There is abundance of shade on lawns and drives, given by rows of fine large cottonwoods planted about forty years ago, and a splendid growth of maples, spruce, poplar and other varieties planted from ten to fourteen years [ago]."[14]

Impressed by this report and by Arthur Lafferty's physical inspection, Tom signed a short-term lease to Wolhurst and moved his family west. He purchased the estate in March 1906 for an estimated $150,000. The family kept 2020 Massachusetts as their Washington home. However, as Walsh told the *Ouray Herald* in June 1906, "Colorado is my home and I am glad to get back here. I have never let two years go by without coming here, and intend to stay here every year now. It is one of the greatest states in possibilities and we have been too busy in developing its purely business opportunities to make it the state it should be. This will be remedied and it will become the center of attraction for the people of America." Such outward optimism, however, could not suppress his personal pain, revealed to Tim Kennedy in a letter the following month. "We are nicely fixed here," Tom told his Worcester family, "and have everything except our dear boy and we feel that he is with his heavenly Father, but the wound will not heal. . . . Evalyn now walks with a cane and limps but little. We hope that will disappear in a short time. We are occupying a beautiful place 14 miles from Denver. Mrs. Walsh and myself are fairly well."[15]

The family suffered one more loss at Wolhurst. Carrie's mother, Arabella Reed, came from her nearby home in Denver to live with them. Her health was failing, and she passed away from pneumonia in December 1907, at age seventy. *The Denver Republican* remembered the mother who had brought her daughter to Leadville twenty-eight years before as a woman "quite vigorous for her years. She took much interest in current events and was greatly interested in the affairs of the Walsh family. . . . She was a most gentle and kindly lady."[16]

Despite the lingering grief, the Walsh family soon returned to their famed social life, now transferred to Wolhurst. They remodeled the large house and filled it with art treasures. Then they brought their new friends and neighbors to see it. The entertainment was lavish, frequently involving two to three bands and a large team of attendants. Caroline Bancroft tells us that on one occasion Walsh entertained top Republican officials at Wolhurst, then a week later entertained Democrats to keep in the latter's good graces. One guest found the host's personality surprisingly unpretentious. It was as if a citizen more fortunate than others felt it was his duty to meet his neighbors and bring credit to his city.[17]

Walsh still loved to show off Colorado to Washington dignitaries. In August 1907 he entertained Secretary of War William Howard Taft at a Wolhurst breakfast meeting with twenty-five guests. Sending his thanks from Yellowstone Park, his next stop, the secretary praised Walsh for agreeing "to be a member of the state delegation in the National Convention on my behalf. I of course cannot be sure what the complexion of the delegation will be, but I fancy from what I heard, that with Mr. Roosevelt's positive declination, it will naturally swing around to me."[18]

With the 1908 success of Walsh and his fellow convention delegates, followed by a resounding victory at the polls, an appreciative President Taft returned to Wolhurst just over two years later for the grandest celebration the estate would ever know. Tom wanted to give his own chosen name to his Colorado home, settling on "Clonmel." The new president was the guest of honor for the September 22, 1909, ceremonies marking the name change. Invitations went out to trainloads of Denver citizens, and the September 23 issue of *The Denver Republican* listed the names of no fewer than 300 prominent citizens "noticed" at the event. Joining President Taft and Mr. and Mrs. Walsh in the receiving line were Governor and Mrs. Shafroth and Captain Archie Butt, a high-ranking member of the Taft administration who later perished on the *Titanic*. Other dignitaries present included Denver mayor Robert Speer, Secretary of the Interior Richard Ballinger, Colorado senator Thomas Patterson, Wyoming senator Francis Warren, and former Colorado governors Charles Thomas, James Orman, and James Peabody. The president expressed his great pleasure on being asked to

> rebaptize . . . this beautiful estate and call it "Clonmel." "Clonmel" is a
> beautiful place in the County Tipperary. The hard headed immigrants from
> Tipperary and from every part of the Emerald Isle have come to the front
> as they deserve to come to the front in America. . . . I consecrate this the
> estate of "Clonmel." I wish I could connect with it in some way the name of

Walsh, but as that goes without saying, both in Denver and throughout the country, it is unnecessary. I congratulate the people of this vicinity that Mr. and Mrs. Walsh are their neighbors. We in Washington feel delighted that they are neighbors of ours. Their generosity and kindly courtesy are known the country over.[19]

The large and jovial Taft could not resist a joke about Tom's Irish origins, probably a continuing banter between the two men, for Tom had once closed a letter to Taft with "the Gods or the Irish (which mean the same) were kind to me." Taft now recalled a story told to him by a high-level Irish judge who had once held court in Tipperary. In a manslaughter case, the court found the defendant guilty of striking another man with a blackthorn stick. The victim's demise was hastened by the fact that he had a "paper skull." Asked if he knew of any reason why the judgment of the court should not be carried out, the guilty party sought the answer to just one question: "I would like to ask what the 'divil' a man with a head like that was doing in Tipperary?" Tom later described the president to Evalyn (who was not present) as "shaking like an earthquake of merriment."[20]

A SENATOR FOR THE COMMON MAN?

No sooner had Walsh returned to Colorado than his name was once again mentioned for high public office. The leading Republican contender in the 1906 U.S. Senate race was the "smelter king" from Pueblo, Simon Guggenheim. Walsh and Guggenheim were personal friends. Nonetheless, Tom hosted a luncheon for leading Republicans at Wolhurst and refrained from declining to be included in the race. His motivation may have been to make certain Guggenheim would know his candidacy was not a sure thing. Evalyn felt her father both talked like a candidate and at the same time let it be known he was not trying to be one.

Later in the year, Walsh served as director general of the Pikes Peak Centennial Celebration in Colorado Springs. On September 27 he presented one of many addresses by dignitaries. He chose for his topic the clouds threatening the country, which might cause the United States to join the ranks of failed civilizations. He found the darkest cloud to be accumulated and concentrated wealth, "crushing from the masses the life of individual ownership, individual independence, and, almost, individual existence." Since no wealth could be created without the assistance of the people, they should receive their proportionate share. He found the greatest cause of the decline of civilizations to be human selfishness. It carried with it the threat of eventual business stagnation, with millions thrown out of work. As a response to the threat, he suggested a graduated tax on accumulating fortunes. He was also concerned about the inability of the masses to receive credit from banks, seeing no reason why the government could not create a department of savings banks to accomplish this end. The masses could also benefit from direct election of public officials, an obvious reference to the political race he was contemplating, for senators were still chosen by state legislatures. Finally, he closed by emphasizing the responsibility the masses must shoulder in return: that of patriotism.[21]

The Denver Post accused Walsh of startling his listeners by advocating "modified Socialism." It feared he had stepped on the toes of at least a few of the millionaires seated before him. In fact, the more inflammatory aspects of the speech, invoking concern for the poor and institution of an income tax as a remedy, were similar to statements Theodore Roosevelt was making at the same time. Evalyn saw a certain appeal to the masses that might have placed her father in serious contention against fellow millionaire Guggenheim. However, Tom Walsh's Senate candidacy went no further. Lack of motivation by Walsh was one reason. An even greater reason was the huge expense Simon Guggenhein was willing to undertake to virtually "buy" the seat. Called the financial "angel" of the Colorado Republican Party, he developed a special relationship with the party's state chairman, John F. Vivian, who could call on him for money at any time.[22]

Therefore, little surprise was evinced when the Colorado legislature picked Guggenheim for the seat later in 1906, with no showing of regret by Walsh. A later account by his old friend General Frank Hall depicts Tom's general frustration with the machinations of politics. Hall predicted failure when approached by an unidentified member of a political syndicate seeking an introduction to the owner of Wolhurst. The proposition was that Walsh should declare as a Senate candidate and then furnish a large campaign fund. The man, whose principles Hall held in low esteem, later returned to complain that Walsh had turned him down cold. Hall felt that Walsh's standing was so high in both Colorado and the nation's capital that a Senate seat would have added little to his reputation.

In 1908, when Walsh served as a delegate to the Republican National Convention in Chicago, he hosted a dinner for other Colorado delegates and senators from other states. The senators impressed upon the Coloradans that they would welcome a Senator Thomas F. Walsh of Colorado, with immeasurable benefits flowing to the state from his election. Nothing further happened. Walsh did serve as a presidential elector in the 1908 election, casting his vote for his friend William Howard Taft. The following year, according to one source, Republicans sought a Walsh candidacy three years in advance of the 1912 expiration of Senator Guggenheim's term. Tom replied, "Unless the people of Colorado tender me the nomination, I will not go into such unseemly campaigns as Colorado has had in the last few years."[23]

If Walsh could not or did not want to aspire to high office, he was certainly willing to aid his friends who did. One such friend was Myron T. Herrick, Ohio politician and millionaire businessman. Following Taft's election, Herrick sought appointment as secretary of the treasury. His friend Tom Walsh wrote a glowing letter to the president-elect about Herrick's qualifications and also defended him against charges of corporate malfeasance in Colorado. At the time, Herrick was serving as president of the Colorado Power Company. Accompanying Walsh's letter to Taft is a newspaper article charging Herrick's company with an attempt to monopolize waterpower in the West. It also charged the company with denying the Reclamation Service access to "perhaps the best reclamation reservoir site on the continent" and accused Herrick of being a tool of Rockefeller interests.

Walsh was no stranger to the circumstances behind the attacks on Herrick. The land in question was the Gore Canyon, where efforts had been made through the Reclamation Service to block the Moffat Road four years before. Walsh was also an investor in the Colorado Power Company, and so he sought to educate Taft on the true facts in his three-page letter of January 5, 1909. Addressing his letter to "My dear Judge," Walsh defended his friend against a gross injustice. He had thoroughly investigated Herrick and his company, Colorado Power, before investing. Walsh's research had convinced him that "my ideas were his exactly, and that he would see to it that no stock should be offered for sale until it was on a paying basis; and further, that the public, under his presidency, would always be kept as fully posted on the affairs and conditions of the company as he was." As for the company's actions in Gore Canyon, "All the Power Company did was to divert the waters, without interfering with the railroad, through a long tunnel parallel with the bed of the river, which gave a big drop to the water volume, and instead of allowing it to run idly to the ocean, harnessed it into use for benefit of human beings. This is what the company has done wherever it has developed power. It has not impaired in any case the use of the water for purposes of irrigation." In regard to his friend's worthiness to assume high office, "[Y]ou will pardon me if I say that it will give me the greatest pleasure to see Mr. Herrick in your cabinet. I know his great ability in matters of business, his pure life, his sterling honesty, his high sense of patriotism and justice, and his broad, liberal and sympathetic soul. I consider him one of God's noblemen; and knowing him as I do, I would, as I said, be delighted to see him a member of your official family."

Myron T. Herrick was no stranger to William Howard Taft. Herrick had made his fortune as a Cleveland banker, then served a term as Ohio's governor before reentering the business world. In the end, Taft picked another of Walsh's friends, Chicago banker Franklin MacVeagh, as his treasury secretary. Taft must have felt no ill will toward Herrick, however, for he later appointed him ambassador to France, where the Ohioan distinguished himself as a friend of that nation in the years leading up to World War I. Herrick was also a long-time associate of another Ohio politician who would become a close friend of the Walsh family, Warren G. Harding. Harding served as Herrick's lieutenant governor, then as a U.S. senator from Ohio. Long after Tom Walsh's death, when Harding ascended to the nation's highest office, his friendship with Evalyn and her family would prove more burden than blessing (as further described in Chapter 17).[24]

FAMILY AND COUNTRY

CHAPTER FIFTEEN

A HONEYMOON TO REMEMBER

Evalyn's on-again, off-again romance with Ned McLean dated back to before her accident. Finally she told him she would accept his latest marriage proposal only if he would quit drinking. Ned agreed (at least for the moment), and soon he won over the skeptical Tom and Carrie as well. Washington and Denver society expected an extravagant wedding of two children from prominent families. Evalyn and Ned decided to save their families the time, trouble, and expense of a large event, and on the afternoon of July 22, 1908, they eloped in a small ceremony with a few friends in Denver. Among those friends were smelting heir Crawford Hill, owner of *The Denver Republican*, and his wife, Louise, "queen" of the Denver social register. Tom was away at the Republican National Convention when the bride and groom returned to Wolhurst. Carrie showed mild displeasure at missing out on the planned musicales, receptions, dinners, and dances. She did order a large wedding feast.

Tom had few regrets that he would not be hosting one more lavish affair. Returning from the convention, he optimistically reported to Tim Kennedy that the "little rascal cupid got in his work and made Evalyn marry the one and only young man she ever loved and who in return adored her. . . . Young Ed McLean is a fine, handsome young man, very unselfish, considerate and kind— as I said, he adores Evalyn and well he might, for she is a beautiful character."[1]

Evalyn and Ned's European honeymoon in September more than made up for the missed formal wedding. The two fathers, Tom Walsh and John McLean, decided, in Evalyn's words, to "match each other in extravagance," giving the couple $100,000 apiece. The newlyweds took along far more than money, as disclosed by the three-page Treasury Department Declaration entitled "List of wearing apparel and personal effects of Mrs. Edward B. McLean, to be taken abroad, sailing on the S/S 'Rotterdam' from the port of New York, N.Y. Sept. 15, 1908, and to be returned to the United States during the year." The jewelry section consisted of:

2 diamond necklaces
2 strings of pearls
13 diamond and emerald rings
1 enameled watch
1 turquoise & diamond brooch
3 diamond pins
2 diamond bracelets
1 diamond studded gold hand bag
1 turquoise and diamond piece
1 diamond and ruby watch

The two-and-a-half-page section of wearing apparel and personal effects contained, among other items:

1 white rabbit coat, 12 silk blouses
1 mink set, 12 linen blouses
1 sable set (coat, etc.), 24 lace blouses
1 chinchilla set (jacket, etc.), 1 black muff and stole
16 high neck afternoon gowns (lace, silk, and linen)
12 dinner gowns (silk)
8 embroidered pillows
27 hats
50 pairs shoes and slippers
150 pairs silk stockings
15 dozen kid gloves (pairs)[2]

Maggie Buggy, Evalyn's lady-in-waiting, and Platt, the chauffeur, accompanied the young couple. A new Mercedes awaited them at the dock in Amsterdam, with Maggie and Platt left to drive the Packard that had crossed the sea with them. They drove through Holland and Germany to Berlin. "Dresden, Leipzig, Cologne, Dusseldorf—each one to me stands for a shopping spree," recalled Evalyn. Along the way they decided one Mercedes was not enough and rushed to Paris to buy another (if for no other reason than to carry all their belongings). In Berlin Ned decided to try his hand at high-level influence. His aunt's husband was a Russian diplomat named George Bakhmeteff, and Ned had learned that Uncle George was under consideration to be the czar's ambassador to Washington. The young nephew wired his uncle of his intention to use money and personal connections to secure the ambassadorship for him. Bakhmeteff immediately wired back that Ned should cease all interference immediately. Ned flew into a rage, not his last in what would prove a stormy marriage.

Vienna followed, then Constantinople. Here the U.S. ambassador, a friend of both fathers, offered his assistance. Evalyn made two requests: to see the sultan and to see his harem. The latter was especially difficult to achieve, yet the ambassador complied. Evalyn's main recollection of both events was of the number of exquisite jewels on display. Egypt was next, where Evalyn confesses to buying "a lot of junk," then the Holy Land, where Ned had to save Evalyn from drowning in the River Jordan. Palestine, the couple decided, did not suit their mood, and ten days later they were back in Paris.

Not enough of the $200,000 was left to pay their Paris hotel bill, so wires went out to their fathers. John McLean balked at further contributions. Tom, however, sent "fresh credit." Evalyn suddenly remembered that she had never picked out the wedding gift her father had promised her. Pierre Cartier Jewelers was just down the street, and there she discovered the 92½-carat Star of the East. One hundred twenty-five thousand dollars later it was hers, deemed by the two to be a combination wedding and Christmas present. Only U.S. customs remained as a potential problem. Evalyn sneaked the jewel past the customs agents and was soon displaying it to the parents in Washington. Tom, she tells us, was impressed and even laughed at the customs deception. The McLeans displayed different reactions. Emily found the stone hideous, and John feared for his reputation as a prominent editor should the customs story leak out. Tom promised to send his lawyer to square everything with the officials. His final comment, she recalls, was, "Hell, I am glad to buy it for Evalyn. There won't be a bit of trouble. I'll send word to the customs men that she is not all there."[3]

Tom and Carrie could not have been overly critical of the young couple's spending habits, for, as disclosed in a letter they wrote right after the start of the honeymoon, the parents were spending plenty on their side of the ocean. Writing from New York's Hotel St. Regis on September 18, 1908, they report:

> My dearest children,
>
> We start for Wolhurst in a few minutes. After your sailing the two Pops and two Moms pooled their issues and went to the theatres and stood bravely shoulder to shoulder in their efforts to look and feel cheerful. They did their "damndest" to comfort each other and succeeded as well as possible. The quartet are fortunately congenial. We are all delightfully healthy and well and all expect to plunge into the doing of great things in the near future. In fact, Mama Carrie Bell took the plunge the day after you left and has been hunting for things for her darlings every day since the only satisfaction I could get when I asked for information was "Wait and see how these darlings' rooms will look when I have finished with [them]."
>
> The papers announce that cholera is raging in St. Petersburg. If so, give it the glad go by. Papa Mac is liable to have things going his way in the Senatorial line, whilst poor amiable Papa Tommy the dear dear boy must continue to be a 0 in things political as he is in other things; that is, unless you two dears come back and boost him, say two or more years from now when he will be more matured. *He is so young.* Well, dear ones, have a good restful time. . . . We will probably attend the Trans-Mississippi Congress in San Francisco from 6 to 10 October. Keep us full posted on your movements so we can reach you by cable at any time; also, where letters will reach you. If you go to Berlin, don't fail to write the de Hagerman Lindecroomes, and the Hills, both good friends of ours. Well dear pets, we miss you, but the best part of us, our hearts' love, is ever and always with you, and our prayers rise to Heaven supplicating for you every possible human happiness, protection from all harm and a safe return to your parents,
>
> Carrie and Tom

While this letter seems to show Carrie's disappointment at Tom's lack of political success, in fact the letter is in Tom's handwriting and unmistakably in his style, frequently given to self-deprecation. John R. McLean did not succeed in becoming a U.S. senator, so the two fathers had one more thing in common.[4]

A parental letter of November 1 to the honeymooners is in Carrie's script and style, written from Wolhurst:

> Dear darling children,
>
> We were so delighted to get your letter yesterday and know you were both so well, happy and amused. Father is playing bridge with Mr. and Mrs.

Hill [Crawford and Louise] and Mr. English, who came out last night to dinner, after which they played till two o'clock in the morning. . . . Are going tomorrow night to the Campions and hear the election returns. . . . We have sent you letters all over Europe to the Credit Lyonnais. Hope you got them. You have not said you got your fur coats but presume you did. How nice you are going to the Holy Land together. So much better than Monte Carlo. I do hope the weather will be good for your trip from Naples to Paris. . . . Father has had a bad cold but is all right again. . . . Father has two new dogs, very nice wolf hounds, named Jack and Jill. They are a lot of company for him when he walks around the place. . . . Well, darling babies, be good and enjoy yourselves and remember we love you always the same,
Mother and Father[5]

HELPING FAMILY ON BOTH SIDES OF THE ATLANTIC

Tom's love of family extended well beyond his wife, daughter, and son-in-law and to both sides of the Atlantic. His other family members frequently struggled to make ends meet. After Patrick died in 1897, his widow, Josephine, and her children continued to live in the little town of Florence, Colorado. Tom had promised to send Josephine money for her son Frank's education, and on August 8, 1904, his anxious sister-in-law wrote him that the young nephew "has fully made up his mind to take up the study of medicine. . . . You know what it costs. I am very nervous and hope you will let me know what you intend doing. Oh, I do wish his father could have lived to raise him. It is hard for a lone mother. With love to all from a fond sister, Joe."

Tom mailed the money in October 1904, although no Dr. Frank Walsh ever emerged. By May 1909, Frank's interest had shifted to motion pictures. His uncle once again sent a stipend, although by the time he had received it in July, Frank had (perhaps wisely) decided to stay at his position as a clerk for the Wells Fargo Company. Later, after Tom's death, Carrie sent more money to help Frank in a business venture, with results unknown. While Frank disappears from the family papers after this point, his sister Minnie Koontz corresponded with her cousin Evalyn for a long time, naming her daughter Evalyn Walsh Koontz. She also sent Evalyn the gift of the crucifix that had belonged to their Grandmother Bridget.[6]

Tom's brother Michael died in Denver in early December 1904. The city's newspapers described Michael Walsh as a successful miner and New Mexico cattle rancher, who had retired to Denver three years earlier because of ill health. Tom had recently given Michael 160 acres of ranch land near Sterling, on Colorado's eastern plains. Michael and his family had been living near Maria and Arthur Lafferty during his last illness. Maria was too distraught to notify Tom of their older brother's death, so a family friend named L. H. Smith conveyed the word to Washington. Tom responded that "Maria must be sensible; whilst death is a very sad event in any family, still living and constant suffering is a thousand times worse." Tom sent John Benson to represent him at his brother's funeral and to pay all the expenses. Evalyn showed little remorse for the passing of the uncle who had inspired others in the family to come to America. Noting that he passed away from dropsy of the liver, she blamed his death as the reason the Walshes could not entertain during the 1904 holidays.

Tom also helped Michael's daughter Marguerite (Maggie) with the education of her son Tom and sent her a new automobile. Unfortunately, her kind uncle's gift exploded as a result of a faulty valve and injured her severely. She later made a full recovery.[7]

Tom's relationship with his brother Michael and with the public might well be summed up in his response to a letter he received at 2020 Massachusetts in May 1904. John W. Doyle of Leadville, Colorado, wrote the former resident of his town, now a well-known millionaire, requesting the sum of twenty-six dollars "due me for labor performed on a claim in Evansville called the John Mitchell. I went to work on it with your brother Mike in February '79, he quit it and went on the police force in Leadville and I got Mike Kennedy, and he quit and I hire [sic] a man name of McGuiggan to finish the work, and paid him his share of the amount I claim due me." Tom Walsh replied, "I have no memory whatever of neglecting having paid every cent on the work we had done in Evans Gulch in the year 1879; on the contrary, I was very particular in settling all of the bills. However, lest I should do you an injustice, and believing you to be an old acquaintance of mine, I remit the amount you say was due you, of $26.00."[8]

With the death of his sister Maria Lafferty in January 1908, Tom had lost all his brothers and sisters except Kate in Ireland. Maria's obituary noted her closeness to Tom, who offered financial and personal aid to Maria, her husband, Arthur, and the foster children the childless couple raised. In a letter from Maria to her brother, probably written in 1904, she thanks Tom for having a beneficial effect on her husband. Writing upon her return from a trip to Ireland, she indicated that "when I came home I found Arthur so good and careful. He has quit playing cards and drink all together. That is the best [it] could be for my health, as I could not ever bear to have him spend your good money foolishly." Arthur's 1916 obituary noted that he was a respected citizen and part-owner of the Columbia Hotel in Denver.

At least three of the foster children raised by Arthur and Maria Lafferty became so close to Tom that they called him "uncle." An undated letter from a girl named Irene, attending Loretto Heights Academy, invites the famous uncle to her Junior Commencement exercise, where "I will play the piano. I hope you will be here in time for it." Tom also took a special interest in brothers Fred and Will Chambers, paying for their education and training. Two 1904 letters from attorney Stephen A. Osborn show Tom supporting the two boys' acceptance into the U.S. Navy. Apparently only Fred, the more promising of the two, actually went into navy training. Later, Fred wrote Tom thanking him for the gift of $100 to pay for room and board at an unnamed school.[9]

Tom never forgot his three Worcester sweethearts, cousins Catherine, Joanna, and Sarah Power, and their families. The Walsh Papers disclose many letters to and from Worcester, mostly from Walsh to Tim Kennedy, Joanna Power's husband. Kennedy often supplied Walsh with coachmen, knowing that kindness to horses was a prime requirement for the job. Walsh in return sent money to the cousins at Christmas and other times of the year as well. A letter Tom wrote just after his brother Michael's death in 1904 is typical:

> My Dear Tim,
>   Christmas is fast approaching and so am I in a humble way asking for a small part in the family gatherings of my three sweethearts in the coming Christmas. Please divide the enclosed check among them and also divide what they will prize far more than the check—lots of my love and sincerest wishes for a happy Christmas.
>   Sincerely yours, Thomas F. Walsh
> P.S. Poor Mike died ten days ago. Is Sexton employed? Pat is a good man around horses but makes a poor showing on the bone—we like him very much otherwise. T.

Through Vinson's death, the Walshes' move to Colorado, and the rising national prominence of their favorite cousin, the Worcester family could still expect regular correspondence and financial assistance. What is perhaps Tom's last letter to them is addressed to Tim Sullivan, an old family friend dating back to their Tipperary days. Tom's cousin Catherine (Kate) had passed away two years before. The absence of Tim Kennedy is not explained, for he lived until 1918. Writing on November 20, 1909, Tom instructs Sullivan:

> My dear Tim,
>   Will you please get the enclosed check cashed and divide it between my two sweethearts and Kate's family. We are all enjoying the blessings of good health. You "Lads of tips" would feel good if you heard President Taft

christen and rename Wolhurst Clonmel when he visited us this September. I am sending you a paper that tells of it. I hope the relatives are all in good health, also Jer Sullivan and family. I am expecting to become a grandfather about Christmas. I am sending lots of love with this little check to all the folks including your dear good self.

Thomas F. Walsh[10]

Tom had not seen his family in Ireland for many years prior to his return in 1899. Evalyn remembered that her father "picked up the threads of many old friendships, and his hand was in and out of his pocket throughout the day; he made no show of his giving, not ever." Evalyn does not mention the names of any Irish relatives she met, concentrating more on a woman who placed an Irish curse on her. Tom returned in 1903 to place his limestone cross on his mother's grave in Kilmurray Cemetery and to remember some of his other beloved Irish relatives as well. His inscription reads:

> In Memory of Bridget Walsh of Baptist Grange Died 12 Oct, 1852 Age 33 years Erected by her affectionate son Thomas F. Walsh of Washington, D.C., U.S.A. His sister Alice aged 10 months, and of his uncle Peter Walsh died 2 Aug. 1883 aged 72. Also his nephews Thomas and William who died young, and his grandfather John Walsh, died 2 Sep. 1848, aged 79 years.[11]

Beginning in 1903, the Walsh Papers disclose an ongoing correspondence between Ireland and Washington. Among the first are letters from Tom's brother-in-law John Healy, his sister Margaret's husband, and from their daughter Annie. The family lived in Boherbue, County Cork, where John had retired after years in the Irish constabulary. The letters sadly report Margaret's passing in 1894. Annie's letter boldly requests aid for her father, two sisters and brother, and herself, "as you sir are placed above the wants of necessity . . . perhaps your recollection of our mother and your relation to her may plead my excuse for stating so much and enlist your kind consideration on our behalf." John Healy asked if his daughter Harriet could come to America. Tom replied in June 1904:

> My dear Mr. Healy:-
> It is . . . a very serious matter to have [a] young girl come to stay in this country without having friends to guide and watch over her. . . . This city, Washington, . . . would not be a desirable place for her to come at all, for it would be very difficult for her to get such a situation that would suit her here.
> We are leaving tomorrow for the West, to be gone all summer. When we return next fall, I will have some inquiries made in New York as to what can be done. In the meantime I beg to enclose draft for twenty pounds for

the children, which you will please distribute amongst them according to your best judgment.

Healy wrote back that the money was most appreciated and that it had paid the fee for his daughter Charlotte to attend a Dublin training college for teachers. He reports on the family in Baptistgrange, noting that Tom's sister Kate had married a man named Shea and was living "in the old farm where you were all reared" and that his brother John's family was next door. Tom also sent a check to Kate in a November 1904 letter. Kate ended up living far longer than the others in her generation, dying around 1951. Tom's pattern of giving continued, although if one family story can be believed, he once sent a particularly large sum of money that was lost and never received.[12]

John, Tom's oldest brother, had remained a farmer in the family's home area. Tom sent him money on a regular basis, both for his family and for the poor in the nearby town of Fethard. By 1903, John Walsh was benefiting from his longtime work with the Irish Land League, for he had the opportunity to purchase the farm he had rented for so many years. Tom sent the money to provide his brother with his dream. Unfortunately, by the time it arrived John was seriously ill, and much of the farm money went for his medical needs. At about the same time, John unwisely signed for the debt of one Mikey Power to the Bank of Ireland. Power soon defaulted on the loan. John Walsh died in June 1903, soon after the death of his wife, Catherine. Several months later their daughter Joanna reported to her generous uncle in Washington that the bank had claimed all that remained of the money for the farm. Joanna, recently married to Peter McGrath, stated her resolve to keep the farm, but the family letters do not disclose if she succeeded.[13]

After John's death, Tom kept up the practice of aiding the area's poor. Before he died, John had asked a local man named Richard McCarthy to administer the fund. On one occasion Joanna McGrath reported that McCarthy had nearly exhausted the fund in burying one recipient. Perhaps for that reason, Walsh wrote a 1904 letter to McCarthy, requesting that he "send me a little statement on the condition of the fund of the poor persons in Fethard which we are assisting." Presumably, Tom found the fund in order at the time. However, later in the year, following a trip to Ireland, Maria Lafferty reported that the fox might be guarding the hen house, for some of the poor were using Tom's gifts to "get drunk at McCarthy's." Walsh also made a contribution to start a library in Fethard. The closeness of his family members no doubt led to his attraction to the small town, but the city of Clonmel a few miles to the south was otherwise dear to his heart.[14]

A PUBLIC-SPIRITED CITIZEN AND PATRON

Walsh's memberships in clubs and societies continued to grow; a list compiled for the years 1907–1908 includes no fewer than forty-nine affiliations. His life memberships included the Aero Club of Washington, American Irish Historical Society, American Mining Congress, American Political Science Association, Archaeological Institute of America, Automobile Club of America, Colorado State Commercial Association, Colorado State Forestry Association, Denver Press Club, El Jebel Association, Friendly Sons of St. Patrick, Littleton Club, National Geographical Society, Sons of Colorado, and Western Stock Show Association. While Denver and Washington groups dominated the list, Walsh belonged to the Chambers of Commerce in New York, Naples, Paris, and London, as well as to the Hellenic Travelers Club of London. He remained a proud member of Ouray's Masonic Lodge No. 37.[15]

Tom's interest in mining now focused on research involving rare western minerals, especially radium. On May 21, 1908, his letter on the subject was read to the House of Representatives in Washington. He asked for government action on the research and exploration of radium, where Europe had taken the lead. "If we want an atom of it [radium]," Walsh stressed, "we must beg for it from the Austrian government." Many areas of the United States, especially in the West, held radium deposits but needed an impetus to start a radium business. In the same letter he also recommended creation of a federal Bureau of Mines, for "[t]he great national industry of mining is worthy of the same governmental encouragement and protection that is given to the other industries, especially in the saving of life." The House approved creation of the bureau by a vote of 222 to 29.[16]

Walsh also donated some of his own money to support the scientific study of radium. On May 22, 1908, he gave the Colorado School of Mines $1,000 for the Vinson Walsh Research Fund. In his speech that year to the school's graduates, he stressed that rarer minerals needed more attention, with particular emphasis on "[r]adium, that miracle of the century. . . . We know little of its properties, but even that little fills us with wonder and amazement, and hints at undreamed of possibilities in this unexplored region of physical science." The School of Mines in turn created the Vinson Walsh Research Department. Its first director, Dr. Herman Fleck, used the endowment to study western radium-bearing ores and to patent the first process to extract the elements radium, vanadium, and uranium. This led to the Colorado radium boom, which lasted into the 1920s, establishing the School of Mines and the Denver area as centers for study of both the potential and the hazards of these rare substances.[17]

Tom's love and appreciation of animals led to his election as president of the Colorado Humane Society. The society's September 1908 newsletter presented a biography of its new leader, noting with favor the signs he had posted at both the Camp Bird Mine and Wolhurst warning employees and others that no bird or other wild creature was to be harmed in any way. Walsh had earlier sent the newsletter a graphic description of an Easter Sunday bullfight in Madrid. He concluded his acceptance speech with the wisdom (which he had not always heeded), "Don't put shotguns into the hands of your boys for them to go out and destroy every little bird or other animal that crosses their path. . . . No, try the better way. Treat all of God's creatures in a gentle, humane way and, believe me, you will be richly rewarded." Evalyn later recalled finding a receipt for $700 worth of birdseed at Wolhurst, an excess, she thought. In 1909 Walsh even criticized his good friend Theodore Roosevelt, who had just concluded a well-publicized African safari after his term as president ended.[18]

While Walsh continued to actively promote western irrigation, others took the lead in on-the-ground development. Overlooked in the publicity about President Taft's 1909 visit to rechristen Clonmel was the fact that one of the president's next stops was to support a cause of longtime interest to Tom Walsh. After leaving Clonmel, the presidential train traveled to Montrose, Colorado. There, on the morning of September 24, 1909, President Taft rang a bell that was electrically wired to open the headgate of the Gunnison Tunnel. The symbolic first water poured from the tunnel, headed for the parched Uncompahgre Valley (although because of a malfunction the initial water flow had to be stopped). Its permanent flow commenced the next day. Many important citizens of Colorado and the nation were present for the historic event, including Chipeta, the widow of Chief Ouray. Tom and Carrie Walsh were also present, joining their friend Governor John Shafroth in the review stand. Otherwise, they were not active participants in the ceremony.

The heroes of the Gunnison Tunnel opening were the engineers who drove the bore through bedrock in an outstanding technological achievement. Other honorees included the area's Colorado legislators and former congressman John Bell, who made the dream a reality by spearheading new state and federal laws. As the 1909 president of the Trans-Mississippi Congress, Tom Walsh played an important role in organizing the event. Amazingly, he is not singled out for praise in the press coverage of the ceremonies at Montrose. One reason was probably his own sense of fundamental fairness. Walsh's speeches on behalf of irrigation never mentioned the Uncompahgre Valley specifically (or any other place, for that matter). He likely saw his job as a promoter of national irrigation generally, while preference shown to any particular area might undermine his credibility. Another reason was his health. Pictures taken at the gala for Clonmel plainly show that the cheerful, ruddy-faced Irishman of earlier days had been replaced by a gaunt and stooped figure with a careworn face, a man who had aged considerably in a short number of years. Obviously, he had little stamina after putting on the elaborate festivities at his home.[19]

Still, Walsh could be heartened by the praise of others. Earlier in the summer he had received a kind letter from Senator Francis Warren of Wyoming, chair of the Senate Committee on Military Affairs. After finishing some business with Walsh before the tunnel's grand opening, Warren concludes, "Colorado may well be proud of having a citizen like you who has the means, the disposition, and the peculiar tact to attract people of prominence, not only to yourself but to the locality for which you have done so much, and which, of course, originally gave you somewhat of a look-in upon her buried treasures."[20]

THE PASSING OF THOMAS F. WALSH

CHAPTER SIXTEEN

THE GOLDEN CRADLE

Evalyn felt that as Tom smiled at his Clonmel guests, they could not see that he was dying. His health was failing rapidly, and he began making end-of-life decisions. He had recently received a very large payment from Camp Bird, Ltd. as one of his last dividends from the sale. He quickly distributed it among family members. Tom gave $15,000 in bonds to his attorney, Stephen Osborn, to be distributed among the families of his sister and two brothers in Colorado. He bought the Sears Estate in Bar Harbor, Maine, for Evalyn and Ned, then furnished Ned's office and continued to shower monetary gifts on the son-in-law that exceeded the tight allowance his own father paid. Earlier in the year, Evalyn and Ned had given Tom and Carrie the joyous news of an expected new arrival in the family. On December 18, 1909, their first child, Vinson Walsh McLean, was born. The newspapers christened him the "hundred-million dollar baby." Tom sent Vinson's parents another $50,000 of his Camp Bird money to celebrate the birth of the only grandchild he would know.

Walsh's old friend King Leopold, learning that the child was on the way, promised to send a golden cradle. The promise was one of the Belgian monarch's last acts. Having "sold" the Congo to his countrymen, the king enjoyed even greater riches and shared at least a few with his friends during the brief life that was left him. On December 17, one day before Vinson's birth, Leopold succumbed to cancer. The golden cradle arrived in Washington the following February, Leopold's promise carried out by the new king, his nephew Albert.[1]

Another of Leopold's final acts was to once again marry Caroline, the Baroness de Vaughan, his companion for many years. Their relationship dated back well before the death of Queen Clementine, the wife Leopold hated. Some sources have suggested that Caroline was once a Paris prostitute. Her chief sin was coming from a level of society lower than that considered acceptable for a liaison with European nobility. Leopold and Caroline had first tried to marry in 1902, not long after Clementine's death, but the ceremony was secret and of doubtful validity. The second marriage was open and intended to legitimize Leopold's two sons with Caroline, probably with the intention that the eldest would become king. The great majority of the Belgian people may have disagreed, yet the friendly Vatican sanctified the marriage. Leopold also tried to leave most of his estate to his two sons, having made every attempt to disinherit his three daughters with Clementine. A threatened crisis over succession to the Belgian throne was averted when the people overwhelmingly supported Albert, who was much more popular than his uncle.

Despite the many efforts of his powerful friends, Leopold's reputation with the U.S. press was very unfavorable. Many Colorado papers painted the king in a strongly negative light in their obituaries. His unsavory human rights record in the Congo was one charge, and another was a promiscuous lifestyle exemplified by his liaison with the Baroness de Vaughan, all of which left his country with a considerable mess.[2] Loudest of all was the acid-tongued David F. Day, former editor of Ouray's *Solid Muldoon*, now pouring forth his venom in the *Durango Weekly Democrat*. In a short editorial comment the day after Leopold's death simply titled, "Belgium's King," Day fomented, "He is dead— again. Leopold was the worst dose of degeneracy that ever blew into a throne. With him virtue was a football; womanhood a door mat; cunning an accomplishment; cruelty a passtime [sic]. . . . The blackest page in Belgium's history, a page of oppression, cruelty and murder, of crime and torture. . . . There were no fig leaves about the loins of Paris when the old degenerate got busy. May he be long dead. We are not used to writing the eiderdown obituaries."[3]

Tom Walsh grieved the death of his friend and made a supportive press statement. Asked to comment on the king's personality, Walsh replied:

> You can put me on record as asserting that no better monarch has lived than King Leopold of Belgium. He was a man who had been greatly traduced, and entirely without reason. He was an entirely different man than many people believed him to be. With Congo atrocities, such as were attributed to him, I know he had nothing to do, for I know him intimately and talked with him at length concerning his interests there. He was not the man of immorality such as has been painted. But on the other hand he was of delightful personality and ever mindful of the welfare of the people of Belgium.[4]

Walsh also sent a cablegram with condolences to the Belgian court, which Charles Thomas described as hastily drawn together. It apparently was not printed in Denver newspapers, which almost universally held Walsh in the highest esteem. These papers did note Walsh as a close friend of the king but printed nothing derogatory about the relationship. Even this gesture may simply have reflected pride that a Colorado man was affiliated with a king, even a controversial one. When it came to the United States, Leopold no doubt had higher regard for the political power of Nelson Aldrich or the incredible wealth of the Guggenheims than for the mining expertise of Tom Walsh. Prominent writings later in the twentieth century on the king's contacts and mining affiliates in the United States do not mention Walsh at all.[5]

David Day, however, felt none of the editorial constraints of his Denver counterparts. He remained an avowed opponent of mine owners, regardless of any redeeming qualities they might possess. While the acid tongue remained, some of Day's other journalistic skills seem to have left him by 1909, as witnessed in his December 24 editorial entitled "To the Rescue":

> Tom Walsh has the glad hand for King Leopold. Leopold was the master degenerate of modern times. His business investment, luck, made him a libertine. Tom Walsh's moral record would not cause the flush of shame to crimson a cold storage egg. Leopold was a money made and titled degenerate. Tom Walsh had the price and the inclination. He poses for senator in Colorado. The love we bear for wife, mother and daughter will enable us to get busy. Tom Walsh's money may make him senator in this state, but we shall be in at the finish. In point of morality Leopold and Walsh were twins. Both should have been still borned [sic].[6]

According to Charles Thomas, other Colorado newspapers (apparently outside Denver) republished Day's attack.[7] Thomas's standing as a former governor and soon a U.S. senator from Colorado, together with his personal and professional closeness to Walsh, makes him a credible source. However, coverage of Day's attack on Walsh in any other newspaper has not survived in the microfilm collections of the Denver Public Library and the Colorado Historical Society.

LAST ILLNESS

Tom Walsh's natural reaction to Day's charges was outrage, although it never reached the press. There is no indication that Walsh and Day had ever met, communicated, or commented on each other. Walsh certainly knew of Day's record in Ouray and might have considered him a kindred spirit as a fellow sponsor of the Miners' Hospital and proponent of workers' rights. However, Tom had little time to dwell on the subject, mourn the death of his friend the king, or enjoy the new arrival in his family. On January 10, 1910, after six weeks of illness, he suffered a serious heart attack. His doctors soon declared him out of danger but recommended a stay in Florida for the remainder of the winter. The illness, nonetheless, could not keep him from accepting, in absentia, another term as president of the Sons of Colorado on January 28. Florida's seaside air did not prove beneficial. Evalyn soon received word that her father had suffered a severe hemorrhage and was diagnosed with the curse of many who had worked the mines: lung cancer.[8]

Next, the medical experts recommended the drier climate of San Antonio, Texas. According to the press, Tom, Carrie, and the doctors traveled to the Texas city and rented a mansion. Evalyn presents a different account, denying that any doctors were present. Carrie had converted to the Christian Science faith, to her daughter's chagrin, and now insisted that one of her friends, a woman of that faith, was sufficient to care for her husband. Evalyn tells of arriving on the scene, taking charge, evicting her mother's friend, and hiring the best doctor in town, along with a team of nurses. Her critically ill father thanked her, and she in turn thanked the doctors who now gave him morphine.

Whichever story is true, Tom continued to decline. He was receiving hundreds of telegrams wishing him a speedy recovery, but by March 21 it was apparent that the San Antonio trip had been to no avail. Despite denials by Turner Wickersham, his secretary, the consensus among reporters was that Tom Walsh had little time to live, for severe pneumonia had set in.[9]

The next day the family began its return to Washington. Tom was carried to the car, his face drawn and colorless, his eyes deep and sunken, his every move made with great difficulty. Still, the March 23 *Denver Times* predicted a fight from a man "young in years, with the possibility of high deeds yet to be done." The doctors at Johns Hopkins, who had once saved his daughter's leg, tried in vain to stop the cancer, which was too far advanced when he arrived on March 24. Visits from his young grandson were all that sustained him for two more weeks. On the evening of April 8, 1910, six days past his sixtieth birthday, Tom Walsh died.[10]

HE HAD OPPRESSED NOT ONE
SINGLE SOUL IN THE ATTAINMENT

Governor John F. Shafroth spoke for many others when he stated that the citizens of Colorado would miss Tom Walsh more than they would any other citizen of the state who had died. Another prominent Denver citizen, Frank C. Goudy, found him "the most generous-hearted man I ever met, ready to do anything to help someone else. A remarkable thing about him was that, with as little school training as he had, he had a scholarly bent and a polish of manner that bespoke his broad mind and innate fineness."[11] David Moffat mourned the man who had come to the aid of his beleaguered railroad as "loyal and honest and a thoroughly good man in every way."[12] John Benson remembered his boss and friend as "good to the men who worked for him, true to those who had entered into possession of his friendship, charitable to the distressed and needy."[13]

Perhaps the crowning statement by the Denver press appeared in *The Rocky Mountain News*, entitled "Miners Loved Walsh as Friend and Benefactor." The author, Alfred Damon Runyon, was embarking on a career that would leave a large mark on journalism. Now he eulogized, "'Honest wealth is the badge of power; it makes possible the pleasure of doing good.' In that sentence, Thomas F. Walsh, that good man who has passed beyond the Great Barrier, epitomized his ideas of his own vast wealth." Yes, Walsh was very rich, "he was rich beyond the dreams of avarice," but that wealth was clean. He had "oppressed not one single soul in the attainment; it was money that washes as clean as mountain water, but the ownership of it meant to this man simply that it had become possible for him to enjoy the pleasure of doing good." That was also true for other men of means,

> but his greatest benefactions, of which the world will never hear, were
> providing a balm for the sores of poverty. . . . The tall, spare, slightly
> stooped figure in the Prince Albert coat; the flowing mustache that veiled
> a smiling mouth; the gray head bowed against the sun—standing by the
> rippling maples at Clonmel, surrounded by men and women of fashion, by
> music and gaiety, and by his friends—it is a picture easy to conjure up in the
> mind of the average Denver citizen because they have so often seen him so,

but the picture of him distributing, with lavish but quiet hand, his helpful aid among the poor and suffering is the one which will always remain in the heart and memory of thousands. . . . Without Tabor, without Stratton, and certainly without Walsh, the history of this state would have lost much. Hear Tom Walsh: "My friends, your first care must be the building up and perfecting of a high and noble character." That is the way he preached; that is the way he believed.[14]

The passing of an important local citizen brought wide coverage in the Washington, D.C., press. While lacking the flowing prose and emotional expression of Denver writers such as Runyon, Washington writers did provide an in-depth look at the man and his accomplishments. *The Washington Post* noted that Walsh was interested in better transportation, as witnessed by his membership in both the Automobile Club of America and the Aero Club of Washington and his presidency of the latter. The paper also credited him with many works in the advancement of science, foremost among them the establishment of the Vinson Walsh Fund. The *Post* also found Walsh popular as an after-dinner speaker, possessed of an inherited Irish wit.[15]

The Walsh story reached other newspaper audiences throughout the nation. In Durango, Colorado, the *Democrat* provided its readers with a short, unbiased obituary, notable only in that it referred to Walsh as the "silver mining king." The story seems to have been the creation of the Associated Press rather than the paper's editor. Four days later, however, David Day appeared with an editorial, reflecting that "Tom Walsh won a fortune by going from Silverton 'over the range.' Let us at least hope that his journey over the divide will win eternity for him."[16]

Elsewhere in the country, similar glowing yet respectful tributes flowed, many repeating the Associated Press appellation of silver mining king. The Birmingham, Alabama, *News* produced perhaps the best of many exaggerations. The town's mayor, Frank P. O'Brien, informed the local press that he was an old friend of the Walshes and that Tom had met Carrie in a little confectionary shop on Second Avenue in the city sometime in 1872. Their Birmingham wedding took place the following year, with Mayor O'Brien, of course, present.[17]

Tom Walsh was laid to rest in Washington's Rock Creek Cemetery, in a family mausoleum where the family had buried his son, Vinson, and Carrie's sister, Lucy Lee. According to his wishes, his funeral was a simple affair held at 2020 Massachusetts. It was a Scottish Rite Masonic service, with former Colorado senator Henry Teller among the delegates from that organization. President Taft attended his friend's service, as did a Colorado political figure who had known Walsh much longer, Charles S. Thomas. Honorary pallbearers included U.S. Supreme Court Justice Joseph McKenna, House Speaker Joseph Cannon, Colorado senator Charles J. Hughes Jr., John R. McLean, Walsh's secretary Turner A. Wickersham, and his old Chicago friend and business partner David Wegg. Evalyn recalled that another pallbearer was Myron Herrick, "whom we loved."[18]

WOULD HE REMEMBER COLORADO?

The value of Tom Walsh's estate was estimated at $8 million. In today's money the estate would be worth approximately $124 million, making Walsh, then as now, very wealthy but not fabulously so. The state of Colorado held at least $3 million of the estate, and the state's citizens eagerly awaited bequests to their favorite causes. Attorney Stephen A. Osborn predicted, "This much I know: Mr. Walsh entertained large plans which would be of interest to Colorado."[19] Osborn made the statement with confidence, for he had drawn a will for Walsh that left $80,000 to charities in the state. It was not to be, however. Walsh had signed a new will in Washington on January 10, 1910, the same day he suffered his heart attack. The new document placed nearly all his property in a trust for ten years, benefiting only Carrie and Evalyn. After that time the trust was to be divided equally between the two. The will also gave Carrie $100,000 in a special fund to be distributed according to her wishes, taking into account her late husband's desires. Colorado's only place in the will was to designate Clonmel as "that place where I am accustomed to spend my summers." Walsh listed Washington as his place of residence. The new will had been prepared in haste, for both Carrie's and Evalyn's names are misspelled.[20]

Colorado newspapers were shocked. One felt Tom had fallen under the wrong kind of outside influence, that which sought to reduce payment of Colorado inheritance tax over all other motivations. Another Denver reporter felt that had Tom lived, recovered his health, and come to his senses, he would once again have remembered his professed love of Colorado and rescinded his recent acts. For all we know, the reporter might have been close to the truth.

Only the papers of his friend Charles Thomas reveal the depth of Tom's indignation over David Day's attack and its seeming support by others in Colorado. It is a subject Evalyn misses (or avoids), as did the news media of the time. Thomas felt Walsh had been mortally wounded by the attack, which was made when he was far from well. Tom told his friend he wanted to leave Colorado and never return. He directed Thomas, as his longtime attorney, to carry out the steps of removing all his personal property from Colorado, selling Clonmel, and making certain no Colorado inheritance tax would be owed on account of his death. According to state law at that time, if Colorado was a person's residence when he or she died, the state inheritance tax would be levied on the value of all that person's property owned in the state and all non–real estate property owned anywhere else in the country. Therefore, for an estate the size of Walsh's, the tax would have been considerable. Thomas begged his friend to reconsider. However, Tom passed away before the two men could return to the subject. Only the will change, performed by a Washington attorney, carried out Walsh's sudden and furious new plans.[21]

While some in Colorado had expected a bequest, others felt the estate's large inheritance tax (estimated at $100,000 to $150,000) might bode well for state projects. Only four days after the millionaire's death, *The Colorado Springs Herald* announced that proceeds from Walsh's death tax would finally allow the state treasurer to pay for the long-awaited automobile road to Cañon City. Attorney General John T. Barnett announced immediate plans to collect the money. In turn, Walsh's family, executor, and trustee sought to carry out his wishes and prevent, or at least minimize, any payment of the tax to Colorado. Charles Thomas and Stephen Osborn represented the estate. Arapahoe County brought suit for collection of the tax, which by law was the duty of a resident's county.[22] Soon a bizarre testimony unfolded in which many of the acts of kindness and generosity Tom Walsh had exhibited toward the people of Colorado were used against the interests of the estate.

On July 27, 1910, in a hearing before a referee in the state capitol building, Walsh's friends, neighbors, and colleagues swore under oath about his Colorado activities. In nearly every case the witness seemed to have felt Walsh had been acting in a very commendable manner toward his state and community. Nonetheless, such actions might also mean he considered Colorado his residence, exactly what the county intended to prove. Neighbors recalled Tom going out of his way to meet them and invite them to his home. John Springer, a noted local political figure of the time, remembered him saying that his last days could not be spent in a better place than Wolhurst (Clonmel) and the beautiful surroundings of Colorado. Springer and Walsh had also served together in the Republican Party, including as Colorado delegates to the 1908 Republican National Convention. Kate Lilley recalled Tom establishing prizes in Littleton to encourage civic pride in its young people. He told her he had the same interest in all Colorado towns, adding, "beautiful Colorado—it's my home."

The secretary of the Sons of Colorado told how Walsh had obtained the land for the organization's headquarters, donating a portion of the purchase price. Tom qualified for membership in the fraternal order since he had come to live in Colorado while it was still a territory. He also served as the group's pres-

ident in 1909–1910. Edward Hanley, a future Colorado secretary of state, testi-
fied to his many activities while acting as Walsh's secretary that, in one way
or another, benefited Colorado. The attorney of Arapahoe County was particularly interested in Walsh's desire to become a U.S. senator from Colorado.
Hanley replied that Tom was seriously interested in running for the office only
once, in 1906, when the political activity might have taken his mind off his son's
death.[23]

Even a case of mistaken identity by the state of Colorado was used against
Walsh. One Thomas F. Walsh, a Chicago native with roots in County Waterford,
had established himself as a leading Denver architect. Late in 1909, Thomas
F. Walsh, mining millionaire, received in his Washington office an Executive
Order from Governor Shafroth appointing him to the State Board of Examiners
of Architects. Accustomed to frequent honors bestowed by Colorado citizens
and officials and knowing something about architecture through his development of impressive residential and commercial structures, he accepted. Tom
believed the position was honorary. Shortly thereafter, Colorado officials sent
a letter of apology. Walsh, the architect, was in fact the intended appointee to
the position, which required an architect's license. Tom replied that the mistake
was no imposition and that he knew the architect of the same name well and
wished him the best. Nonetheless, Tom had accepted the erroneous nomination, a fact now used as further evidence that he considered himself a Colorado
resident.[24]

Carrie gave her deposition on May 15, 1912, in the office of the clerk of
the Probate Court for the District of Columbia, represented by an associate
of Charles Thomas named Nye. In a very lengthy session, she tried to evade
every attempt by John Helbig, the lawyer for Arapahoe County, to prove that
Clonmel was the Walshes' residence. Yes, the Walshes had voted in Arapahoe
County, but only because District of Columbia residents had no vote at the time.
At best, Colorado was their home for only a few summer months. Otherwise,
Washington was their residence, with additional stays in other homes on the
East Coast, as well as in Europe. When the family left Clonmel in the fall of
1909, they did not intend to return for some time, possibly years. The following
summer was to be spent at Bar Harbor, Maine, where the couple could be near
the McLeans and their young grandchild. When Helbig asked Carrie if they
had once been poor, Nye objected on materiality because it was not a discredit
to have once worked for a day's pay. "I know that," Helbig replied. "It is the
greatest credit in the world that Mr. Walsh had the success that he did and he
is a man and a citizen much respected by everybody in the State of Colorado. I
think I have the right to protect the honor of his memory among our people."

Carrie responded that Tom was a comparatively rich man when she married him. She finished by stating that she could not recollect Tom ever saying that Clonmel was to be their Colorado home.[25]

In the end, the Arapahoe County Court found in favor of its own county, and the Walsh estate was ordered to pay a very substantial Colorado inheritance tax (which, nonetheless, it could afford). The estate had sold Clonmel in late 1910. Horace Bennett, a millionaire who made his money in Cripple Creek, was the buyer. Bennett promptly renamed the estate "Wolhurst." Thus Tom Walsh's intent to liquidate his Colorado interests and leave the state forever was finally carried out, although not exactly in the manner he had planned. To the extent he cared about the vast estate where he had entertained William Howard Taft and many others, he would have been saddened by its fate. Bennett turned Wolhurst into a country club. Then the property passed to an unsavory character named Charlie Stephens, who ran a casino frequently charged with illicit gambling. Stephens had a clever method for evading the law. As his Wolhurst casino lay directly on the line between Arapahoe and Douglas counties, he introduced gaming machines on wheels, which could literally be rolled into the next county when the other's law enforcement officers arrived.

The estate later saw duty as both a country club and a nightclub before falling on hard times in the 1970s. A 1976 fire destroyed what was left of the great Wolhurst home. However, the name Wolhurst survives to this day in a residential community developed around the lake and among the huge cottonwoods. The gazebo built by Wolcott, and often used by the Walshes in entertaining, still graces the lakeshore. Nearby, the ruins of a fireplace are all that remain of the mansion. Most residents probably do not know that a U.S. president once visited and rechristened the estate "Clonmel."[26]

THE WALSH FAMILY AND THE WALSH MINE

CHAPTER SEVENTEEN

CARRIE

Carrie Bell Walsh lived another twenty-two years at 2020 Massachusetts Avenue, surrounded by Washington wealth and near her daughter and her family. A woman who left no diaries and few letters, Carrie remains a bit of a mystery. It seems undisputed that, like many others of her era, she was the quiet but strong right arm of a successful husband who emerged in her own right during the final years of her life. She carried on Tom's philanthropy after his death. Her relief work for Belgian orphans of World War I attracted international attention. Carrie also sent clothing and blankets to the poor of Cracow, Poland, earning a commendation from the Ladies of the Polish Society St. Vincent a Paolo. She opened her home for use by Washington volunteers who made garments for victims of the war. Carrie worked alongside the others, who frequently complained that they could not accomplish more. Their efforts were nonetheless appreciated in the highest quarters.

In October 1919 the Walsh Palace finally welcomed royal visitors from Belgium. King Albert and Queen Elizabeth came to personally thank Carrie Walsh for her work and present her with the Order of Elizabeth, Queen of the Belgians. They stayed for three days. The mansion was acting as a stand-in for the White House on this occasion because President Woodrow Wilson had just suffered a stroke. Carrie offered her home and deferred to Vice President and Mrs. Thomas R. Marshall as hosts for a state dinner, which also included the French ambassador, a Supreme Court justice, cabinet members, senators, and representatives. Everything possible was Walsh gold, from the chrysanthemums and candelabra to the table service forged from Camp Bird ore.[1]

Carrie distributed nearly all the special fund from Tom's will to build a treatment and care center for victims of leprosy. Then, after the death of her grandson Vinson, she founded a sewing circle in his honor to benefit poor children. In her philanthropy, she is said to have contributed both thought and money. Her qualities are best summed up in her listing in *The National Cyclopedia of American Biography*:

> She was a woman of great force of character and attractive personality, possessed of great refinement and delicacy of feeling, and through her extensive reading and travel, became well informed on a wide range of subjects. She was a music lover and was herself an accomplished pianist. Art also found in her a patron and admirer. She had a democratic, kindly nature, was fond of flowers and gardening, intensely loyal in her friendships, devoted to her family and her home, and was a gracious hostess. Her religious affiliation was with the Christian Science Church.[2]

The latter fact once again brought her daughter misgivings, as it had during Tom's last illness. Evalyn mentions the quiet and accepting Carrie only twice after Tom's death, first to briefly describe her mother's war work. Later, the daughter breaks from a discussion of her own jewels to describe her mother's passing. Carrie was in great pain when she sent for Evalyn, who promptly brought in doctors. They diagnosed cancer of the lungs, yet Carrie would not accept their treatment and insisted on using a religious healer she had known for years. Evalyn brought the woman from Chicago to Washington and let her perform her trade for a while. One day Carrie called for her daughter and told her, "Please give me something for my pain and don't let her come to me any more." From that time forward, Evalyn gave her mother morphine whenever she needed it. Carrie Walsh died on February 25, 1932.[3]

EVALYN, NED, AND A LARGE BLUE DIAMOND

One day in 1911, jeweler Pierre Cartier reentered Evalyn and Ned's lives. He arrived at their Paris hotel room carrying a tightly wrapped package with wax seals. Cartier convinced Evalyn that she had seen the package's deep blue treasure once before, resting against the throat of the sultan's favorite harem member in Constantinople (although later she seems to have had some doubts). Tales of the history of the Hope Diamond vary so widely as to make it impossible to separate fact from fiction. Cartier's account to Evalyn, passed on to her readers, seems as credible as any. Like most of the stories, it begins in the seventeenth century when a Frenchman named Tavernier purloined the gem from a Hindu god or idol, thereby creating the curse. Tavernier in turn sold the stone to the French king Louis XIV, only to be killed by a pack of dogs. The stone, now called the Tavernier blue, was later worn by Queen Marie Antoinette. After her trip to the guillotine, French revolutionaries inventoried the great blue gem, then lost it. The Tavernier blue had weighed an impressive $67^2/_{16}$ carats. In 1830 a diamond dealer named Daniel Eliason offered a big blue diamond for sale in London, weighing $44\frac{1}{4}$ carats. His buyer was London banker Henry Thomas Hope. Later, in 1874, a stone called the Brunswick blue came on the market. It was probably the smaller part of the Tavernier blue, which had been broken in two by a party unknown.

The Hope family gave the larger stone their name and in return suffered nothing worse than financial ruin and embarrassment. The original Lord Hope died, and his widow later left a life estate in the diamond to her grandson, Lord Francis Pelham Clinton Hope. The younger Hope squandered his fortune and married an American actress named May Yohe, who often used his jewels in her acts. May later eloped with an American captain, Lord Hope was declared bankrupt, and the stone once again disappeared. It was returned to the Hope estate, then sold to a U.S. syndicate and resold to one Selim Habib, most likely of Turkey. Cartier could not tell Evalyn if this led to its possession by Sultan Abdul-Hamid, her host in Constantinople. The jeweler would only say that his firm purchased the diamond from a man named Rosenau in Paris. One other doubtful version of the story has Selim Habib acting as an agent for the sultan (and then drowning), after which the sultan gave the gem to his favorite in the harem, who Evalyn saw wearing it and who was stabbed to death a short time later.[4]

Cartier told the story with great effect, slowly unfolding the package as he went. Evalyn conferred with Ned, who was equally transfixed, and she recalls her husband's response was "How much?" She adds, "I do not know why [he asked the question], since he almost never paid for things until forced by threats of suit." Evalyn rejected the stone, only to have Cartier reappear in Washington a few months later with the simple request that she borrow it for the weekend. The diamond "stared" at her for much of the weekend. Still, the process took several more months. At last, probably in late 1911 by her account, they came to terms: $154,000, payable in the sum of $40,000 "before long" and the remaining $114,000 over three years. Ned remained true to the financial behavior his wife described (possibly abetted by her). Evalyn tells of an occasion in February 1912, "the same day we settled a lawsuit with Cartier and paid a part of the $154,000 for the Hope Diamond." However, an invoice sent by Cartier in 1918 lists the purchase price as $180,000, for "1-Head ornament composed of oval shaped links all in brilliants, containing in center, the 'Hope Diamond' weighing $^{44}/_{50}$. Price agreed following terms of contract signed February 1, 1912." Either Evalyn has her dates and amounts wrong, the head ornament cost an additional $26,000, or the $180,000 represents a settlement amount including substantial interest and penalties for the earlier nonpayment. The rest of the payment period consumed more than three years, for the 1918 invoice shows a balance still owed of $58,500. Presumably, it was all paid later, for Pierre Cartier continued to find Evalyn a trustworthy buyer for his lavish goods.[5]

Evalyn also tells us that not long after they acquired the Hope Diamond, she told Ned's mother and her friend, Mrs. Robert Goelet, about the purchase. Both strongly advised her to call off the deal. She returned the diamond to Cartier, and he immediately sent it back. Mrs. McLean and Mrs. Goelet both died within the next year, making them the first two victims of the stone after it came into Evalyn's possession. She received letters from many persons, often conveying ominous messages. Former owner May Yohe wrote frequently, pleading with her to throw the stone away. Finally, she had it blessed by Catholic Monsignor Russell. Her description of the ceremony comes complete with thunder suddenly crashing and knocking down a nearby tree. Evalyn, however, concludes the episode on a positive tone. The luckiest thing about the stone was that she could always hock it.[6]

Bad luck, nevertheless, continued for Evalyn and her family, although they did their best to live and entertain in the most extravagant manner possible. Her morphine habit returned during her grief over her father's death, but she tells us she mastered it once and for all with the help of her doctors. Ned, however, could not carry out his pledge to quit drinking. His problem continued, with two episodes in the summer of 1914 that Evalyn recalled as particularly painful. Both occurred in Newport, a town that already provided enough sad memories.

In the first episode, a very inebriated Ned lost heavily at a casino, and Evalyn charged the establishment with contributing to her husband's condition. In the second event, his drunken behavior at a party insulted such Newport stalwarts as the Astors and the Fishes. John R. McLean removed his son from Newport soon after this incident.

Two more sons were born to the McLeans, John Roll (Jock) in 1916 and Edward Beale Jr. (Neddie) in 1918. Then in 1919, while the couple attended the Kentucky Derby, tragedy struck their oldest son. Always protected by family and servants, on this day ten-year-old Vinson managed to break away and bolt into the street in front of the family's Washington home. A car that had nearly come to a halt merely pushed the boy so he fell. While he seemed only shaken at first, Vinson died within a few hours. Despite racing home in a train specially chartered for the emergency, Vinson's parents did not arrive in time to be at his bedside.[7]

Ohio senator Warren Harding and his wife, Florence, joined the McLeans' circle of friends in 1916, meeting them at a poker party given by Alice Roosevelt Longworth and her Ohio congressman husband, Nick. The friendship became so close that in 1921 the new President Harding appointed Ned chair of his Inauguration Committee. Unfortunately, Ned's elaborate plans for the event came to naught when Congress questioned the expense, and the festivities were called off. Evalyn and Ned did their best to make it up to the First Couple with an elaborate private party. Later the same year, they named the Hardings godparents to their daughter Evalyn Washington (Evie).

Tom and Carrie Walsh, and their daughter after them, could now count five straight U.S. presidents as friends, and Evalyn would befriend four more. The relationship with the Hardings was perhaps the closest of all and in the end the most stressful. The president frequented the golf course located at Friendship, the McLeans' family estate in Virginia where Evalyn and Ned spent much of their time. Evalyn found Harding quite jovial on these occasions but otherwise not particularly up to the demands of his lofty position. One Christmas, after the president had received a number of threatening letters, Evalyn and Ned let the Hardings hide out at their I Street house. Soon the McLeans were also close to some of Harding's associates. One of them, Jess Smith, called Evalyn in early 1923 to ask if he might come to the family's Leesburg, Virginia, farm to relax. He never arrived, and the next day's news told of his suicide in a Washington hotel in the wake of a growing scandal over his misuse of certain privileges as a close assistant and confidant to Attorney General Harry Daugherty.[8]

Warren Harding died suddenly later that year while returning from a trip to Alaska. Evalyn tells of staying at the White House to console her friend

Florence, who lived only a few months more. Harding had seemed to know that his world might be caving in, for earlier he had told Evalyn he wished he could walk out and slam the door to the White House and never go back. What he had feared came to pass the next year. Teapot Dome and other scandals brought a long round of congressional hearings and trials involving Harding administration insiders.

The McLeans might still have escaped the furor but for an early 1924 meeting between Ned and the embattled former secretary of the interior, Albert M. Fall. Senator Thomas J. Walsh of Montana, no relation to Evalyn's father, was hounding Fall at Senate hearings over gifts he might have received from oil interests seeking preference on federal leases. Fall was having a particular problem explaining how he had obtained $100,000. He asked his friend Ned McLean to lie and say he had loaned Fall the money. Ned complied, instructing his lawyer to tell the tale to the Senate committee, then later telling it himself to Senator Walsh. When Evalyn asked him to recant his lie, Ned responded, "I won't go back on Al Fall." Soon, he had to. Oilman Edward L. Doheny admitted that he was the real donor of the money, seriously harming Fall's case and pinning Ned with a charge of perjury before the U.S. Senate. In the end the senators decided not to punish Ned, which Evalyn attributed "to [his] childlike manner when responding to questions, to a squad of high-priced lawyers, and to some other factors."[9]

The marriage was already on a downhill course, and this deception did not help. Ned was a consistent failure at his business of running the newspapers he had inherited from his late father and could not curb his drinking problem. He made little effort to hide the fact that he had a mistress. The couple separated in 1928, and Evalyn filed for a divorce, which she never obtained. Ned's drinking eventually led to insanity, and he was placed in a Maryland sanitarium. Despite their estrangement, Evalyn continued to be Ned's sole source of emotional support. Ned is described at this time as hostile to all other outsiders, insistent that he was not Ned McLean, and given to flying into rages when so addressed. He died in the hospital in 1941, at age fifty-five. Evalyn also had to spend much of those last years dealing with Ned's many creditors. Suits against his estate continued for several more years, with his estranged wife winning only support payments.[10]

Meanwhile, Evalyn was trying to make it on her own, but her generous yet impulsive nature kept getting in the way. In 1932, while mourning the death of her mother, she heard about the kidnapping of the Lindbergh baby. Evalyn decided to mount an all-out effort to find the baby. In her emotion-driven haste, she picked the wrong man for the job. Evalyn had known Gaston

Bullock Means since the days of the Harding administration, when he was a minor functionary in the scandal-ridden office of Attorney General Daugherty. Another law enforcement agent of the time, J. Edgar Hoover, called Means the "worst crook I ever knew." Hoover thought firing Means was one of his best acts as the new FBI director. Means had bragged that he had been accused of every crime, from murder on down, but convicted of none. Obviously, he had been convicted of at least one, for he had spent time in prison. During Teapot Dome, Means had spied on Ned when the former was employed in Daugherty's department.

Now Evalyn sent for Gaston Means, believing him devious enough to carry out the job of finding the Lindbergh baby. Means, short on cash as usual, told the trusting Evalyn a story about how his underworld contacts (bootleg criminals he had met in prison) could lead him to the kidnappers. She paid him $100,000, raised by a mortgage on her Oxford Hotel property. It was the last she ever saw of the money. Means had fabricated all his contacts, as well as his efforts to find the baby. He did convince Evalyn to travel all the way to El Paso to receive the baby. Gaston Means later went to federal prison on a charge of larceny and died there. Despite her loss and the obvious embarrassment attached, Evalyn still felt "glad in my heart that there was something that compelled me to try my best to take part in the effort to ransom the Lindbergh baby."

Evalyn probably harbored similar feelings when she led Alice Longworth on a night tour of Depression-era Washington in the middle of a blizzard, handing out money so the poor could eat. Some time later, another nighttime expedition with Cissy Patterson led her to order 1,000 sandwiches and 1,000 packs of cigarettes for the Bonus Army of unemployed veterans who had marched to the nation's capital. Then, noticing that her personal financial affairs were not in the best of shape, Evalyn turned to the best prescription for the blues she had ever found. Soon thereafter, Pierre Cartier agreed to her purchase of the $135,000 "Star of the South," with $50,000 down and the remainder of the payments spread over a two-year period.[11]

When Little, Brown and Company published *Father Struck It Rich* in 1936, the press was ready for a good poverty-to-riches story. At least two of its members came away disappointed. *New York Times* reviewer C. G. Poore found it "apparent that one is reading another version of the Midas Follies— cf. Recent books by Cornelius Vanderbilt, Jr. and Mrs. Harry Lehr." While criticizing Evalyn for raising no new social issues in her book, he offered praise at the personal level for the woman who "has done a great many kind things for other people, from helping young waifs and strays to feeding and defending the veterans who went to Mr. Hoover's Washington with the Bonus Expeditionary Force." *The New Republic's* critic, Edwin Tribble, thought her jewel-buying tendencies spoke the loudest of any aspect of her character. However, he also praised Evalyn's accounting abilities, proclaiming, "Mrs. McLean threw away her millions, but she knows where they went. Her autobiography is an itemized account of a forty-year spending jag." Tribble found Gaston Means the most fantastic way to dispose of $100,000. While noting her confession that their money brought on the family's many problems, Tribble concluded that "the Hope diamond still glitters on the breast that is heaving with sorrow."[12]

The year after her book was published, Evalyn tried her hand at a different kind of writing. Her old friend Cissy Patterson persuaded her to write a column for Cissy's *Washington Times Herald.* For the next five years, Evalyn's "My Say" appeared in the paper, as she took on a wide variety of topics and fielded many questions about her Hope Diamond. Soon she had many readers, although the columnist herself thought it was "an awful waste of white paper." Evalyn needed the money and worked long hours, sometimes writing late at night after one of her parties.

Her financial condition in the early Depression years had caused Evalyn to cut back on entertaining, to the disappointment of her admirers. By the end of the decade she was back at it. Family events such as her children's birthdays got her started. Her son Jock received the grandest possible twenty-first birthday party. Friendship was remodeled for the event, which included three orchestras, an all-night buffet, and breakfast at dawn, all for a thousand guests.[13] In the end, she eclipsed her father's reputation for extravagant entertaining.

World War II gave Evalyn a new venue for entertaining. While the public waited for rationing to take its toll on the society queen, she acted almost as if nothing had happened. "Rationing Holds Few Bounds for Mrs. McLean's Dinners," wrote correspondent Helen Essary in April 1942. While claiming that Evalyn had hosted 3,000 party meals the previous year, the reporter noted, "Those hospitable days are not gone, not at Friendship. The doors of the big yellow mansion are still opening wide three or four times a week for ambassadors, war-effort stars, cabinet members, Supreme Court justices, writers, New Dealers and hopeful Republicans. Plus the ladies of the same." Only the menu had changed, for now "grapefruit, spaghetti with mushroom sauce, fresh asparagus, egg salad, vanilla ice cream and cake is the favorite menu. Beer, ginger ale and other soft drinks are served in abundance. Wines and whiskeys are omitted." Essary also noted that Evalyn paid little regard to having adversaries at the same table. Britain's ambassador sat next to Finland's minister (whose nation had just joined the German side), while the chair of the Maritime Commission smiled at the chair of the Senate committee investigating his shipbuilding program. In this interview, Evalyn claimed she showed the Hope Diamond to her guests but never let them touch it, for "it's bad luck to everybody but me." Soon Evalyn's guests included many wounded servicemen and their wives, sweethearts, and nurses. Weddings of veterans were held at her new Georgetown mansion, Friendship II (in 1944 Evalyn had surrendered the first Friendship, her country estate, for the war effort). At these events she relaxed the Hope Diamond rules, lending the blue stone to the brides. No tales of their bad luck have surfaced.[14]

Lucius Beebe found Evalyn perhaps the most lovable of all the eccentrics he covered in his social columns. He loved her fascination with electrical wiring, an interest so intense that she joined the electricians' union and clipped her union cap badge to the Hope Diamond. After one Christmas party for members of the diplomatic corps, she felt her ballroom needed rewiring. U.S. Court of Appeals judge Thurman Arnold and Cissy Patterson had stayed after the festivities and were recruited for the project. They spent the rest of the night handing tape and wire to their hostess, who was standing at the top of a ladder. Beebe was known for his flamboyance, and this incident is not mentioned in either Patterson's biography or Arnold's autobiography, yet it still seems believable. Evalyn's friends and guests loved her with all her eccentricities and could easily have been talked into a little late-night wiring. Arnold especially liked her simple, down-home nature, which brought the atmosphere of a mining camp to Washington. He also recalled that she "had the gift of originality, sympathy for people in distress, the love of jovial companionship, and [a] desire to bring people of all sorts of positions and ideas together." Writing after her death, he found Evalyn and her parties to have been irreplaceable.[15]

After expressing a desire in her book to see the family fortunes turn around, more tragedy ensued for Evalyn. Her daughter Evalyn, the wife of Senator Robert Reynolds, died in 1946 at age twenty-four. She had locked herself in her room after arguing with her husband and was later found to have succumbed to a combination of sleeping tablets and alcohol. Her death was never determined to be a suicide. She left a daughter not yet four years of age.

Evalyn Walsh McLean died from pneumonia the following year at age sixty-one, having never recovered from her daughter's death. Her passing came on April 24, 1947. The fortune from the Camp Bird Mine had shrunk considerably from what her parents had left her, and much of it was in jewels. Evalyn's friend, Judge Thurman Arnold, was present at her death and was soon named one of her executors (along with Supreme Court Justice Frank Murphy, also present at the deathbed). Cissy Patterson was there, too, with Frank Waldrop, her managing editor. Father Edmund A. Walsh of Georgetown University, Evalyn's favorite priest, gave her the last rites, but her family did not arrive in time to be with her when she died.

Arnold later recalled that his immediate problem was what to do with an unguarded house full of precious stones when the banks had already closed. He gathered up the jewels, including the Hope Diamond, put them in a shoebox, and drove around Washington trying to find a safe location. Waldrop, who accompanied him, finally suggested J. Edgar Hoover's office. The FBI director, probably used to being interrupted at odd hours, agreed to have his office hold the box until the estate could be opened. New York jeweler Harry Winston later purchased the Hope Diamond from Evalyn's estate, allegedly for $1 million. After years of displaying the stone, Winston donated it to the Smithsonian Institution in 1958. His method of delivery was inauspicious; he placed the priceless gem in the U.S. mail. It remains at the Smithsonian to this day, one of the Institution's main attractions.[16]

On December 19, 1951, the government of the new Republic of Indonesia purchased 2020 Massachusetts Avenue from Carrie's estate, paying $335,000, considerably less than what the Walshes had spent to build and furnish their palatial home a half-century before. It has served as the nation's embassy to this day. Its Indonesian owners have preserved much of "2020's" architecture and retain a deep respect for the mansion's former owners, history, and traditions.[17]

Her errors and poor judgment aside, Evalyn Walsh McLean had at least inherited her parents' generosity and congeniality and perhaps a dose of their common sense. She stood up to the supposed curse of her diamond, correctly identifying the source of family misfortune as nothing more than their wealth. Evalyn gives herself credit for assisting those less fortunate, but she spends remarkably little time telling readers how she acquired her reputation as a hostess to the rich and famous. Jewels are mentioned too often in her book, her family's history far too little. However, the book is a good part confessional, and the jewels were undeniably a much more recent and memorable part of her life in 1936. The reader of *Father Struck It Rich* may too quickly relegate the author to the status of spoiled child, defensive, unappreciative, and not truly interested in a family history other than her own. Evalyn was more than that. Like her father, she would have welcomed Smoky Jones of Deadwood. Unlike her father, she would have invested in his mine.

THE CAMP BIRD AFTER WALSH

It was not uncommon for eastern or European investors to pay a fortune for a western mine, only to find that it was past its peak. The Camp Bird was a notable exception. To Walsh's estimated profit of $2.4 million over his six-year stay, the new owners added their own of over $15 million from 1902 to 1916. During this period the mine withstood a devastating 1906 avalanche that destroyed the mill. A new mill was rapidly built. By 1910 it became apparent that the grade of ore along the Camp Bird vein was dropping. The trend continued, and by 1914 the mill operated at only 40 percent capacity. As miners followed the vein deeper and deeper into the mountain, the cost of pumping water from the lower levels became a major expense. All this prompted the 1916 decision to suspend operations and drive a new, lower adit. The owners decided to economize by running all operations from the lower level. They mothballed the boarding-house and other 3-level buildings and dismantled the aerial tram line. The new adit, at the 14-level, took nineteen months to complete and finally reached the Camp Bird vein 11,000 feet in from the portal. Even so, results were discouraging, and the mine was shut down again in early 1920.

After it reopened in October 1925, the focus of mining returned to the 3-level, and the mine operated continually until 1929. In that year operations passed to King Lease, Inc., which both continued year-round operation and established a permanent camp at the 3-level utilizing the old buildings. Soon thereafter, author David Lavender arrived for a tour of duty as a hard-rock miner. His observations in his 1956 book, *One Man's West*, provide as good a glimpse of mining life as is found anywhere and one of the few accounts of Camp Bird life told by a miner. Some of that life probably had changed very little since the time of Tom Walsh more than thirty years earlier, while in other ways the miners' lot was worse. By Lavender's account, "Men began to paw over the old bones. The lease company for whom I was about to work re-opened the Camp Bird. But not in its former glory. Those beautiful basin mills stayed silent. Ore had originally been brought down to them from the mine three miles farther up the mountain via an aerial tramway, but this had fallen into ruin and would have cost an enormous sum to rebuild."[18]

Lavender lived in what had been the grand Walsh boardinghouse, now fallen on harder times but still a cut above most mine accommodations. Where 300 workers had once lived, 40 men and 2 women occupied one corner of the building (rats occupied the rest). Lavender arrived by horse and found that shipments of concentrate were hauled by mule train down to the 9,500-foot level of the former mill. From that location, freight sleighs carried the load the rest of the way to Ouray, at least in winter, which it was when he arrived. Other mules worked inside the mine. He found no labor problems and no union membership, even though some men did possess union cards. It was, after all, the Depression, and any job was a privilege. Lavender marveled that no one complained about the appalling living conditions. The marble basins and tubs of the Walsh era had disappeared, replaced by a single washbasin per floor. Filthy work clothes were taken off in an unheated change room, to be discovered frozen stiff when it came time to put them back on. The food, however, was excellent, and a miner named Hughie ran a well-equipped store. The miners were mostly from other shores, dominated by Swedes, Finns, and Slavs; a few Irish, Cornishmen, and Norwegians; one Frenchman; and "a scattering of native Americans." Ethnic strife was rare, as was any other kind of strife. Everyone seemed to accept the situation and go about their work.

In the mine itself, workers had followed the Camp Bird vein far down into the earth, until such a course became too expensive. Then another horizontal tunnel was cut in from the side of the mountain, and more soon followed. By this time the mine's vertical depth was twice the height of the Empire State Building, with horizontal drifts stretching for miles. Lavender's job was hoist man, raising and lowering the buckets that held both ore and men. Sometimes he worked with the miners on the 4-level. Despite the use of blower fans, the air was foul from the daily dynamite blasts, which occurred at 3:30 each morning and afternoon. After each blast the workers pried loose any rock not dislodged by the explosion (some of which landed on the miners' heads), then the muckers shoveled the ore into a car. Lavender always found the gagging stench of powder present, even after the ore pile had been sprayed with water.

David Lavender stayed through the warm season, taking his one bath in Ouray at Easter time. He had to survive an avalanche to obtain this luxury. Once the weather turned cold again, he retired from mining and went off to add ranch work to his western experience. Soon after Lavender's departure, a fire gutted the boardinghouse. A new, more modern building (with a heated change room) replaced it, only to witness more disaster. On February 25, 1936, an avalanche hit the camp at 3-level. The mill and new boardinghouse were destroyed, and three persons were killed, including the mill superintendent. The mill was rebuilt within a few months, but no boardinghouse ever again graced the mountainside.

From 1937 on, King Lease shifted attention back to the lower levels and, in a series of year-to-year leases, mined on a continual basis until 1956. The World War II requirement that nonessential gold mining be discontinued had no effect on Camp Bird. It merely replaced gold with production of base metals such as copper, lead, and zinc. This type of operation continued well into the 1950s. When King did not renew its lease for 1957, Camp Bird, Ltd. resumed control and made some major improvements to the mine, including a modern mill built in 1960. The Camp Bird Mine was sold in 1963 to Federal Resources, which added more improvements in connection with its ownership of the neighboring Revenue and Virginius properties. However, as the mining drove deeper, water removal became a greater and greater expense. Finally, in 1978, the owners decided to allow the lower levels, which had reached as far as the 21-level, to flood. From this point forward, the decision of whether the Camp Bird was mined depended entirely on fluctuations in the prices of gold and silver. Continual mining no longer made good economic sense for the great mine, whose glory days were behind it.[19]

"Bye, bye Bird-ie," eulogized Ouray's *Plaindealer* on the morning of August 3, 1995. Ninety-nine years after Tom Walsh's discovery, the Camp Bird Mine was shut down for good. Its 1960 mill was dismantled and shipped to Mongolia, a sure sign of mining's shift in emphasis from the much-explored western United States to the new frontiers of the Third World. From its inception, the mine had produced more than 1.5 million ounces of gold, together with large amounts of silver, lead, copper, and zinc. The new owners of the mining site, a New Jersey investment group interested in tailings reclamation, predicted no more mining for the Camp Bird.[20] As with any great and long-lived mine, though, the question lingers as to what riches remain in the earth and what conditions, be they economic or environmental, it might take for miners to renew the search.

CONCLUSION: THE LEGACY OF THOMAS F. WALSH

The end of the nineteenth century and the first part of the twentieth might be termed the "Golden Age of the American Eulogy." The flowing prose that poured forth to extol the deeds and personal character of Thomas F. Walsh was not unlike that extended to others in prominent positions at the time. Author Edwin P. Hoyt Jr., covering the 1905 death of Meyer Guggenheim, reported, "The praise was fulsome, for it was not yet the time when millionaires were excoriated except by anarchists, socialists, and syndicalists."[1] Often, death or other misfortune resulted in high praise that brushed aside any indiscretions engaged in along the road to success. Still, Walsh should not be subjected to many of the charges that could be levied against other businessmen of his time. His fortune was not based on abuse of laborers or on misrepresentation to investors, matters on which many of his contemporaries stand guilty. At worst, he failed to tell "the whole truth" when approaching sellers of mining property, from the owners of the cabin on the Frying Pan to those of the abandoned workings of the Imogene Basin. This practice, nonetheless, continues to this day as a standard in the business of natural resource extraction (and is argued by some to be a necessity for a profit-making venture). In all other respects, Tom's conduct of business was nothing short of exemplary, for his or any time.

Once Tom had obtained his fortune, he used it lavishly yet still maintained it. His philanthropy deserves all the high praise given it, but in retrospect, did he really do enough? The ever-generous Walsh felt his donations should reach a substantial number of persons, but especially his immediate family. Tom's laborers repaid his generosity by working hard and never striking. Did his family repay that generosity as well? Carrie continued his philanthropy and meaningful course of life. Writing in 1936, after her tale of woe Evalyn exhorts her family that it is time for Tom Walsh's descendants to cast aside luxury and learn how to work. In hindsight, might her tale have been far more satisfying had her father provided his children with a secure yet modest lifestyle while passing on the bulk of his millions to the many causes he supported? We will never know, but it is fair to say that for all his love and loyalty toward family, Tom both spoiled and misjudged his children. Evalyn, it seems, would agree, for at the end of her book she moralizes:

> If Ned McLean and I had been born into average-income families and normal environments, given just what we were born with, we probably should have been average citizens to-day, leading normal lives with normal faults and virtues, reading this story with the same emotions you have felt. Character or environment? The world has never settled that argument. I think we each had enough character to have met the negative tests of such an environment. The very circumstances of normal life encourage self-discipline, punish self-indulgence.[2]

Two pages later she pays final tribute to the father who made it all possible:

> I can hear my father talking now of "clean money." His came directly from the earth, not from other men, whether fairly or unfairly. He took great pride in that. A generous man and one who liked people, he taught me that there was no true generosity in giving money if the giver has much money; that unless I gave something of myself as well, it cost me nothing; therefore, meant nothing. This I have tried to practise, hope to practise more. That he did not teach me more, I cannot find it in my heart to reproach his memory. He had not, after all, experienced the evil side of money. He knew little of weakness. A strong character himself, it would have been natural for him to take for granted the strength of his children, to fail to realize the

different circumstances of money earned and money inherited. It is I myself
I reproach; most of all, because he would be disappointed in me.[3]

Misguided loyalty also explains Tom's unflinching defense to the end of
an unworthy King Leopold. If he had a blind spot for the faults of Evalyn and
Vinson, it was magnified in his attachment to his royal friend. Walsh, who
had little need for more money, enjoyed no significant economic benefit from
his closeness to Leopold. He was also astute enough to avoid any close business ties, especially in the Congo. Rather, he sought exposure to a high-level
world ruler, and he found a man he liked personally but one who did not respect
others, as did the trusting Walsh. When he defended his friend, Walsh paid the
price, if only briefly. In that short time, however, his Irish temper burst forth
in all its fury. At other times it soon subsided, with little lasting effect. We
can only guess that the same would have happened except for his death. To his
friend Charles Thomas, his outburst was a mere aberration resulting from his
strong tendency to honor old ties. Thomas, of course, had found in Walsh the
overriding characteristics of generosity and geniality, a man seemingly loved
by all.[4] Apparently, most others who encountered Tom Walsh felt the same
way.

For all this, has Walsh left any lasting legacy or proven to be a visionary?
The Camp Bird likely will never reopen, at least not if current economic conditions and expectations for environmental protection continue. The small city
of Ouray honors one of its foremost citizens in a variety of ways, particularly in
the historical museum found in the hospital he once saved. The Walsh example
of diligence in finding rich ore is still sound and can be readily enhanced by
modern technology. However, in a modern society that values a clean environment above all else, ore finders, for all their talents, have little status outside
the shrinking U.S. mining industry.

Therefore, if one seeks something truly unique and perhaps visionary about
Tom Walsh, it must be his attitude toward the treatment of workers and others
less privileged than himself. At least one source attributes Walsh's motivation
to mere political ambition. However, this is difficult to grasp, considering the
continuing and unerring support for the working class expressed in his actions
and words over a long period of time. At the same time, Walsh displayed an
unmistakably lukewarm attitude toward running for political office. With
his standing and influence, when the Republicans found him unpalatable as a
candidate, he could have switched to the Democrats or run as an independent.
He chose not to do either. The words of his 1906 Colorado Springs speech were
prophetic. They still resonate in a world of rapid technological change, charges

of corporate misbehavior, and a growing gap between rich and poor. His recommendations, controversial in his own time, were nonetheless enacted long ago. If the teachings of certain modern-day business/labor experts catch hold, a phrase such as "as employers, treat your men [and women] with humanity and justice" might become standard fare in labor relations. Indeed, business author David Batstone, in his 2001 book *Saving the Corporate Soul, & (Who Knows?) Maybe Your Own*, titles one chapter "Valuing the Worker" and begins with Principle Five: "The worker will be treated as a valuable team member, not just a hired hand."[5] Later in the chapter, Batstone praises Massachusetts industrialist Aaron Feuerstein, who kept his entire workforce on the payroll even after a fire destroyed the firm's plant. Aaron's values are summarized as follows:

> A worker is an asset, not an expense.
> Skilled labor offers a sharper competitive edge than cheap labor.
> A business has a moral responsibility to sustain its community.
> Workers accept justifiable layoffs but resent job weeding.
> Management commitment yields worker loyalty.
> Customers respond to quality and innovation above price.
> Profit is only one of the many values a company strives to maximize.[6]

Batstone does not quote Thomas F. Walsh in his book, but he could easily have done so.

Perhaps the tall, genial Irishman who loved people and animals and still amassed a fortune will appear in future studies which stress that financial success and simple humanity can readily work together.

GLOSSARY OF MINING TERMS

These definitions are taken from *Dictionary of Mining, Mineral and Related Terms*, published by the American Geological Institute, 1997; Eric Twitty, *Riches to Rust: A Guide to Mining in the Old West*, Western Reflections, Montrose, CO, 2002; Duane A. Smith, *Staking a Claim in History*, 2001; and Ed Raines, "Colorado Gold: Part 2—The Discovery, Mining History, Geology, and Specimen Mineralogy of Selected Occurrences in Central Colorado and the San Juans," *Rocks and Minerals* 72, 5, September–October 1997.

Adit—A horizontal or nearly horizontal passage driven from the surface for the working or unwatering of a mine. If driven through the hill or mountain to the surface on the opposite side, it would be a tunnel. The two terms are often confused.

Amalgam—A pasty alloy of gold (and/or silver) and mercury, about one-third gold by weight.

Amalgamation—The process by which mercury is alloyed with gold and/or silver to produce an amalgam. It was used at one time for the extraction of gold and silver from pulverized ores, now superseded by the cyanide process.

Apex—The highest or top point of a vein.

Bleichert Aerial Tramway—Aerial tramways provided an efficient way to haul ores down a steep mountain slope from a mine to a mill or loading terminal. They were also used to haul men and supplies in both directions. They consisted of a moving wire rope circuit supported by large wooden towers. The first aerial tramways in the West were Hallidie tramways, named for Scotsman Andrew Hallidie, who also originated the San Francisco cable car system. They used a single-wire rope. German engineers Theodore Otto and Adolph Bleichert developed a double-rope system first used in Europe in 1874. It became the standard in U.S. mining by the 1890s (at least for mines having sufficient capital to afford it). Single-wire rope systems had ore buckets fixed to the rope, requiring that they be loaded and unloaded while in motion. The double-wire rope system (the ropes were called the track rope and the traction rope) provided for longer tramways carrying larger ore loads. The traction rope employed a releasable mechanical clamp called a grip to attach ore buckets, allowing the buckets to be temporarily released for easier and more efficient loading and unloading. Aerial tramways used many of the same principles as modern-day ski gondolas and chairlifts.

Concentration—The separation and accumulation of economic minerals from waste (also called gangue). The concentration of ores always proceeds by steps or stages, and the ore must first be crushed before the minerals can be separated. Further methods of concentration vary with minerals and even localities where used.

Crosscut—A small passageway that extends from an adit, shaft, or drift to a vein.

Cyanide Process—A process for extracting gold from finely crushed ores, concentrates, and tailings by means of cyanide of potassium or sodium used in dilute solutions. The gold is dissolved by the solution and removed from other minerals. It is then recovered, usually by being deposited on metallic zinc. All this is accomplished in a cyanide mill.

Diamond Drill—A drilling machine with a rotating, hollow, diamond-studded bit that cuts a core. The core provides a sample of the rock. This is a common method for exploring and studying a mineral deposit.

Drift—A horizontal passage underground that parallels the vein, as distinguished from a crosscut, which intersects it, or a level or gallery, which may do either.

Frue Vanner—A vanner is any machine that separates ore from waste rock. It could be a gold pan or a shovel in a miner's hand. A Frue vanner is a specialized machine consisting of a rubber belt traveling up a slight incline. The material to be treated is washed by a constant flow of water while the entire belt is shaken from side to side. The type of Frue vanners used at the Camp Bird Mine contained plates to catch the free gold separated by the washing and shaking.

Gangue—Undesired minerals, mostly nonvaluable, associated with valuable ore; waste rock.

Level—A main underground roadway or passageway to provide access to stopes or working areas in a mine. They are commonly numbered by their depth, such as the 1–21 levels found in the Camp Bird Mine.

Lode—In ordinary miners' usage, a lode (also called a vein, lead, or ledge) is a deposit of valuable minerals enclosed between definite boundaries. Most boundaries consist of quartz or other rock in place. Not a placer deposit.

Mill—While this term has many uses in mining, when applied to ore treatment it generally means the plant where machines crush, grind, and concentrate the valuable minerals in an ore. A great variety of crushing and grinding mills exist, with ball, rod, and stamp mills the most common in the American West. Smelting is the next step after milling. The goal of milling is to enrich a low-grade ore that cannot be smelted at a profit into a concentration that can be smelted to yield a profit.

Mining Claim—A unique form of property ownership used to define mining rights, as codified by the U.S. Mining Law of 1872 and further defined by state laws. The claims are said to be "located" when the claimant follows the procedures of staking on the ground and recording the claim in county and federal offices. The claims are usually lode and placer, corresponding to the type of mineral deposit located. Mill-site and tunnel claims may also be located to facilitate development. Lode claims can encompass a maximum area of 1,500 feet along a vein and 300 feet on either side of the vein (subject to being extended by use of extra-lateral rights). Placer claims are defined by acreage using government subdivisions (e.g., quarter sections or portions thereof). Initially, mining claims are referred to as "unpatented." Mining claimants can obtain a patent through a governmental administrative procedure, involving such matters as a mineral survey and proof that the claimants have discovered a valuable mineral deposit. A patented mining claim is a form of fee-simple real estate title, subject to the terms of the patent document.

Ore—A naturally occurring rock from which at least one mineral can be mined profitably.

Placer—A deposit in which gold in its free state has been concentrated by stream action. Not a vein or a lode deposit. State and federal mining laws provide for vein and lode mining claims as a method for securing legal right to minerals.

Raise—A vertical or inclined opening in a mine driven upward from a level to connect with an ore body or the level above or to explore the ground for a limited distance above one level. After two levels are connected, the connection may be a winze or a raise, depending upon which level is taken as the point of reference.

Shaft—A vertical or inclined excavation made for finding or mining ore or coal; raising water, ore, rock, or coal; hoisting or lowering men or material; or ventilating underground workings. The term specifically applies to a vertical excavation as opposed to a horizontal adit or tunnel.

Smelting—Any metallurgical operation in which metal is separated by fusion (melting) from those impurities with which it is chemically combined or physically mixed, as in ores.

Stamp Mill—A mill in which rock is crushed by descending pestles (or stamps) operated by water, steam, or electric power. Amalgamation is usually combined with crushing when gold or silver is the metal sought, further enhanced by the use of mercury.

Stope—An excavation from which ore is being, or has been, excavated in a series of steps. Usually applies to highly inclined or vertical veins. Frequently used incorrectly as a synonym for a room, which is a wide working place in a flat mine.

Tailings—The neutralized, very finely crushed material discarded after economically recoverable metals have been extracted from the ore.

Timbering—The operation of setting timber supports in mine workings or shafts. The term can also cover the setting of timber, steel, concrete, or masonry.

Vein—A sheetlike or tabular mineralized filling of a fracture or fault in a host rock. In common usage, the same thing as a lode.

Winze—A vertical or inclined opening, or excavation, connecting two levels in a mine and driven downward. A winze differs from a raise only as to point of construction. When completed, if one is standing at the top looking down, it is a winze; if at the bottom looking up, it is a raise.

GEOLOGY OF THE CAMP BIRD MINE

This diagram of the geology of the Camp Bird Mine is from Tom Rosemeyer, "Camp Bird Mine, Ouray County, Colorado," *Rocks and Minerals* 65, 2, March–April 1990; and Ed Raines, "Colorado Gold: Part 2—The Discovery, Mining History, Geology and Specimen Mineralogy of Selected Occurrences in Central Colorado and the San Juans," *Rocks and Minerals* 72, 5, September–October 1997.

Formation	Era	Period/Epoch	Valuable Minerals Found
Silverton— volcanic	Cenozoic	Tertiary/Oligocene 24–38 million years ago (mya)	Gold-quartz base metal where ore shoots have penetrated from below
San Juan Tuff— volcanic	Cenozoic	Tertiary/Oligocene, 24–38 mya	Gold-quartz base tuff—breccias metal shoots, thickness 2,500 feet
Telluride— conglomerate	Cenozoic	Tertiary/Eocene, 38–55 mya	Lead, copper, zinc
Entrada— sandstone	Mesozoic	Jurassic, 140–205 mya	none
Dolores— sandstone	Mesozoic	Triassic, 205–240 mya	none
Cutler—shales, siltstones, and sandstones	Paleozoic	Permian, 240–290 mya	none

WALSH FAMILY TREE[1]

Michael Walsh, of County Tipperary, Ireland
(dates of birth and death unknown, lived in
eighteenth century)

John Walsh, 1769–1848
County Tipperary

continued on next page

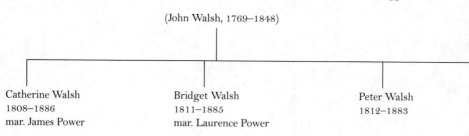

(John Walsh, 1769–1848)

Catherine Walsh
1808–1886
mar. James Power

Bridget Walsh
1811–1885
mar. Laurence Power

Peter Walsh
1812–1883

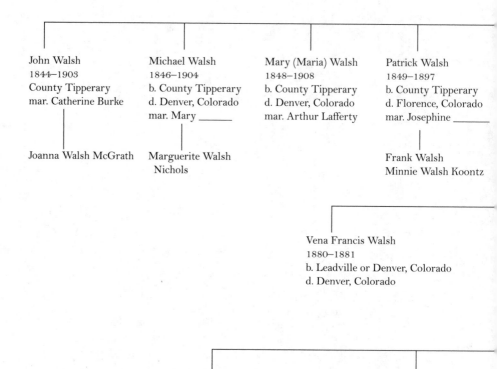

John Walsh
1844–1903
County Tipperary
mar. Catherine Burke

Joanna Walsh McGrath

Michael Walsh
1846–1904
b. County Tipperary
d. Denver, Colorado
mar. Mary _____

Marguerite Walsh
Nichols

Mary (Maria) Walsh
1848–1908
b. County Tipperary
d. Denver, Colorado
mar. Arthur Lafferty

Patrick Walsh
1849–1897
b. County Tipperary
d. Florence, Colorado
mar. Josephine _____

Frank Walsh
Minnie Walsh Koontz

Vena Francis Walsh
1880–1881
b. Leadville or Denver, Colorado
d. Denver, Colorado

Vinson Walsh McLean

John Roll McLean

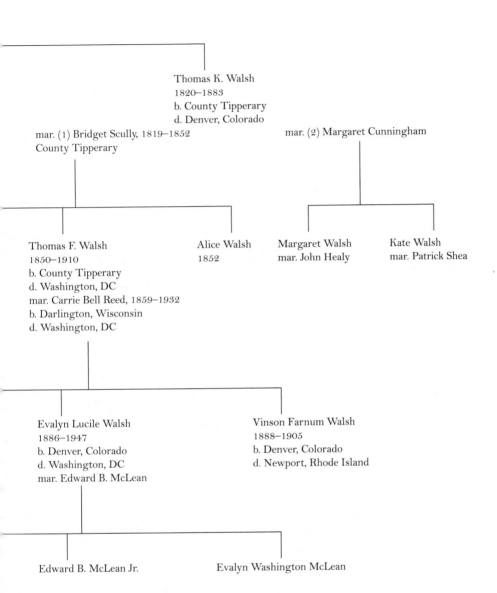

Thomas K. Walsh
1820–1883
b. County Tipperary
d. Denver, Colorado

mar. (1) Bridget Scully, 1819–1852
County Tipperary

mar. (2) Margaret Cunningham

Thomas F. Walsh
1850–1910
b. County Tipperary
d. Washington, DC
mar. Carrie Bell Reed, 1859–1932
b. Darlington, Wisconsin
d. Washington, DC

Alice Walsh
1852

Margaret Walsh
mar. John Healy

Kate Walsh
mar. Patrick Shea

Evalyn Lucile Walsh
1886–1947
b. Denver, Colorado
d. Washington, DC
mar. Edward B. McLean

Vinson Farnum Walsh
1888–1905
b. Denver, Colorado
d. Newport, Rhode Island

Edward B. McLean Jr.

Evalyn Washington McLean

Note: 1. For background materials for Walsh family tree, see Kennedy, "The Family History"; Inscription
on family memorial, Kilmurray Cemetery; and Rapp, Epilogue to *Queen of Diamonds*. It is not known if
Thomas K. Walsh had additional siblings beyond those listed.

NOTES

INTRODUCTION: IN SEARCH OF TOM WALSH

1. "Colorado Grief-Stricken over Death of Tom Walsh," *The Rocky Mountain News*, Denver, April 9, 1910; Charles S. Thomas, "A Famous Carpenter," unpublished manuscript in the Charles S. Thomas Collection, MSS 626, Box 10, Colorado Historical Society, Denver; see also the articles of April 9, 1910, on Walsh's death in *The Denver Post*, *The Denver Times*, and *The Denver Republican*.

2. Evalyn Walsh McLean, with Boyden Sparkes, *Father Struck It Rich* (1st ed. Boston: Little, Brown, 1936; 2nd ed. Ouray, CO: Bear Creek, 1981; commemorative ed. under the title *Queen of Diamonds*, Franklin, TN: Hillsboro, 2000). All page references in this book refer to the 2nd edition.

CHAPTER 1: ORIGINS IN IRELAND

1. Quote from Richard Dowling and other background materials are from Sean O'Donnell, *Clonmel 1840–1900, Anatomy of an Irish Town* (Dublin: Geography Publications, n.d.), 1, 11–18.

2. Edward MacLysaght, *The Surnames of Ireland* (Dublin: Irish Academic Press, n.d.), 296; Margaret Kennedy, "The Family History," unpublished and undated manuscript in the possession of Kathleen O'Brien of Worcester, Massachusetts, a cousin of Thomas F. Walsh. In the manuscript, the name Michael Walsh is presumed correct. However, Kennedy incorrectly refers to John Walsh as "Patrick" and to Thomas K. Walsh as "Michael." Correct names are from the inscription on the family memorial in Kilmurray Cemetery, Ballyneale Parish, County Tipperary, Ireland, erected by Thomas F. Walsh in 1903. See also Dennis Clark, *Hibernia America: The Irish and Regional Cultures* (New York: Greenwood, 1986), 4.

3. Kennedy, "Family History," 2–3. The birth record for Peter Walsh is from the family memorial. The birth date for Thomas K. Walsh is from the burial records of Mount Olivet Cemetery, Golden, Colorado. While father and son may both have been known as Tom Walsh, for convenience this book refers to Thomas K. or Thomas as the father and Thomas F. or Tom as the son who is the main subject of the book.

4. Emily Hahn, *Fractured Emerald: Ireland* (Garden City, NY: Doubleday, 1971), 216–229; O'Donnell, *Clonmel*, 29; Kennedy, "Family History," 2.

5. O'Donnell, *Clonmel*, 153–158; Hahn, *Fractured Emerald*, 246–259; Cait Ni Mhannin, "The Famine Around Slievenamon," in *Slievenamon in Song & Story*, Sean Nugent, ed. (Waterford: Telecom Eireann, n.d.), 71–72.

6. Ages of the family members are from the inscription on the family memorial at Kilmurray Cemetery and the Baptismal Record of Powerstown Parish records compiled by the Bru Boru Heritage Center, Cashel, County Tipperary. All dates are of baptisms, which followed shortly after birth. For instance, Thomas F. Walsh was born on April 2, 1850, and baptized on April 28.

7. Kennedy, "Family History," 2–3; McLean, *Father*, 27; interview with Mary Ryan, great-great niece of Thomas F. Walsh, July 2000. See also Mary Ryan, *Hope* (London: Headline, 2001), 595. While this book is a fact-based novel, the information cited is in the author's notes at the conclusion and establishes that Margaret Cunningham was Thomas K. Walsh's second wife and the great-great-grandmother of author Mary Ryan.

8. The Walsh quote is in "The Fair at Seville," unpublished manuscript in Box 100, Evalyn Walsh McLean Collection, Manuscript Division, Library of Congress, Washington, DC (hereafter "Walsh Papers"). The crucifix is mentioned in a letter from Minnie [Walsh] Koontz to Evalyn Walsh McLean, undated, Box 3, Walsh Papers. The letter was probably written around 1936, when Minnie Koontz was giving the crucifix to her cousin Evalyn.

9. O'Donnell, *Clonmel*, 41–42; interview with Mary Ryan. The Walsh quote is in *The Denver Post*, April 9, 1910.

10. Interview with Mary Ryan. There are few, yet conflicting, reports of the early work experiences of Tom Walsh. O'Donnell, *Clonmel*, 116, provides background on the area's economy at the time.

11. O'Donnell, *Clonmel*, 22–24; Homer E. Socolofsky, *Landlord William Scully* (Lawrence: Regents Press of Kansas, 1979), 50, 121–130. It is not known if William Scully and Bridget Scully Walsh, the mother of Thomas F. Walsh, were related.

12. McLean, *Father,* 28; K. Theodore Hoppen, *Ireland Since 1800: Conflict and Conformity,* 2nd ed. (New York: Longman, 1999), 56, 101–106; *The Denver Post,* April 9, 1910. My telephone interview with Michael O'Brien of Clonmel, Ireland, grandson of Kate Walsh Shea, half-sister of Thomas F. Walsh, August 2001, established the estrangement of Thomas K. Walsh from his wife, Margaret, and other family information. Information on the life of John Walsh is in his obituary in *The Nationalist and Tipperary Advertiser,* Clonmel, Ireland, June 24, 1903. The marriage of John Walsh to Catherine Burke on September 10, 1868, is recorded in the Marriage Record of the Powerstown Parish.

CHAPTER 2: TO AMERICA AND THE WEST

1. Kennedy, "Family History," 16. See letters from Thomas F. Walsh to Tim Kennedy, December 17, 1904, and September 5, 1908, both in Box 9, Walsh Papers. Kennedy was the husband of Walsh's cousin Joanna Power. The Walsh quote is in *The Denver Post,* April 10, 1910.

2. Ron Chernow, *Titan: The Life of John D. Rockefeller, Sr.* (New York: Random House, 1998), 52.

3. *The Denver Post,* April 10, 1910; letter Katherine Kennedy to Walsh, April 23, 1904, Box 11, Walsh Papers.

4. Morris H. Cohen, "Worcester's Ethnic Groups, a Bicentennial View," in *Worcester People and Places,* ch. V (Worcester: Bicentennial Commission, Worcester, MA, 1976), 7, 13–14; Lorraine Michele Laurie, *The Island That Became a Neighborhood: A History of Green Island in Worcester, Massachusetts, 1826–1985* (Worcester: self-published, 1985), 1–7.

5. *The Denver Post,* April 10, 1910; McLean, *Father,* 28; James E. Fell Jr., *Ores to Metals: The Rocky Mountain Smelting Industry* (Lincoln: University of Nebraska Press, 1979), 1–75.

6. Carl Ubbelohde, Maxine Benson, and Duane A. Smith, *A Colorado History,* 7th ed. (Boulder: Pruett, 1995), 41–122; Thomas J. Noel, "All Hail the Denver Pacific: Colorado's First Railroad," *Colorado Magazine* 50, 2, Colorado Historical Society, Denver, Spring 1973.

7. The estimated time and cost of Walsh's 1871 journey came from the *Travelers Official Guide of the Railway and Steam Navigation Lines in the U.S. and Canada,* 2 vols., 1874 (publisher unknown), Archives of the Colorado Railroad Museum, Golden. Moffat's earlier journey is described in Steven F. Mehls, *David H. Moffat, Jr.: Early Colorado Business Leader,* PhD dissertation, University of Colorado at Boulder, 1982, Western History Department, Denver Public Library, 15–16. See also Forest Crossen, "Thomas Fitzpatrick, Railroadman," in *Western Yesterdays,* Vol. 6 (Boulder: Paddock, 1968), 3–4.

8. Gary Morgan, *Three Foot Rails: A Quick History of the Colorado Central Railroad* (Colorado Springs: Little London, 1974), 3–11.

9. Ibid.; Duane A. Smith, *Henry M. Teller: Colorado's Grand Old Man* (Boulder: University Press of Colorado, 2002), 20–21; Robert C. Black III, *Railroad Pathfinder: The Life & Times of Edward L. Berthoud* (Evergreen, CO: Cordillera, 1988), 77–78.

10. McLean, *Father*, 28; Ubbelohde, Benson, and Smith, *Colorado History*, 63–64.

11. *The Denver Republican*, April 9, 1910; Robert L. Brown, *Central City and Gilpin County, Then and Now* (Caldwell, ID: Caxton, 1994), 120, 134–135.

12. Robert M. Utley, *Cavalier in Buckskin: George Armstrong Custer and the Western Military Frontier* (Norman: University of Oklahoma Press, 1988), 128–147; Richard B. Hughes, *Pioneer Years in the Black Hills*, 2nd ed., Agnes Wright Spring, ed. (Rapid City: Dakota Alpha, 1999), 1–41; *Rocky Mountain News*, April 9, 1910.

13. *Black Hills Daily Times*, Deadwood, September 9, 1876, microfilm records of the Hearst Library, Lead, SD.

14. *Black Hills Pioneer*, Deadwood, October 1 and October 7, 1876, March 10 and July 6, 1877, microfilm records of the Hearst Library, Lead, SD.

15. Mildred Fielder, *Silver Is the Fortune* (Aberdeen, SD: North Plains, 1978), 202–212.

16. Ibid. *The Rocky Mountain News*, April 9, 1910, tells of Tom's carpentry feats in Deadwood. Hughes, *Pioneer Years*, and John S. McClintock, *Pioneer Days in the Black Hills* (1st ed. 1939, 2nd ed. 1966, 3rd ed. Norman: University of Oklahoma Press, 2001), provide coverage of early history and the 1879 fire. McClintock also tells of conflict between mineral locations and town lots. The tale by Albert Gushurst is in "Some Lawrence County History" (Deadwood, SD: Lawrence County Historical Society, 1981), 9–10, Archives of the Adams Museum, Deadwood, SD. No record of Walsh as a proprietor of a local business is found in *Collins' Deadwood Business Directory of 1878–79*, but Walsh had probably left the area by the time of its publication.

17. McLean, *Father*, 29–30, 114. McClintock, *Pioneer Days*, 120–128, and Hughes, *Pioneer Years*, 118, discuss the Smith murder. McClintock raises the possibility that it was perpetrated by non-Indians, while Hughes places the blame squarely on the Indians. Neither Walsh nor Crawford is mentioned as a member of the posse. McClintock also discusses Bullock and his connection to Roosevelt. See also Edmund Morris, *Theodore Rex* (New York: Random House, 2001), 233, regarding the Roosevelt-Bullock relationship. John W. "Captain Jack" Crawford was a colorful local character who gained national renown on the Chautauqua circuit. Darlis A. Miller, *Captain Jack Crawford: Buckskin Poet, Scout and Showman* (Albuquerque: University of New Mexico Press, 1993) is a biography that includes his friendship with Walsh. Crawford is also described by McClintock and Hughes, the latter noting him as a member of the Custer Minute Men, employed by locals for protection from the Indians.

18. McLean, *Father*, 30–32. *The Rocky Mountain News*, April 9, 1910, gives the Walsh quote on Smoky Jones. See also Duane A. Smith, *Staking a Claim in History: The Evolution of Homestake Mining Company* (Walnut Creek, CA: Homestake Mining Company, 2001), 8, 21–24; Herbert S. Schell, *History of South Dakota*, 3rd ed. (Lincoln: University of Nebraska Press, 1975), 147–148. The Location Certificate for the Homestake Lead was recorded January 4, 1880, in Book 1 of Certs., p. 398, Office of the Clerk and Recorder of Lawrence County. The account of Moses Manuel, told to Bruce C. Yates, appears in McClintock, *Pioneer Days*, 235–238.

19. Hughes, *Pioneer Years*, 42–43, 91; McLean, *Father*, 29–32. Evalyn was not the only party to pass along the Homestake tale, which made its way to the Colorado press not long after her father became famous. See, for example, *Ouray Herald*, Ouray, CO, January 12, 1899, and *The Denver Times*, April 9, 1910. *The Rocky Mountain News*, April 9, 1910, quotes Walsh himself telling the tale.

20. McLean, *Father*, 32, gives Evalyn's figure for Tom's earnings, while the *News Gazette*, Colorado Springs, April 11, 1910, provides the sum of $100,000. See *The Denver Post*, April 10, 1910, for the estimate of $10,000 made from carpentry work. *The Denver Post*, April 9, 1910, and Fielder, *Silver*, 204–207 concur on the sale of the mine to Asmus.

CHAPTER 3: LIFE IN THE
SILVER BOOMTOWN OF LEADVILLE

1. Duane A. Smith, *Horace Tabor: His Life and Legend* (Niwot: University Press of Colorado, 1989), 53; Don L. Griswold and Jean Harvey Griswold, *History of Leadville and Lake County, Colorado*, 2 vols. (Boulder: Colorado Historical Society in cooperation with University Press of Colorado, 1996), introduction by James E. Fell Jr., 189 (*Mining Record* representative quote).

2. Griswold, *Leadville*, 163; Sewell Thomas, *Silhouettes of Charles S. Thomas, Colorado Governor and United States Senator* (Caldwell, ID: Caxton, 1959), 31.

3. Griswold, *Leadville*, 281 (quote regarding Miss Reed); McLean, *Father*, 33–35. Evalyn refers to her grandmother as "Anna," which could be an error but might also be a term of endearment.

4. *History of Lafayette County*, 1881, Lafayette County Historical Society, Darlington, Wisconsin, 525–530, covers Stephen S. Reed and Darlington's early history. The Affidavit of Stephen S. Osborn (a Darlington native and later a Denver attorney and close associate of Walsh), Box 109, Walsh Papers, establishes that Arabella Beckwith was his first schoolteacher in Darlington. U.S. Censuses 1860 and 1870 for Darlington, Johnson Library, Darlington, establish the names, ages, places of birth, and net worth of the Reed family. A deed recorded January 20, 1859, Book U, pp. 29–30, Office of the Register of Deeds for Lafayette County, conveys the E1/2 of Lot 7, Block 6, Darlington, from Fassett to Reed. The current Register of Deeds for the county verifies that the street address of the property was the house taken down for the firehouse. See also Arabella L. Reed's obituary in *The Denver Republican*, December 6, 1907, regarding her and her family's lives. See also stories in *The Denver Times*, November 11, 1898, and *The Rocky Mountain News*, October 30, 1955, about brothers Elton and Edwin Beckwith and their cattle operations and Elton's mansion near Gardner, Colorado. Evalyn incorrectly calls Elton her mother's brother.

5. All quotes from Griswold, *Leadville*, 379.

6. Stories of religious friction in the family are in McLean, *Father*, 25, also in my interviews with Kathleen O'Brien, September 2000, and Mary Ryan. A letter from John Healy to Thomas F. Walsh, May 19, 1904, Box 9, Walsh Papers, estab-

lishes that Thomas K. Walsh had lived in Denver and corresponded with his Irish relatives. More than one Thomas Walsh (none with middle initial K) is found in T. B. Corbett, W. C. Hoye, and J. H. Ballenger, *Denver City Directory*, microfilm, Western History Department, Denver Public Library, for the years 1869–1883. According to burial records in Golden's Mount Olivet Cemetery, Thomas K. Walsh died in 1883 and is buried next to his daughter Maria Lafferty, who died in 1908. Bodies buried at Mount Calvary Cemetery were moved to Mount Olivet in the 1950s to make way for the Denver Botanic Gardens. In this case, the headstones seem to have been lost in the move.

7. William J. Convery III, *Pride of the Rockies: The Life of Colorado's Premiere Irish Patron, John Kernan Mullen* (Boulder: University Press of Colorado, 2000), 71–83, 113–122, 171–183, 195–202; Stephen Birmingham, *Real Lace, America's Irish Rich* (New York: Harper & Row, 1973), 28–30, 247–248, 277–279.

8. Press quoted in Griswold, *Leadville*, 418; McLean, *Father*, 33.

9. Griswold, *Leadville*, 466; McLean, *Father*, 36.

10. Marshall Sprague, *Money Mountain: The Story of Cripple Creek Gold* (Lincoln: University of Nebraska Press, 1953), 113, 164; Smith, *Horace Tabor*, 307, 334. The Little Pittsburg is most commonly spelled without the final "h," although some spellings conform to that of its namesake city in Pennsylvania. Frank Waters, *Midas of the Rockies: The Story of Stratton and Cripple Creek* (New York: Covici-Friede, 1937), 98–99.

11. McLean, *Father*, 37; *The Rocky Mountain News*, April 9, 1910. My search of the public records of Lake, Pitkin, and Summit (now Eagle) counties, those comprising the Frying Pan District, failed to turn up Walsh's name in the district.

12. Griswold, *Leadville*, 540; McLean, *Father*, 83–84; *Ouray Herald*, January 12, 1899. See Mining Deeds made between Thomas and Patrick Walsh and recorded in the Office of the Clerk and Recorder, Lake County, Colorado, February 13, 1884, Book 105, p. 389, and October 27, 1883, Book 105, p. 55. See also Patent to Mining Lodes, April 18, 1887, Book O, p. 20, issued by the U.S. General Land Office to grantees Thomas F. Walsh, Patrick Walsh, S. Vinson Farnum, and A. W. Duggan for the Gerald Griffin Claim. See Deed, Walsh to Wegg, April 13, 1886, Book 112, p. 264, Lake County Records, noting an early dealing between the two men. See also the obituaries of Michael Walsh, *The Denver Post*, December 6, 1904, and Arthur Lafferty, *The Denver Post*, September 7, 1916.

13. Smith, *Horace Tabor*, 72–75, 109–115; Mehls, *David Moffat*, 57–60; Joseph E. King, *A Mine to Make a Mine: Financing the Colorado Mining Industry 1859–1902* (College Station: Texas A&M University Press, 1977), 87–88.

14. Smith, *Horace Tabor*, 72–75, 109–115; Mehls, *David Moffat*, 57–60; King, *A Mine*, 87–88.

15. Smith, *Horace Tabor*, 127–132; Mehls, *David Moffat*, 57–60; King, *A Mine*, 87–88, 92–94.

16. Mehls, *David Moffat*, 58–60; King, *A Mine*, 104–106, 164–168; letters O. H. Harker to D. H. Moffat, December 14, 1884, and January 15 1885, Agnes Wright Spring Collection, Colorado Historical Society, Denver.

17. In the letter William Dunham to Walsh, February 23, 1903, Box 77, Walsh Papers, promoter Dunham states that his own promotions are taking into account Walsh's aversion to the "mining stock business." Further discussion of the subject is in Richard H. Peterson, *The Bonanza Kings* (Lincoln: University of Nebraska Press, 1971), 97. See *Colorado Springs Gazette*, April 9, 1910, for a thorough discussion of Walsh's early self-education.

CHAPTER 4: DENVER, SMELTING, AND THE SILVER CRASH

1. The oldest known letter between Carrie and Tom is dated June 4, 1880, and is in Box 4, Walsh Papers. Another letter from Tom to Carrie, June 22, 1888, also in Box 4, refers, among other things, to Steve Reed still being a problem. See also McLean, *Father*, 34, 38 (Evalyn's quote regarding Steve Reed), 114.

2. The obituary of Vena Walsh is in *The Rocky Mountain News*, January 23, 1881, listing Vena's middle name as "Francis," which could be a misspelling of "Frances"; McLean, *Father*, 15–16, 37–38; Corbett, Hoye, and Ballenger, *Denver City Directory*, for the years 1882–1885; Griswold, *Leadville*, 1267, 1445, 1884; *The Rocky Mountain News*, April 9, 1909. The records of the Clerk and Recorder for Denver (then part of Arapahoe County) show numerous real estate transactions involving Walsh between the years 1880 and 1900.

3. McLean, *Father*, 37–38. See undated (probably 1910) and unpublished document entitled "To the Best of Mrs. Walsh's Recollection," Thomas F. Walsh Collection, E. S. Bird Library, Syracuse University, New York (hereafter "Walsh Syracuse Papers"). At the time, Carrie was supplying the family's lawyers with evidence that the family did not and had not for some time considered Colorado their home in an effort to avoid paying inheritance tax on her late husband's estate. Therefore, she would have been motivated to make their time outside the state seem as lengthy as possible. The letters from Tom Walsh to Carrie Walsh are dated July 22 and July 30, 1888, written from the Atlantic, Nantasket Beach, Massachusetts, Box 4, Walsh Papers. See letters that deal with the Birmingham properties from Hagood and Thomas to Walsh, September 3 and September 24, 1892, Box 1, Arthur Redman Wilfley Papers, Archives, University of Colorado at Boulder Libraries (hereafter "Wilfley Papers").

4. McLean, Father, 23; Diane Wilk, *The Wyman Historic District* (Denver: Historic Denver, Inc., in cooperation with Denver Museum of Natural History, 1995), 48. Thomas J. Noel and Barbara S. Norgren, *Denver: The City Beautiful and Its Architects, 1893–1941* (Denver: Historic Denver, Inc., 1987), 208–209, describes the life of the brilliant but unfortunate William A. Lang.

5. Jay E. Niebur, in collaboration with James E. Fell Jr., *Arthur Redman Wilfley: Miner, Inventor and Entrepreneur* (Denver: Western Basin Historical Research Center, Colorado Historical Society, 1982), 56–58; letter Austin to Walsh, January 24, 1892, Box 1, Wilfley Papers.

6. Articles of Incorporation of the Summit Mining and Smelting Company, Index to Domestic Corporations, Book 32, pp. 529–530, Colorado State Archives, Denver;

letters Maria Lafferty to Walsh, July 13, 1892, and Farnum to Walsh, September 30, 1892, both in Box 1, Wilfley Papers.

7. Stanley Dempsey and James E. Fell Jr., *Mining the Summit: Colorado's Ten Mile District, 1860–1960* (Norman: University of Oklahoma Press, 1986), 191–193, 230–231; McLean, *Father*, 37–38; letters Farnum to Walsh, July 5, 1892, and Austin to Walsh, November 15, 1892, both in Box 1, Wilfley Papers; Niebur and Fell, *Wilfley*, 58–61.

8. Ubbelohde, Benson, and Smith, *Colorado History*, 211–219.

9. Smith, *Horace Tabor*, 281–315; Noel and Norgren, *Denver: The City Beautiful*, 209; Charles S. Ryland, "Golden's Resourceful Merchant," *The Denver Westerners Roundup* 28, 9, November–December 1972.

10. Dempsey and Fell, *Mining the Summit*, 193, 231–233; Sprague, *Money Mountain*, 1–120. See deeds to the Deer Horn, Deer Horn #2, and Pride of the Rockies claims, dated October 29, 1892, recorded at Book 150, p. 47; dated December 21, 1892, recorded at Book 152, p. 56, all in the Records of the Office of the Clerk and Recorder, El Paso County, Colorado (the area did not become a part of newly formed Teller County until 1899). Grantees in each of the mining deeds are Arthur R. Wilfley ⅓, Ethan Byron ⅙, Samuel Lee ³⁄₃₂, Thomas F. Walsh ³⁄₃₂, David Wegg ⁹⁄₃₂, and Amos Henderson ¹⁄₃₂. T. A. Rickard, "Two Famous Mines—II," *Mining and Scientific Press*, December 30, 1911.

CHAPTER 5: A BONANZA IN THE SNOWY SAN JUANS

1. Richard K. Young, *The Ute Indians of Colorado in the Twentieth Century* (Norman: University of Oklahoma Press, 1997), 19–30; Charles Marsh, *People of the Shining Mountain* (Boulder: Pruett, 1982), 7–8, 56–57; Duane A. Smith, *Song of the Hammer & Drill: The Colorado San Juans 1860–1914* (Golden: Colorado School of Mines Press, 1982), 7–9; P. David Smith, *Mountains of Silver: The Story of Colorado's Red Mountain District* (Boulder: Pruett, 1994), 93; Val J. McClellan, *This Is Our Land* (New York: Vantage, 1976), 74, 398, 412.

2. Young, *Ute Indians*, 30–43. See Griswold, *Leadville*, 339, for this and other newspaper articles fanning the flames of Ute hatred. Reference is to the 1864 Sand Creek Massacre of Cheyenne and Arapaho Indians (many of them women, children, and the elderly) by the Colorado militia led by Colonel John Chivington. While largely vilified today, Chivington was still a hero to many whites in 1879.

3. Young, *Ute Indians*, 30–43.

4. Doris H. Gregory, *History of Ouray: A Heritage of Mining and Everlasting Beauty*, Vol. 1 (Ouray, CO: Cascade, 1995), 1–4, 38, 42; McLean, *Father*, 39.

5. Smith, *Mountains of Silver*, 88–191; Tom Rosemeyer, "Camp Bird Mine, Ouray County, Colorado," *Rocks and Minerals* 65, 2, March–April 1990, 116–117; "The True Story of the Camp Bird Discovery," *Engineering and Mining Journal*, Denver Correspondence, June 18, 1910, 1266; "William Weston Tells," *Ouray Herald*, December 8, 1911; Doris H. Gregory, *The Great Revenue and Surrounding Mines* (Ouray, CO: Cascade, 1996), 9–12; "One of America's Greatest Gold Mines—The Camp Bird," *The Victor Herald*, Victor, CO, October 6, 1936. The term "adit" is used here with reference to

horizontal mine passages having one opening to the mountainside. The term used in reporting at the time was "tunnel," which technically means a passage driven through the mountain to the other side. See "Glossary of Mining Terms," Appendix A.

6. "The True Story of the Camp Bird Discovery," 1266; "William Weston Tells"; Gregory, *The Great Revenue*, 9–12; Rosemeyer, "Camp Bird Mine," 117; T. A. Rickard, *Across the San Juan Mountains* (1st ed. San Francisco: Dewey, 1907; 2d ed. Ouray: Bear Creek, 1980), 28–29; Frances Melrose, "Tom Walsh's Lucky Hunch," *The Rocky Mountain News*, February 2, 1947, B-1–B-8; Theodore Calvin Peas and James G. Randall, eds., *The Diary of Orville Hickman Browning*, Vols. 20 and 22 (Springfield: Illinois Historical Collections, Illinois State Library, 1925), xxi–xxii, 362, 472, 504, 518. See Jack L. Benham, *Camp Bird and the Revenue* (Ouray: Bear Creek, 1980), 19–20, for more on fraudulent schemes perpetrated by Orrin Skinner.

7. *Solid Muldoon*, Ouray, CO, August 17, 1883. See also Smith, *Mountains of Silver*, 73–75, 85.

8. Gregory, *History of Ouray*, 51, 61–63.

9. *Solid Muldoon*, November 21 and November 28, 1879, and July 17, 1885. See also Smith, *Mountains of Silver*, 152.

10. Editions of the *Solid Muldoon* are in the microfilm collection of the Colorado Historical Society, Denver, Colorado. See also coverage of the illustrious Ouray career of David F. Day in Smith, *Mountains of Silver*, 73–75, 85, 152, 181, and Gregory, *History of Ouray*, 51, 61–63. See also Kathleen P. Chamberlain, "David F. Day and the *Solid Muldoon*: Boosterism and Humor on Colorado's Mining Frontier," *Journal of the West*, Denver, October 1995. Day died in 1914 and was buried in Denver's Riverside Cemetery. See "David F. Day, Noted Editor, Buried Today," *The Rocky Mountain News*, June 25, 1914, 3.

11. Smith, *Mountains of Silver*, 186; Gregory, *History of Ouray*, 107. See letters Walsh to Wegg, May 6, November 8, and December 26, 1894, all in Box 77, Walsh Papers. The public records of Ouray, Dolores, and San Juan counties, as well as records of the U.S. Bureau of Mines, disclose few operations by Walsh in the San Juan area prior to his finding the Camp Bird Mine in 1896. He likely leased all mines he operated at the time he was manager of the Silverton smelter.

12. McLean, *Father*, 36–46. Letter Hagood and Thomas to Walsh, September 24, 1892, Box 1, Wilfley Papers, discusses the problems with the Birmingham properties. The Walsh house in Ouray no longer exists.

13. Letters Walsh to Wegg, August 2, August 18, and August 29, 1895, March 25, 1896, and May 29, 1897, all in Box 77, Walsh Papers. No letters from Wegg to Walsh appear in the papers of this time.

14. Letters Walsh to Davies, January 31, 1903, Box 9; Osborn to Walsh, September 5, 1903, Box 77; Walsh to Benson, April 17, 1904, Box 78; and Abstract of Testimony, John A. Thompson Against Thomas F. Walsh, U.S. Circuit Court of Appeals, S. Dist. of New York, 1905 (hereafter "Thompson Case Testimony"), 2–3, Box 103, all in Walsh Papers. See Mining Lease, dated October 8, 1894, recorded in Book 91, p. 464, Office of the Clerk and Recorder of San Juan County, Colorado, in which George S. Orth

leases the Ben Butler and other claims to Thomas F. Walsh ³/₆, John A. Thompson ¹/₆, E. E. Byron ¹/₆, and W. R. Williams ¹/₆; also Mining Deed from Wegg and Farnum to Walsh, February 28, 1885, Book 74, p. 63 for a ¹/₈ interest in the American Lode, same county.

15. McLean, *Father*, 42–49; Rickard, "Two Famous Mines—II."

16. Walsh almost certainly misinterpreted his find, for while petzite and hessite (gold and silver telluride minerals) are occasionally observed in Camp Bird vein ore, they are not the main ore minerals of value. Gold, as the native metal, alloyed with between 5 percent and 20 percent silver, is by far the most valuable mineral in the vein. See Rosemeyer, "Camp Bird Mine," and Ed Raines, "Colorado Gold: Part 2—The Discovery, Mining History, Geology and Specimen Mineralogy of Selected Occurrences in Central Colorado and the San Juans," *Rocks & Minerals* 72, 5, September–October 1997; see also my discussions with Ed Raines on the subject. The story of the discovery of the rich vein in the Gertrude claim from Walsh's viewpoint is in his speech to the 1908 graduating class of the Colorado School of Mines, Golden, Colorado. The text of the speech and other tales of the discovery are in "Yield of Millions and Millions More Assured," *The Denver Times*, April 9, 1910. Both Walsh quotes are from that speech.

17. *The Denver Times*, April 9, 1910. Evalyn's account is very similar in McLean, *Father*, 49–54. Richardson concurs that Walsh took his own samples and found rich ores. See "Andy Richardson's Story: The Camp Bird Mine," undated issue of the *Ouray County Historian*, Archives of the Ouray County Historical Society. See also Rickard, "Two Famous Mines—II" and "The True Story of the Camp Bird Discovery," *Engineering and Mining Journal*, June 18, 1910. The story of the deception of assayer Strout and the use of outside assayers is in the *Silverite/Plaindealer*, Ouray, Colorado, December 14, 1910, and *The Denver Republican*, December 3, 1899.

CHAPTER 6: THE FABULOUS CAMP BIRD MINE

1. Sources on the geology of the Camp Bird Mine are Rosemeyer, "Camp Bird Mine," 133 (quote on gold deposits); Raines, "Colorado Gold: Part 2"; Chester W. Purinton, Thomas H. Woods, and Godfrey D. Doveton, "The Camp Bird Mine, Ouray, Colorado, and the Mining and Milling of the Ore," *American Institute of Mechanical Engineers Transactions* 33, 1902; H. A. Titcomb, "The Camp Bird Gold Mine and Mills," *School of Mines Quarterly* 24, Columbia University, New York, November 1902; Frederick Leslie Ransome, "A Report on the Economic Geology of the Silverton Quadrangle, Colorado" (Washington, DC: U.S. Geological Survey, 1901); Rickard, "Two Famous Mines—II"; R. H. Downer and Ralph E. DeCou, "A Description of the Working Mines of Ouray County, Colorado," *The Bulletin*, Technical and Engineering Society of the State School of Mines, Golden, Colorado, December 1901; A. Chester Beatty, "Report on the Camp Bird Mine," unpublished report dated February 1902, Archives of the Colorado School of Mines. See *Precious Metals Digest*, Malden House Publishers, 1983, for the 1900 gold prices. See also Sprague, *Money Mountain*, 1–107.

2. Various estimates of how much Walsh had to spend are in *The Rocky Mountain News*, Denver, April 9, 1910; *Silverite-Plaindealer*, Ouray, December 14, 1900; and Peterson, *Bonanza Kings*, 48. See various deeds of record listing Thomas F. Walsh as grantee in the Office of the Clerk and Recorder for Ouray County, 1896–1910. See also Rickard, *Across the San Juan Mountains*, 29; "William Weston Tells," *Ouray Herald*, December 8, 1911.

3. Rosemeyer, "Camp Bird Mine," 117; Melrose, "Tom Walsh's Lucky Hunch," *The Rocky Mountain News*, February 2, 1947, B-7; "Ouray Mourns the Death of the Discoverer of the Camp Bird Mine," *Plaindealer*, Ouray, CO, April 15, 1910. The card catalog of the Denver Public Library's Western History Department lists the names of all mines referenced in the department's extensive collection.

4. *Silverite-Plaindealer*, November 12, 1897. The *Engineering and Mining Journal*, August 14, 1897, discloses that the smelter Walsh had run in Silverton closed in 1897. See also discussion in Ransome, "Silverton Quadrangle," 22–23.

5. Rosemeyer, "Camp Bird Mine," 118; *Silverite-Plaindealer*, November 12, 1897, and November 17, 1899; *The Denver Republican*, December 3, 1899; Benham, *Camp Bird and Revenue*, 44–45.

6. *The Denver Republican*, December 3, 1899, 25. Letter Walsh to Benson, December 28, 1904, Box 78, Walsh Papers, establishes their common origins in Ireland. See Will Meyerriecks, *Drills and Mills: Precious Metal Mining and Milling Methods of the Frontier West*, 2nd ed. (Tampa, FL: Self-published, 2003), 180–183, for a good discussion of the use of quicksilver.

7. *Engineering and Mining Journal*, January 29, February 6, October 9, and December 10, 1898; Ransome, "Silverton Quadrangle," 42, 203–204; Rosemeyer, "Camp Bird Mine," 118; *The Denver Republican*, December 3, 1899, 25; *The Denver Times*, September 23 and October 3, 1898; *Mining Reporter*, Denver, September 29, 1898; Benham, *Camp Bird and Revenue*, 46–47; Purinton, Woods, and Dovetone, "Camp Bird Mine," 533.

8. *Engineering and Mining Journal*, January 28, February 11, August 19, and December 30, 1899; *The Denver Times*, February 9, August 14, October 8, and December 31, 1899; *The Denver Republican*, December 3, 1899. Here the reporter, like Walsh before him, had overemphasized the importance of the tellurides and failed to note that gold in its native state is the most important mineral in the vein.

9. *Engineering and Mining Journal*, June 16, September 22, October 6, and December 1, 1900; Rosemeyer, "Camp Bird Mine," 120; *Mining Reporter*, March 1, August 9, and November 1, 1900; *The Denver Times*, April 15 and November 23, 1900; Rickard, "Two Famous Mines—II."

10. Charles W. Henderson, "Mining in Colorado," Prof. Paper 138, U.S. Department of the Interior, United States Geological Survey, Washington, DC, 1926; Rickard, "Two Famous Mines—II"; *Engineering and Mining Journal*, August 10, 1901; *The Denver Times*, February 26 and June 12, 1901, and February 23, 1902; *Mining Reporter*, February 21, 1901; McLean, *Father*, 78–86.

11. Peterson, *Bonanza Kings*, 97; letter William Dunham to Walsh, February 23, 1903 (quote about flotations of property on a stock basis), and letters Walsh to Wegg, May

12 and 13, 1897 (both on Camp Bird Mine letterhead), all in Box 77, Walsh Papers; *The Rocky Mountain News*, April 9, 1910; *The Denver Post*, April 9, 1910; *The Denver Republican*, September 3, 1899 (quote on Walsh having "cleaned up a neat little fortune").

CHAPTER 7: WALSH ON LABOR

1. *Twelfth Census of the United States*, State of Colorado, County of Ouray, Imogene and Sneffels Precincts, 1900, microfilm, Western History Department, Denver Public Library. I performed all calculations of average ages.

2. Letter Walsh to Wegg, July 10, 1894, Box 77, Walsh Papers; Peterson, *Bonanza Kings*, 76.

3. McLean, *Father*, 63; Rosemeyer, "Camp Bird Mine," 120; *The Denver Republican*, December 3, 1899; *Silverite-Plaindealer*, November 1, 1901; Benham, *Camp Bird and Revenue*, 48; Rickard, *Across the San Juan Mountains*, 8; *Miners' Magazine*, Western Federation of Miners, Denver, Colorado, Archives, University of Colorado at Boulder Libraries, March 1901.

4. Titcomb, "The Camp Bird Gold Mine and Mills"; *The Denver Republican*, December 3, 1899; Rosemeyer, "Camp Bird Mine," 120; Purinton, Woods, and Doveton, "Camp Bird Mine," 525–526.

5. *The Denver Post*, June 6, 1904; Gregory, *The Great Revenue*, 147–150, 171–178; Sprague, *Money Mountain*, 133–156; Thomas J. Noel, "William J. Haywood," *Colorado Heritage* 2, 1984, 2–12; William Philpott, *The Lessons of Leadville* (Denver: Colorado Historical Society, 1994); Ubbelohde, Benson, and Smith, *Colorado History*, 245–259.

6. *The Denver Times*, September 23, 1901.

7. John Hays Hammond, *The Autobiography of John Hays Hammond* (New York: Farrar & Rinehart, 1935), 2 vols., vol. 2, 493–494; *The Denver Times*, September 26, 1903; Peterson, *Bonanza Kings*, 76; "Directors' Report and Statement of Accounts to 30 April 1903, Camp Bird Limited," Ouray County Historical Society Papers; John W. Taylor, "Interview with Harry T. Cook," MS, 1934, Colorado Historical Society, 2; Richard H. Peterson, "Thomas F. Walsh and Western Business Elitism: The Lifestyle of a Colorado Mining Magnate, 1896–1910," *Red River Valley Historical Review* 6, 4, Fall 1981, 55. The quote on Walsh's leadership style is in the *Ouray Herald*, January 12, 1899.

8. Peterson, "Thomas F. Walsh," 55 (including Eben Smith quote); Philpott, *Leadville*, 50.

9. Thomas J. Noel and Cathleen M. Norman, *A Pikes Peak Partnership: The Penroses and the Tutts* (Boulder: University Press of Colorado, 2000), 34–46, 60–62; Edwin P. Hoyt Jr., *The Guggenheims and the American Dream* (New York: Funk & Wagnalls, 1967), 50–57, 120–121, 224–240, 331–350; Fell, *Ores to Metals*, 228–229.

10. Peterson, *Bonanza Kings*, 74–86; Walsh quoted in *The Rocky Mountain News*, April 9, 1910.

11. Peterson, *Bonanza Kings*, 74–86.

12. *Miners' Magazine*, April, July, September, October, and November 1900; January and September 1901; April and September 1902; March 10, 1904; April 7, 1910.

CHAPTER 8: WHAT TO DO WITH MILLIONS OF DOLLARS

1. Gregory, *History of Ouray*, 79–81; *The Colorado Miner*, Denver, December 1900; *The Denver Times*, November 21, 1900; *Plaindealer*, Ouray, December 22, 1905; letter Ferrari to Walsh, January 14, 1903, and letter Darley to Walsh, January 15, 1903, both in Box 9, Walsh Papers; *Silverite-Plaindealer*, December 14, 1900; McLean, *Father*, 77; *The Denver Post*, August 4, 1901. The miner's quote is in General Frank Hall, "Thomas F. Walsh Entertains His Friends at His Camp Bird Mine," *The Denver Post*, August 4, 1901. The Walsh tribute is in *Trail Magazine*, 2, April 1910; see also Peterson, "Thomas F. Walsh," 56.

2. Gregory, *History of Ouray*, 132, 238–241. Walsh quote in Hall, "Thomas F. Walsh." Vinson Walsh was actually thirteen at the time.

3. *The Denver Republican*, October 4, 1897. Evalyn's account is in McLean, *Father*, 59–66. Other newspaper accounts are in *The Rocky Mountain News*, *The Denver Post*, and the *Chieftain*, Pueblo, Colorado, all dated October 4, 1897.

4. Two letters Minnie Koontz to Evalyn Walsh McLean, undated, Box 3, Walsh Papers. Other information in the letters indicates that they were written about 1936. Little else is known about the life of Patrick Walsh. *The Rocky Mountain News*, April 9, 1910, gives the date of Patrick's death.

5. McLean, *Father*, 66–68.

6. Thomas, "A Famous Carpenter," 6.

7. Lucius Beebe, *The Big Spenders* (New York: Pocket Books, Division of Simon & Schuster, 1967), 317. See also discussion in Peterson, "Thomas F. Walsh," 325–327.

8. McLean, *Father*, 68–71; *The Denver Times*, December 22, 1898.

9. *The Denver Times*, November 22, 1902; *Denver Daily News*, June 26, 1904; *The Denver Post*, June 26, 1904; *Ouray Herald*, November 16, 1899, and July 29, 1904; Smith, *Henry M. Teller*, 213–223; McLean, *Father*, 72–73.

CHAPTER 9: A PROMINENT
MEMBER OF NATIONAL SOCIETY

1. Official Communication signed by President William McKinley, Box 3, Walsh Papers.

2. Richard D. Mandell, *Paris 1900: The Great World's Fair* (Toronto: University of Toronto Press, 1967), xi, 62–83.

3. Ibid.

4. Ibid.; *The Denver Times*, June 25, 1900, and March 13, 1901; Henry Adams, *The Education of Henry Adams* (Boston: Privately printed, 1918), 379–383.

5. From an abstract of a document entitled "International Universal Exposition, Paris 1900, Report of the Commissioner-General of the United States, Vol. IV, February 28, 1901," Box 3, Walsh Papers; McLean, *Father*, 87–88.

6. *The Denver Times*, June 25, 1900; *Ouray Herald*, September 14, 1900; *Chicago American*, August 21, 1900; *The New York Times*, October 19, 1900; *The Nationalist and Tipperary Advertiser*, Clonmel, Ireland, August 9, 1900.

7. McLean, *Father*, 87–99; *The World*, New York, November 11, 1900.

8. Letter Walsh to Cortelyou, March 27, 1901, Microfilm Reel 55, William McKinley Papers, Manuscript Division, Reference Department, Library of Congress, Washington, DC (hereafter "McKinley Papers").

9. *The Denver Times*, May 5, May 29, and June 6, 1901; letters Walsh to Cortelyou, May 17, 1901, and Cortelyou to Walsh, April 22 and June 6, 1901, Microfilm Reels 56, 77, and 79, McKinley Papers. Interestingly, George Cortelyou went on to hold the positions of commerce secretary and treasury secretary in the Theodore Roosevelt administration but was accused of taking too many corporate contributions; therefore, the gifts from Walsh were only a start. See Morris, *Theodore Rex*, 207–209, 357–358, 488; Beebe, *The Big Spenders*, 317–318; letter John Hay to Thomas Walsh, October 17, 1902, and letter Clara Hay to Carrie Walsh, May 25, 1903, both in Walsh Syracuse Papers.

10. *The Denver Post*, October 5, 1902. See also *The Denver Post*, April 12, 1903, regarding the World's Fair appointment. But see the letter from the Polly Pry Publishing Company to Walsh, April 18, 1904, Box 10, Walsh Papers, which requests permission to do a biographical sketch of Walsh for $1,000, and the reply of Walsh's secretary (undated), also in Box 10, declining on the grounds of privacy. This did not lead to any negative press by Polly Pry.

11. Smith, *Henry Teller*, 228–229. The photograph of the Camp Bird gold badge presented to Roberta M. Wright, sponsor of the cruiser *Denver*, is in Box 110, Walsh Papers.

12. Caroline Bancroft, *The Melodrama of Wolhurst, Celebrated Colorado Show Place* (Denver: Golden Press, 1952), 12–13, 16 (listing Roosevelt as a guest and Walsh as a frequent guest during Wolcott's ownership of Wolhurst). See letter Walsh to Roosevelt, September 21, 1901, Microfilm Reel 19, Theodore Roosevelt Papers, Manuscript Division, Reference Department, Library of Congress, Washington, DC.

13. Charles J. Bayard, "Theodore Roosevelt and Colorado Politics: The Roosevelt-Stewart Alliance," *Colorado Magazine*, Colorado Historical Society, Denver, 42, 1, Winter 1965, 311–319; Morris, *Theodore Rex*, 155–169; Ubbelohde, Benson, and Smith, *Colorado History*, 245–247; letter Murphy to Roosevelt, July 8, 1904, Microfilm Reel 45, Roosevelt Papers.

14. Letter Roosevelt to Walsh, May 5, 1904, Microfilm Reel 334, Roosevelt Papers (appointing Walsh a delegate to the American Mining Congress); McLean, *Father*, 120. See newspapers articles of June 26, 1904, in *The Denver Post*, *The Denver Republican*, *Denver Daily News*, and *Colorado Springs Telegram*, all regarding Walsh's speech at the Brown Palace. Copies of the articles from the Denver papers are also in Microfilm Reel 45, Roosevelt Papers. Either Roosevelt or an aide had penned in notations as to the party affiliation of each paper as follows: *Post*, Democratic; *Daily News*, Democratic; *Republican*, Republican.

15. Letter Walsh to Roosevelt, July 3, 1904, Microfilm Reel 45, Roosevelt Papers; Noel, "Haywood," 2–12; report of John G. Brooks to Commissioner Carroll D. Wright, July 4, 1904, Microfilm Reel 45, Roosevelt Papers, apparently an individual report incorporated into the Bureau of Mines' official report. Roosevelt's receipt of Wright's

report in Bayard, "Theodore Roosevelt," 318–319. See Agnes Wright Spring, "Theodore Roosevelt in Colorado," *Colorado Magazine*, Colorado Historical Society, Denver, 35, 4, October 1958, 247–250, discussing candidate Roosevelt's 1900 support of the gold standard (which, among other things, caused him to narrowly avoid a riot in Victor, Colorado), as well as his long friendship with the controversial Sherman Bell.

16. Morris, *Theodore Rex*, 226–227, 304–307. Roosevelt's May 4, 1903, speech in Denver in support of irrigation is in *Presidential Addresses and State Papers of Theodore Roosevelt*, Part One (New York: P. F. Collier & Son, 1920), 361–364. See also "Thomas Francis Walsh," *National Cyclopedia of American Biography*, 191; Ubbelohde, Benson, and Smith, *Colorado History*, 184, 256–257; "History of the Uncompahgre Project," unpublished document in the records of the Uncompahgre Valley Water Users Assn., Montrose, Colorado.

17. *The Denver Times*, March 1, 1901, and October 9, 1902; *Ouray Herald*, June 29, 1904; "Address of Thomas F. Walsh, President of the National Irrigation Association," delivered at the Colorado Springs Convention, October 5, 1902, Western History Department, Denver Public Library.

18. Spring, "Theodore Roosevelt in Colorado," 261; *The Denver Times*, November 21, 1900; *Mining American*, Denver, November 18, 1916; "Mr. Walsh on Good Roads," *The Denver Republican*, October 24, 1906; *Congressional Record*, 57th Cong., 2nd sess., 1903, Vol. 36, 1396; *Congressional Record*, 60th Cong., 1st sess., 1908, Vol. 42, 6715–6724; letter Burnett to Walsh, March 5, 1908, Walsh Syracuse Papers.

CHAPTER 10: THE PRICE OF AFFLUENCE

1. Financial Statements, Box 103, Walsh Papers. In a typical month, January 1905, of Walsh's total expenses of $15,601, $1,311 went for lawyers' fees. *The Denver Times*, March 24, 1910; *Ouray Herald*, December 12, 1911.

2. *Plaindealer*, December 13, 1901; *Ouray Herald*, June 27, 1902; *Mining Reporter*, January 31 and October 31, 1901, August 21, 1902, and November 12, 1903; *Engineering and Mining Journal*, January 20 and December 1, 1900, February 9 and August 10, 1901; letters Robin to Walsh, August 31, 1892, and Walsh to Robin, September 3, 1892, both in Box 1, Wilfley Papers; Judgments, District Court for Ouray County, Colorado, all dated January 6, 1908, Case Nos. 1072, 1087–1101, 1137; Bond Between Walsh and Camp Bird, Ltd., May 6, 1902, Box 103, Walsh Papers (evidencing Walsh's continuing commitment to defend title to the Camp Bird properties); Thomas, "A Famous Carpenter," 5; Thompson Case Testimony, 74–75.

3. *Ouray Herald*, June 27, 1902; letter Hughes to Walsh, November 16, 1903, Box 77, Walsh Papers; Decree, *Cosmopolitan Mining Company v. Thomas F. Walsh*, Pleas in the Circuit Court of the United States for the District of Colorado, Sitting at Denver, June 23, 1902, recorded May 12, 1904, in Book 82, p. 74, Office of the Clerk and Recorder for Ouray County; Decree, *Cosmopolitan Mining Company v. Thomas F. Walsh*, Supreme Court of the United States, dated March 21, 1904, recorded May 12, 1904, in Book 82, p. 74, Office of the Clerk and Recorder for Ouray County.

4. Thompson Case Testimony, 70–78; letters Thompson to Walsh, December 12, 1900, and January 9, 1901, Box 9, Walsh Papers; letters Thomas to Walsh, November 2 and November 8, 1901.

5. Complaint, *John A. Thompson Against Thomas F. Walsh*, Supreme Court for New York County, June 25, 1903; letter Walsh to Davies, July 25, 1903; and Answers of Thomas F. Walsh to Complaint of John A. Thompson, n.d., all in Box 103, Walsh Papers; letter Davies to Walsh, October 22, 1903, Box 9, Walsh Papers.

6. Amended Bill of Complaint, *Thompson v. Walsh*, U.S. Circuit Court of Appeals, S. Dist. of New York, December 24, 1903, Box 103, Walsh Papers; letter Wegg to Walsh, November 2, 1901, Box 77; letter Walsh to Davies, July 25, 1903, Box 103; letter Byron to Walsh, September 17, 1903, Box 9; letter Benson to Walsh, February 19, 1904, Box 78; letter Walsh to Osborn, April 10, 1904, Box 78; letter Curran to Walsh, April 21, 1904, Box 11; letter Wickersham to Curran, April 27, 1904, Box 11; letter Walsh to Story, April 23, 1904, Box 78; letter Prentice to Walsh, June 16, 1904, Box 78; letter Leavick to Walsh, November 10, 1904, Box 78; and Thompson Case Testimony, 1–78, all in Walsh Papers.

7. Invoice, the Davies, Stone & Auerbach firm to Walsh, November 23, 1905; "Thomas F. Walsh, Engagements," prepared by the Davies firm, n.d.; Thompson Case Testimony, 13–14, all in Box 103, Walsh Papers; letters Davies to Walsh, March 12 and April 3, 1906, both in Box 12, Walsh Papers.

CHAPTER 11: THE WALSH PALACE

1. Carol M. Highsmith and Ted Landphair, "Embassy of Indonesia," in *Embassies of Washington*, ed. Alan Burnham (Washington, DC: Preservation Press, National Trust for Historic Preservation, 1992), Vol. 2, 47–49; "2020 Massachusetts Avenue," in *Massachusetts Avenue Architecture*, Vol. 1 (Washington, DC: Commission of Fine Arts, 1970), 124–125; McLean, *Father*, 111–114; *The Denver Times*, October 18, 1901.

2. Pamela Scott and Antoinette J. Lee, *Buildings of the District of Columbia* (New York: Oxford University Press, 1993), 328–329.

3. Highsmith and Landphair, "Embassy of Indonesia," Vol. 2, 49; undated statement from Mrs. A. Jenness Miller to Walsh, Box 190, Walsh Papers. Evalyn's quote is in McLean, *Father*, 112.

4. Thorstein Veblen, *The Theory of the Leisure Class* (Boston: Houghton Mifflin, 1973), 60–62; Peterson, "Thomas F. Walsh," 58.

5. "15 Dupont Circle, N.W.," in *Massachusetts Avenue Architecture*, Vol. 1, 95–102; Ralph G. Martin, *Cissy: The Extraordinary Life of Eleanor Medill Patterson* (New York: Simon & Schuster, 1979), 328–329; McLean, *Father*, 105; Beebe, *The Big Spenders*, 341; "2020 Massachusetts Avenue, N.W.," Vol. 2, 121–124; Cleveland Amory, *Who Killed Society?* (New York: Harper Bros., 1960), 520; "1401 Sixteenth Street, N.W.," in *Sixteenth Street Architecture*, Vol. 2 (Washington, DC: Commission on Fine Arts, 1988), 279–283; Socolofsky, *Landlord William Scully*, 128; *St. Louis Post Dispatch*, March 31, 1901; *Kansas*

City Star, January 2, 1905; "1913 Massachusetts Avenue, N.W.," in *Massachusetts Avenue Architecture,* Vol. 2, 109–115.

6. "2020 Massachusetts Avenue," 128; McLean, *Father,* 11, 119–120.

7. *The New York Times,* January 28, 1968; "2020 Massachusetts Avenue," 128; McLean, *Father,* 72. Walsh quote in Miller, *Captain Jack Crawford,* 254.

8. Marguerite Cassini, *Never a Dull Moment* (New York: Harper Bros., 1956), 174.

9. *The Denver Times,* February 18, 1903; McLean, *Father,* 113–114.

10. Highsmith and Landphair, "Embassy," 47, 51.

CHAPTER 12: A KING FOR A FRIEND

1. *The Denver Times,* October 20, October 24, and October 26 and November 15 and November 19, 1900.

2. Joseph Conrad, *Heart of Darkness: An Authoritative Text: Backgrounds and Sources; Criticism,* Robert Kimbrough, ed., Norton Critical Edition, 3rd edition (New York: W. W. Norton, 1988).

3. Adam Hochschild, *King Leopold's Ghost* (Boston: Houghton Mifflin, 1999), 33–34, 42–87, 140–199; W. T. Stead and Rev. E. M. Morrison, "The Congo Free State and Its Autocrat," *American Monthly Review of Reviews,* July 1903, 33–42; Edmund D. Morel, "The Belgian Curse in Africa," *The Contemporary Review,* London, vol. 81, January 6, 1902.

4. Hochschild, *King Leopold,* 123–131, 225–234.

5. Ibid., 192–208, 225–234, 259–265, 292–306; Stead and Morrison, "The Congo Free State," 39–41.

6. Hochschild, *King Leopold,* 292–306. Writing about King Leopold's death on December 17, 1909, two Denver newspapers, *The Rocky Mountain News* and *The Denver Times,* state that Walsh acted only as Leopold's adviser and refused to go to the Congo. *The Denver Post* of the same day incorrectly states that he made the trip.

7. Two issues of *The Denver Times,* August 28, 1902, and November 9, 1903, describe Leopold's work with and praise for Walsh. See also Jerome L. Sternstein, "King Leopold, Senator Nelson W. Aldrich, and the Strange Beginnings of American Economic Penetration of the Congo," *African Historical Studies,* African Studies Center of Boston University, Brookline, Massachusetts, 1969, 189–204.

8. Hochschild, *King Leopold,* 101–114.

9. Unpublished, handwritten draft entitled "King Leopold as I Know Him," Box 100, Walsh Papers; letter Curtis to Walsh, January 20, 1902, Walsh Syracuse Papers. See the positive account of Leopold in Demetrius C. Boulger, "The Congo State and Central-African Problems," *Harpers' New Monthly Magazine,* New York, Vol. C, January 1900. See also *Miners' Magazine,* August 1902.

10. David Northrup, *Beyond the Bend in the River* (Athens: Ohio University Center for International Studies, 1988), 93–115, 161; Sternstein, "King Leopold," 189–204; F. Scott Bobb, *Historical Dictionary of Democratic Republic of the Congo (Zaire)* (Lanham, MD: Scarecrow, 1999), 281–282.

11. McLean, *Father,* 97–98.

12. Hoyt, *The Guggenheims,* 151–152; *The Rocky Mountain News,* December 17, 1909; letter Benson to Walsh, May 13, 1904, Box 78, Walsh Papers.

CHAPTER 13: SELLING THE CAMP BIRD MINE

1. Hammond, *Autobiography,* 180–196, 482–485.

2. Ibid., 483.

3. Ibid., 484–485; McLean, *Father,* 103–108.

4. *The Denver Times,* July 29, 1900, and August 26, 1903. Periodic coverage of the proposed sale of the Camp Bird Mine is in *The Denver Times,* September 12, 27, and 30, October 9, 12, 14, 19, 23, and 28, and November 5 and 6, 1900; *Mining Record,* August 9, 1900; *Engineering and Mining Journal,* September 22, October 6, and December 1, 1900.

5. Warranty Mining Deed, Thomas F. Walsh to Camp Bird, Ltd., dated May 6, 1902, recorded May 12, 1902, Book 78, p. 219, in the Office of the Ouray County Clerk and Recorder; *The Denver Times,* May 13 and May 29, 1902; *Engineering and Mining Journal,* May 31, 1902; Rosemeyer, "Camp Bird Mine," 120.

6. Copies of the checks written by Walsh to Thomas and Benson, as well as many others written by Walsh and not chronologically organized, are in the Walsh Syracuse Papers. See also "Reminiscences of Days When Walsh Was Prospecting," *The Denver Post,* April 10, 1910; Petition Walsh to Roosevelt, October 18, 1904, Box 10, Walsh Papers; *Ouray Herald,* June 1, 1906; Virginia McConnell Simmons, *Bayou Salado* (Boulder: Fred Pruett, 1966), 216–222.

7. Letters Leavick to Walsh are as follows, all in the Walsh Papers: December 29, 1903, Box 9; March 28 and September 13, 1904, Box 10; September 2, 1905, Box 12; November 9, 1905, Box 11; and June 24, 1909, Box 79. Letter Richardson to Walsh, November 22, 1909, Box 13; letter Wegg to Walsh, July 21, 1903, Box 77, both in Walsh Papers. Foreign investment offers are in Boxes 78, 79, and 101 of the Walsh Papers. Agreement between Walsh and Dunham, January 20, 1903, Box 103, Walsh Papers (which provides that Dunham will search for mining properties and Walsh will pay him expenses and a ⅛ interest in anything acquired by Walsh); letter Benson to Walsh, September 7, 1903, Box 77, Walsh Papers.

8. *Ouray Herald,* June 1, 1906; "Statement Colorado Building," as of October 31, 1904, Box 103, Walsh Papers. Boxes 10 and 103 of the Walsh Papers, as well as the Walsh Syracuse Papers, disclose purchases by Walsh of several hundred thousand dollars in bonds in the years 1902–1904.

9. *Plaindealer,* September 6, 1901; *The Denver Times,* July 31, 1902; letter Story to Walsh, February 5, 1903, Box 103, Walsh Papers (all rights in the railroad to be transferred to J. J. Burns. It is not known if the transfer was actually made and very doubtful that Burns developed the line further).

10. P. R. Griswold, *The Moffat Road* (Denver: Rocky Mountain Railroad Club, 1995), 49–159; Robert Athearn, *Denver and Rio Grande Western Railroad* (Lincoln:

University of Nebraska Press, 1962), 201–205, 298–299; Mehls, *David Moffat,* 213–216; letter Cavender to Thom, March 7, 1912, Box 80, Walsh Papers (noting that the Walsh investment in thirty-three Moffat Road bonds is now substantially valueless).

CHAPTER 14: DEATH, AND A RETURN TO COLORADO

1. McLean, *Father,* 143–144; Hammond, *Autobiography,* 486.

2. Letter Louis Hooper to Walsh, December 15, 1903, Box 9, Walsh Papers; *The Denver Times,* August 25, 1901; letter C. R. Haugh to Vincent [sic] Walsh, November 7, 1904, Box 78, Walsh Papers; McLean, *Father,* 143–145.

3. Letter Walsh to C. F. Wetzel, December 2, 1904, Box 11, Walsh Papers.

4. Letter Wetzel to Vinson Walsh, December 19, 1904, Box 11, Walsh Papers; McLean, *Father,* 144.

5. McLean, *Father,* 133–139; letter Vinson Walsh to Carrie Walsh, Friday 28 [sic], 1905, Box 1, Walsh Papers.

6. Cleveland Amory, *The Last Resorts* (New York: Harper Bros., 1948), 197–198.

7. Ibid., 198; McLean, *Father,* 143–147.

8. McLean, *Father,* 143–154.

9. Letter Walsh to Roosevelt, September 5, 1905, Microfilm Reel 59, Theodore Roosevelt Papers.

10. Letter Walsh to Tim Kennedy, October 20, 1905, Box 1, Walsh Papers.

11. McLean, *Father,* 148–152; letters Walsh to Kennedy, December 16, 1905, and January 26, 1906, both in Box 1, Walsh Papers.

12. McLean, *Father,* 150–152; *The Rocky Mountain News,* April 9, 1910; letter Chisholm to Walsh, January 20, 1906, Box 78, Walsh Papers.

13. Thomas Felton Dawson, *Life and Character of Edward Oliver Wolcott* (New York: Knickerbocker, 1911), 586–595; Bancroft, *Wolhurst,* 5–15.

14. Letter Chisholm to Walsh, January 20, 1906, Box 78, Walsh Papers.

15. Letter Chisholm to Walsh, March 2, 1906, Box 78, Walsh Papers; *Ouray Herald,* June 1, 1906; letter Walsh to Kennedy, July 19, 1906, Box 1, Walsh Papers.

16. *The Denver Republican,* December 6, 1907.

17. *The Denver Times,* February 2, 1906; *The Rocky Mountain News,* April 15, 1910; Bancroft, *Wolhurst,* 14.

18. Invitation Walsh to Taft, August 3, 1907, Reel 68, William Howard Taft Papers, Manuscript Division, Reference Department, Library of Congress, Washington, DC (hereafter "Taft Papers"); letter Taft to Walsh, September 5, 1907, Reel 69, Taft Papers.

19. Unpublished manuscript entitled "Remarks of President Taft," September 22, 1909, Box 80, Walsh Papers.

20. *The Denver Republican,* September 23, 1909; letter Walsh to Taft, July 21, 1908, Reel 88, Taft Papers; McLean, *Father,* 184.

21. Hoyt, *The Guggenheims,* 184–185; McLean, *Father,* 155–156; "Complete Address of Hon. Thomas F. Walsh," *Ouray Herald,* October 12, 1906; Morris, *Theodore Rex,* 444, 472, 504–507.

22. *The Denver Post*, September 28, 1906.

23. "Testimony of John Springer," Case No. 143, Arapahoe County, Colorado, July 27, 1910, Box 104, Walsh Papers; letter Freeman to Wickersham, June 29, 1908, Box 78, Walsh Papers; *The Denver Post*, April 9, 1910, containing the Walsh quote.

24. Letter Walsh to Taft, January 5, 1909, Reel 116, Taft Papers. Before ascending to the presidency, Taft was often called "Judge" by his friends, for he had been a judge in Ohio before his work on the national scene. Interestingly, Taft confided in his friends that he would rather be chief justice of the Supreme Court than president. He ended up being both. See Morris, *Theodore Rex*, 543; Francis Russell, *The Shadow of Blooming Grove: Warren G. Harding in His Times* (New York: McGraw-Hill, 1968), 147–175, 441–442; Col. T. Bentley Mott, *Myron Herrick, Friend of France* (Garden City, NY: Self-published, 1929).

CHAPTER 15: FAMILY AND COUNTRY

1. Beebe, *The Big Spenders*, 327–328; McLean, *Father*, 167–168; letter Walsh to Kennedy, September 5, 1908, Box 1, Walsh Papers.

2. Evalyn's quote is in McLean, *Father*, 169. See also Treasury Department Document, Box 103, Walsh Papers.

3. McLean, *Father*, 167–181.

4. Letter Tom and Carrie Walsh to Evalyn and Ned McLean, September 18, 1908, Box 1, Walsh Papers.

5. Letter Tom and Carrie Walsh to Evalyn and Ned McLean, November 1, 1908, Box 4, Walsh Papers.

6. Letters Josephine Walsh to Tom Walsh, August 8 and November 20, 1904, May 9 and July 12, 1909, all in Box 1, Walsh Papers; *The Denver Post*, April 9, 1910; telegram Frank Walsh to Mrs. Thomas F. Walsh, December 2, 1910, Walsh Syracuse Papers; letter Koontz to McLean, undated, Box 3, Walsh Papers.

7. Letters L. H. Smith to Tom Walsh, December 7, 1904, and Tom Walsh to L. H. Smith, December 10, 1904, both in Box 10, Walsh Papers; letter Michael Walsh to Tom Walsh, June 3, 1904, Box 11, Walsh Papers; Michael Walsh obituary, *The Denver Post*, December 6, 1904; McLean, *Father*, 132; letter Benson to Tom Walsh, December 8, 1904, Box 78, Walsh Papers. Article on the "exploding gift" is in *The Denver Times*, July 2, 1904. See also letter Maggie Walsh Nichols to Tom Walsh, July 20, 1909, Box 1, Walsh Papers.

8. Letters Doyle to Tom Walsh, May 23, 1904, and Walsh to Doyle, June 11, 1904, both in Box 78, Walsh Papers.

9. The quote about Arthur Lafferty is in a letter from Maria Lafferty to Tom Walsh, October 12, 1904[?], Box 4, Walsh Papers. See also letters from Maria to Tom, August 31, 1894, and July 11, 1903, both in Box 1, Walsh Papers. Maria Lafferty's obituary is in *The Rocky Mountain News*, January 8, 1908; Arthur's is in *The Denver Post*, September 7, 1916. See also letter Irene ____ to T. F. Walsh, undated, Box 4, Walsh Papers. Regarding Walsh's support of the other foster children, see letters Maria

Lafferty to Tom Walsh, October 12, 1904, Box 4, Walsh Papers; letters S. A. Osborn to Walsh, January 15 and 16, 1904, and undated letter Fred J. Chambers to Walsh, all in Box 10, Walsh Papers.

10. Letter Walsh to Kennedy, December 17, 1904, Box 1, Walsh Papers. See also letters from Walsh to Kennedy, December 6, 1901, Box 9, and Kennedy to Walsh, April 23, 1904, Box 11, both in Walsh Papers and dealing with the coachmen. See also letter Walsh to Sullivan, November 20, 1909, Box 1, Walsh Papers.

11. McLean, *Father*, 74–75. I copied the inscription on my visit to Kilmurray Cemetery in July 2000.

12. Letters Annie Healy to Walsh, September 29, 1903; John Healy to Walsh, May 19, 1904; Walsh to John Healy, June 18, 1904; and John Healy to Walsh, July 21, 1904, all in Box 9, Walsh Papers; letter Kate Shea to Walsh, November 15, 1904, Box 1, Walsh Papers. Michael O'Brien of Clonmel, grandson of Kate Shea, gave me the approximate date of her death in a 2001 telephone interview. My interview with Mary Ryan in July 2000 established the story of the lost gift.

13. Letters Joanna A. Walsh to Thomas F. Walsh, July 16, 1903, and Joanna Walsh McGrath to Walsh, December 16, 1903, both in Box 9, and McGrath to Walsh, February 7, 1904, Box 1, all in Walsh Papers; obituary of John Walsh, *The Nationalist*, Clonmel, Ireland, June 24, 1903; letter Kate Shea to Walsh, July 20, 1903, Box 9, Walsh Papers.

14. Letters Walsh to McCarthy, April 25, 1904, Box 11; M. Lafferty to Walsh, October 12, 1904, Box 4; and Murphy, Fethard Town Clerk to Walsh, April 1, 1903, Box 9, all in Walsh Papers.

15. Unpublished document entitled "Clubs and Societies," Walsh Syracuse Papers.

16. May 21, 1908, reading of Walsh letter in the *Congressional Record*, 60th Cong., 1st sess., 1908, Vol. 42, 6715–6724.

17. Stephen S. Hart, "The Denver Radium Boom and the Colorado School of Mines," *Mines Magazine*, Colorado School of Mines, Golden, February 1986, 9–11; letters Victor C. Alderson (Colorado School of Mines) to Walsh, April 19 and June 30, 1909, Box 80, Walsh Papers.

18. "Thomas F. Walsh," *Child and Animal Protection*, Colorado Humane Society, Denver, September 1908, 1–3; "Trip to Spain," unpublished manuscript, Box 100, Walsh Papers; McLean, *Father*, 165 (for Walsh's criticism of Roosevelt); "Thomas Francis Walsh," *The National Cyclopedia of American Biography*, 51 vols. (New York: James T. White, 1892–1969), Vol. 15, 191.

19. *The Rocky Mountain News* and *The Denver Times*, both September 24, 1909; letters Francis to Walsh, May 11, 1909; Catlin (chairman of the Gunnison Tunnel Opening) to Walsh, July 15, 1909; and Brown to Walsh, August 10, 1909, all in Box 13, Walsh Papers.

20. Letter Warren to Walsh, June 19, 1909, Walsh Syracuse Papers.

CHAPTER 16: THE PASSING OF THOMAS F. WALSH

1. McLean, *Father*, 185; *The Rocky Mountain News*, April 9, 1910; *The Denver Times*, February 5, 1910.

2. Hochschild, *King Leopold*, 265–267; *The Denver Post*, December 17, 1909; *The Rocky Mountain News*, December 17 and December 19, 1909.

3. *Durango Weekly Democrat*, December 18, 1909.

4. *The Rocky Mountain News*, December 17, 1909.

5. Thomas, "A Famous Carpenter," 8. Apparently the cablegram has not survived. *The Rocky Mountain News*, December 17, 1909; *The Denver Times*, December 17, 1909. See, for example, Hochschild, *King Leopold*, 243–244, 278–279; Sternstein, "King Leopold"; and Northrup, *Beyond the Bend in the River*, 93–115, none of which mentions Walsh. See also Hoyt, *The Guggenheims*, 151, which asserts that Daniel Guggenheim was the only American to whom Leopold and Thomas Fortune Ryan could have turned for both natural resource expertise and investment power in 1906.

6. *Durango Weekly Democrat* and *Durango Daily Democrat*, December 24, 1909.

7. Thomas, "A Famous Carpenter," 8.

8. McLean, *Father*, 185–192; *The Denver Times*, January 11, January 12, and January 28, 1910.

9. *The Denver Times*, February 24 and March 21, 1910.

10. *The Denver Times*, March 23, March 25, and March 26, 1910; *The Rocky Mountain News*, April 9, 1910.

11. "Colorado Grief-Stricken over Death of Tom Walsh," *The Rocky Mountain News*, April 9, 1910; "Thomas F. Walsh Loses in Brave Fight for Life at Capital," *The Denver Post*, April 9, 1910.

12. *The Rocky Mountain News*, April 9, 1910.

13. Ibid.

14. Ibid.

15. *The Washington Post*, April 9, 1910.

16. *Durango Democrat*, April 13 and April 17, 1910.

17. *Birmingham* [Alabama] *News*, April 9, 1910.

18. *The Washington Post*, April 11, 1910; McLean, *Father*, 191–192.

19. Estate information and Osborn quote are in *The Denver Post*, April 9, 1910.

20. Osborn was presumably referring to the unpublished document dated March 6, 1903, and entitled "To My Heirs at Law and Next of Kin," signed by Thomas F. Walsh, Box 104, Walsh Papers. The document admitted to probate was "Will of Thomas F. Walsh," filed in the Estate of Thomas F. Walsh, Case No. 143, County Court, in Probate, Arapahoe County, Colorado, which was dated January 10, 1910, and admitted to probate April 27, 1910. The names are misspelled "Carry" and "Evelyn." Thomas, "A Famous Carpenter," 9.

21. *The Denver Times*, April 15, 1910; Thomas, "A Famous Carpenter," 9; letter S. A. Osborn to E. B. McLean, August 15, 1910, Box 80, Walsh Papers.

22. *The Colorado Springs Herald*, April 13, 1910; *The Denver Times*, April 15, 1910.

23. Transcript of Testimony, July 27, 1910, Box 104, Walsh Papers.

24. Ibid.; *The Rocky Mountain News*, January 22, 1948 (obituary of Thomas F. Walsh, architect).

25. Testimony of Mrs. Carry [sic] Bell Walsh, County Court, Case No. 143, Arapahoe County, Colorado, May 15, 1912, Box 104, Walsh Papers.

26. *The Denver Post*, January 4, 1913; letter S. A. Osborn to Mrs. Thomas F. Walsh and Mrs. Edward McLean, July 11, 1910, Box 80, Walsh Papers; Bancroft, *Wolhurst*, 16–34; Phil Goodstein, *The Seamy Side of Denver* (Denver: New Social Publications, 1993), 127–129.

CHAPTER 17: THE WALSH FAMILY AND THE WALSH MINE

1. Highsmith and Landphair, "Embassy," 49; "2020 Massachusetts Avenue," 129; McLean, *Father*, 330. The commendation from the Polish society is in Box 97, Walsh Papers.

2. "Carrie Belle Reed Walsh," *The National Cyclopedia of American Biography*, Vol. 26, 319.

3. Bruce A. Gustin, "Mrs. Thomas F. Walsh, Widow of Colorado Mining King, Dies," *The Denver Post*, February 25, 1932, 1; McLean, *Father*, 330.

4. McLean, *Father*, 196–200; Beebe, *The Big Spenders*, 334–335.

5. McLean, *Father*, 196–202, 216; Invoice, Cartier to Mr. and Mrs. Edward B. McLean, August 1, 1918, Box 97, Walsh Papers.

6. McLean, *Father*, 202–204.

7. Ibid., 264–268.

8. Ibid., 269–308; Russell, *The Shadow of Blooming Grove*, 2, 260–263, 410–423, 446–448, 568–570; unpublished document entitled "Senator Thomas J. Walsh Examination of Ned McLean," Box 97, Walsh Papers.

9. McLean, *Father*, 306–316; Russell, *The Shadow of Blooming Grove*, 609–616.

10. Carol Ann Rapp, Epilogue to *Queen of Diamonds* (Franklin, TN: Hillsboro, 2000), 307–310. *Queen of Diamonds* is the 3rd edition of McLean, *Father Struck It Rich*. It also includes a foreword by Joseph Gregory, great-great-grandson of Thomas F. Walsh and great-grandson of Evalyn Walsh McLean.

11. Rapp, Epilogue to *Queen of Diamonds*, 311; Russell, *The Shadow of Blooming Grove*, 517–520, 641; McLean, *Father*, 313, 331–337 (quote regarding her efforts to find the baby is on 334).

12. C. G. Poore, "Two Views from Red Gap," *The New York Times Book Review*, March 15, 1936; Edwin Tribble, "The Hope Springs Eternal," *New Republic*, April 12, 1936.

13. Rapp, Epilogue to *Queen of Diamonds*, 311–313; Martin, *Cissy*, 389–390.

14. Helen Essary, North American Newspaper Alliance, news release entitled "Rationing Holds Few Bounds for Mrs. McLean," Monday, April 19 (presumably 1942), Box 97, Walsh Papers; Rapp, Epilogue to *Queen of Diamonds*, 313.

15. Beebe, *The Big Spenders*, 341–343; Thurman Arnold, *Fair Fights and Foul: A Dissenting Lawyer's Life* (New York: Harcourt, Brace & World, 1965), 251.

16. Rapp, Epilogue to *Queen of Diamonds*, 320–321; Arnold, *Fair Fights*, 250–251.

17. Interview with Ratmoko Ratmansuyu, Press and Information Division, Indonesian Embassy, and tour of the embassy, September 2000.

18. David Lavender, *One Man's West* (Garden City, NY: Doubleday, 1956), 3.

19. Rosemeyer, "Camp Bird Mine," 120–128; Lavender, *One Man's West*, 3–78.

20. *Plaindealer*, August 3, 1995.

CONCLUSION: THE LEGACY OF THOMAS F. WALSH

1. Hoyt, *The Guggenheims*, 148.

2. McLean, *Father*, 341.

3. Ibid., 343.

4. Thomas, "A Famous Carpenter," 9.

5. David Batstone, *Saving the Corporate Soul, and (Who Knows?) Maybe Your Own* (San Francisco: Jossey-Bass, 2001), 125. See similar theories of corporate management in C. William Pollard, *The Soul of the Firm* (New York: HarperBusiness, 1996), and Alan Downs, *Corporate Executions* (New York: American Management Association), 1995.

6. Batstone, *Saving the Corporate Soul*, 135.

BIBLIOGRAPHY

BOOKS

Adams, Henry. *The Education of Henry Adams*. Privately printed, Boston, 1918.

Amory, Cleveland. *The Last Resorts*. Harper Bros., New York, 1948.

———. *Who Killed Society?* Harper Bros., New York, 1960.

Arnold, Thurman. *Fair Fights and Foul: A Dissenting Lawyer's Life*. Harcourt, Brace & World, New York, 1965.

Athearn, Robert. *Denver and Rio Grande Western Railroad*. University of Nebraska Press, Lincoln, 1962.

Bancroft, Caroline. *The Melodrama of Wolhurst, Celebrated Colorado Show Place*. Golden Press, Denver, 1952.

Batstone, David. *Saving the Corporate Soul, and (Who Knows?) Maybe Your Own*. Jossey-Bass, San Francisco, 2001.

Beebe, Lucius. *The Big Spenders*. Pocket Books, Division of Simon & Schuster, New York, 1967.

Benham, Jack L. *Camp Bird and the Revenue*. Bear Creek, Ouray, Colorado, 1980.

Birmingham, Stephen. *Real Lace: America's Irish Rich*. Harper & Row, New York, 1973.

Black, Robert C., III. *Railroad Pathfinder: The Life & Times of Edward L. Berthoud.* Cordillera, Evergreen, Colorado, 1988.

Bobb, F. Scott. *Historical Dictionary of Democratic Republic of the Congo (Zaire).* Scarecrow, Lanham, Maryland, 1999.

Brown, Robert L. *Central City and Gilpin County, Then and Now.* Caxton, Caldwell, Idaho, 1994.

Cassini, Marguerite. *Never a Dull Moment.* Harper Bros., New York, 1956.

Chernow, Ron. *Titan: The Life of John D. Rockefeller, Sr.* New York: Random House, 1998.

Clark, Dennis. *Hibernia America: The Irish and Regional Cultures.* Greenwood, New York, 1986.

Collins, Charles. *Collins' Deadwood Business Directory of 1878–79.* Self-published, Deadwood, SD, 1879.

Convery, William J., III. *Pride of the Rockies: The Life of Colorado's Premiere Irish Patron, John Kernan Mullen.* University Press of Colorado, Boulder, 2000.

Dawson, Thomas Felton. *The Life and Character of Edward Oliver Wolcott.* Knickerbocker, New York, 1911.

Dempsey, Stanley, and James E. Fell Jr. *Mining the Summit: Colorado's Ten Mile District 1860–1960.* University of Oklahoma Press, Norman, 1986.

Downs, Alan. *Corporate Executions.* American Management Association, New York, 1995.

Fell, James E., Jr. *Ores to Metals: The Rocky Mountain Smelting Industry.* University of Nebraska Press, Lincoln, 1979.

Fielder, Mildred. *Silver Is the Fortune.* North Plains, Aberdeen, South Dakota, 1978.

Goodstein, Phil. *The Seamy Side of Denver.* New Social Publications, Denver, 1993.

Gregory, Doris H. *The Great Revenue and Surrounding Mines.* Cascade, Ouray, Colorado, 1996.

———. *History of Ouray: A Heritage of Mining and Everlasting Beauty,* Vol. 1. Cascade, Ouray, Colorado, 1995.

Griswold, Don L., and Jean Harvey Griswold. *History of Leadville and Lake County, Colorado.* Colorado Historical Society in cooperation with the University Press of Colorado, Boulder, 1996.

Griswold, P. R. *The Moffat Road.* Rocky Mountain Railroad Club, Denver, 1995.

Hahn, Emily. *Fractured Emerald: Ireland.* Doubleday, Garden City, New York, 1971.

Hammond, John Hays. *The Autobiography of John Hays Hammond.* Farrar & Rinehart, New York, 1935.

Hochschild, Adam. *King Leopold's Ghost.* Houghton Mifflin, Boston, 1999.

Hoppen, K. Theodore. *Ireland Since 1800: Conflict and Conformity,* 2nd ed. Longman, New York, 1999.

Hoyt, Edwin P., Jr. *The Guggenheims and the American Dream.* Funk and Wagnalls, New York, 1967.

Hughes, Richard B. *Pioneer Years in the Black Hills,* 2nd ed., Agnes Wright Spring, ed. Dakota Alpha, Rapid City, South Dakota, 1999.

King, Joseph E. *A Mine to Make a Mine: Financing the Colorado Mining Industry 1859–1902.* Texas A&M University Press, College Station, 1977.

Laurie, Lorraine Michele. *The Island That Became a Neighborhood: A History of Green Island in Worcester, Massachusetts, 1826–1985.* Self-published, Worcester, 1985.

Lavender, David. *One Man's West.* Doubleday, Garden City, New York, 1956.

MacLysaght, Edward. *The Surnames of Ireland.* Irish Academic, Dublin, n.d.

Mandell, Richard D. *Paris 1900: The Great World's Fair.* University of Toronto Press, Toronto, 1967.

Marsh, Charles. *People of the Shining Mountain.* Pruett, Boulder, 1982.

Martin, Ralph G. *Cissy: The Extraordinary Life of Eleanor Medill Patterson.* Simon & Schuster, New York, 1979.

McClellan, Val J. *This Is Our Land.* Vantage, New York, 1976.

McClintock, John S. *Pioneer Days in the Black Hills,* 3rd ed. University of Oklahoma Press, Norman, 2001.

McLean, Evalyn Walsh, with Boyden Sparkes. *Father Struck It Rich.* 1st ed. Little Brown, Boston, 1936; 2nd ed. Bear Creek, Ouray, Colorado, 1981; 3rd ed. Hillsboro, Franklin, Tennessee (published under the title *Queen of Diamonds,* Foreword, Joseph Charles Gregory; Epilogue, Carol Ann Rapp), 2000.

Meyerriecks, Will. *Drills and Mills: Precious Metal Mining and Milling Methods of the Frontier West,* 2nd ed. Self-published, Tampa, Florida, 2003.

Miller, Darlis A. *Captain Jack Crawford: Buckskin Poet, Scout and Showman.* University of New Mexico Press, Albuquerque, 1993.

Morgan, Gary. *Three Foot Rails: A Quick History of the Colorado Central Railroad.* Little London, Colorado Springs, Colorado, 1974.

Morris, Edmund. *Theodore Rex.* Random House, New York, 2001.

Mott, Col. T. Bentley. *Myron Herrick, Friend of France.* Self-published, Garden City, New York, 1929.

Niebur, Jay E., in collaboration with James E. Fell Jr. *Arthur Redman Wilfley: Miner, Inventor and Entrepreneur.* Western Basin Historical Research Center, Colorado Historical Society, Denver, 1982.

Ni Mhannin, Cait. "The Famine Around Slievenamon." In *Slievenamon in Song & Story,* Sean Nugent, ed. Waterford: Telcom Eireann, n.d.

Noel, Thomas J., and Barbara S. Norgren. *Denver: The City Beautiful and Its Architects, 1893–1941.* Historic Denver, Inc., Denver, 1987.

Noel, Thomas J., and Cathleen M. Norman. *A Pikes Peak Partnership: The Penroses and the Tutts.* University Press of Colorado, Boulder, 2000.

Northrup, David. *Beyond the Bend in the River.* Ohio University Center for International Studies, Athens, 1988.

Nugent, Sean, ed. *Slievenamon in Song & Story.* Telcom Eireann, Waterford, n.d.

O'Donnell, Sean. *Clonmel 1840–1900: Anatomy of an Irish Town.* Geography Publications, Dublin, n.d.

Peas, Theodore Calvin, and James G. Randall, eds. *The Diary of Orville Hickman Browning,* Vols. 20 and 22. Illinois Historical Collections, Illinois State Library, Springfield, 1925.

Peterson, Richard H. *The Bonanza Kings.* University of Nebraska Press, Lincoln, 1971.

Philpott, William. *The Lessons of Leadville.* Colorado Historical Society, Denver, 1994.

Pollard, C. William. *The Soul of the Firm.* HarperBusiness, New York, 1996.

Rickard, T. A. *Across the San Juan Mountains.* 1st ed. Dewey, San Francisco, 1907; 2nd ed. Bear Creek, Ouray, Colorado, 1980.

Russell, Francis. *The Shadow of Blooming Grove: Warren G. Harding in His Times.* McGraw-Hill, New York, 1968.

Ryan, Mary. *Hope.* Headline, London, 2001.

Schell, Herbert S. *History of South Dakota,* 3rd ed. University of Nebraska Press, Lincoln, 1975.

Scott, Pamela, and Antoinette J. Lee. *Buildings of the District of Columbia.* Oxford University Press, New York, 1993.

Simmons, Virginia McConnell. *Bayou Salado.* Fred Pruett, Boulder, 1966.

Smith, Duane A. *Henry M. Teller: Colorado's Grand Old Man.* University Press of Colorado, Boulder, 2002.

———. *Horace Tabor: His Life and Legend.* University Press of Colorado, Niwot, 1989.

———. *Song of the Hammer & Drill: The Colorado San Juans 1860–1914.* Colorado School of Mines Press, Golden, 1982.

———. *Staking a Claim in History: The Evolution of Homestake Mining Company.* Homestake Mining Company, Walnut Creek, California, 2001.

Smith, P. David. *Mountains of Silver: The Story of Colorado's Red Mountain District.* Pruett, Boulder, 1994.

Socolofsky, Homer E. *Landlord William Scully.* Regents Press of Kansas, Lawrence, 1979.

Sprague, Marshall. *Money Mountain: The Story of Cripple Creek Gold.* University of Nebraska Press, Lincoln, 1953.

Thomas, Sewell. *Silhouettes of Charles S. Thomas, Colorado Governor and United States Senator.* Caxton, Caldwell, Idaho, 1959.

Ubbelohde, Carl, Maxine Benson, and Duane A. Smith. *A Colorado History,* 7th ed. Pruett, Boulder, 1995.

Utley, Robert M. *Cavalier in Buckskin: George Armstrong Custer and the Western Military Frontier.* University of Oklahoma Press, Norman, 1988.

Veblen, Thorstein. *The Theory of the Leisure Class.* Houghton Mifflin, Boston, 1973.

Waters, Frank. *Midas of the Rockies: The Story of Stratton and Cripple Creek.* Covici-Friede, New York, 1937.

Wilk, Diane. *The Wyman Historic District.* Historic Denver, Inc., in cooperation with Denver Museum of Natural History, Denver, 1995.

Young, Richard K. *The Ute Indians of Colorado in the Twentieth Century.* University of Oklahoma Press, Norman, 1997.

THESES

Mehls, Steven F. *David H. Moffat, Jr.: Early Colorado Business Leader.* PhD dissertation, University of Colorado, 1982, Western History Section, Denver Public Library.

NEWSPAPERS, PERIODICALS

Birmingham News, Birmingham, Alabama

Black Hills Daily Times, Deadwood, South Dakota

Black Hills Pioneer, Deadwood, South Dakota

Chicago American, Chicago, Illinois

Chieftain, Pueblo, Colorado

Colorado Miner, Denver, Colorado

Colorado Springs Gazette, Colorado Springs, Colorado

Colorado Springs Herald, Colorado Springs, Colorado

Colorado Springs Telegram, Colorado Springs, Colorado
Denver Daily News, Denver, Colorado
The Denver Post, Denver, Colorado
The Denver Republican, Denver, Colorado
The Denver Times, Denver, Colorado
Durango Daily Democrat (also called *Durango Democrat* and *Durango Weekly Democrat*),
     Durango, Colorado
Engineering and Mining Journal, Denver, Colorado
Kansas City Star, Kansas City, Missouri
Leadville Chronicle, Leadville, Colorado
Miners' Magazine, Western Federation of Miners, Denver, Colorado (Archives, University of Colorado at Boulder Library)
Mining American, Denver, Colorado
Mining Record, Denver, Colorado
Mining Reporter, Denver, Colorado
The Nationalist (also called *The Nationalist and Tipperary Advertiser*), Clonmel, Ireland
New York Times, New York, New York
News Gazette, Colorado Springs, Colorado
Ouray Herald, Ouray, Colorado
Ouray Herald and Plaindealer, Ouray, Colorado
Ouray Times, Ouray, Colorado
Plaindealer, Ouray, Colorado
The Rocky Mountain News (also called *Denver Daily News*), Denver, Colorado
Silverite-Plaindealer, Ouray, Colorado
Solid Muldoon, Ouray, Colorado
St. Louis Post Dispatch, St. Louis, Missouri
The Trail Magazine, II, Denver, Colorado
Victor Herald, Victor, Colorado
Washington Post, Washington, D.C.
The World, New York, New York

ARCHIVES, RECORDED DOCUMENTS, COURT PROCEEDINGS

Adams Museum Archives, Deadwood, South Dakota
Colorado Railroad Museum Archives, Golden, Colorado
Colorado School of Mines Archives, Golden, Colorado
Colorado State Archives, Denver, Colorado
County Court, in Probate, Arapahoe County, Colorado
District Court, Ouray County, Colorado
Records of the Office of the Clerk and Recorder for Lawrence County, South Dakota
Records of the Office of the Clerk and Recorder for these Colorado counties: Denver,
     Dolores, El Paso, Gilpin, Lake, Ouray, Park, San Juan, and Teller
Records of the Register of Deeds for Lafayette County, Wisconsin
University of Colorado Archives, Boulder, Colorado
Western History Department, Denver Public Library, Denver, Colorado

MICROFILM COLLECTIONS

T. B. Corbett, W. C. Hoye, and J. H. Ballenger. *Denver City Directory, 1869–1883*. Denver, Colorado, Denver Public Library, Western History Department.

William McKinley Papers. Microfilm, Manuscript Division, Reference Department, Library of Congress, Washington, D.C.

Theodore Roosevelt Papers. Microfilm, Manuscript Division, Reference Department, Library of Congress, Washington, D.C.

William Howard Taft Papers. Microfilm, Manuscript Division, Reference Department, Library of Congress, Washington, D.C.

Tenth and Eleventh Censuses of the United States. State of Wisconsin, County of Lafayette, Town of Center (1860), Village and Town of Darlington (1870), Johnson Library, Darlington, Wisconsin.

Twelfth Census of the United States. State of Colorado, County of Ouray, Imogene and Sneffels Precincts, Denver Public Library, Western History Department.

MAGAZINE ARTICLES,
PROFESSIONAL PUBLICATIONS, ANTHOLOGIES

Bayard, Charles J. "Theodore Roosevelt and Colorado Politics: The Roosevelt-Stewart Alliance." *Colorado Magazine* 42, 1, Colorado Historical Society, Denver, Winter 1965.

Boulger, Demetrius C. "The Congo State and Central-African Problems." *Harpers' New Monthly Magazine*, New York, Vol. C, January 1900.

"Carrie Belle Reed Walsh." *The National Cyclopedia of American Biography*, Vol. 26. James T. White, New York, 1937.

Chamberlain, Kathleen P. "David F. Day and the *Solid Muldoon*: Boosterism and Humor on Colorado's Mining Frontier." *Journal of the West*, Denver, October 1995.

Cohen, Morris H. "Worcester's Ethnic Groups: A Bicentennial View." *Worcester People and Places*, ch. V. Worcester: Bicentennial Commission, Worcester, Massachusetts, 1976.

Crossen, Forest. "Thomas Fitzpatrick, Railroadman." *Western Yesterdays*, Vol. 6. Paddock, Boulder, 1968.

Downer, R. H., and Ralph E. DeCou. "A Description of the Working Mines of Ouray County, Colorado." *The Bulletin*, Technical and Engineering Society of the State School of Mines, Golden, Colorado, December 1901.

Hart, Stephen S. "The Denver Radium Boom and the Colorado School of Mines." *Mines Magazine*, Colorado School of Mines, Golden, Colorado, February 1986.

Henderson, Charles W. "Mining in Colorado." Prof. Paper 138, U.S. Department of the Interior, U.S. Geological Survey, Washington, D.C., 1926.

Highsmith, Carol M., and Ted Landphair. "Embassy of Indonesia." In *Embassies of Washington*. Preservation Press, National Trust for Historic Preservation, Washington, D.C., 1992.

History of Lafayette County. Archives of the Lafayette County Historical Society, Darlington, Wisconsin.

Massachusetts Avenue Architecture. Alan Burnham, ed. Vols. 1 and 2. Commission of Fine Arts, Washington, D.C., 1984.

Morel, Edmund D. "The Belgian Curse in Africa." *Contemporary Review*, London, 80, no. 81, January 6, 1902.

Noel, Thomas J. "All Hail the Denver Pacific: Colorado's First Railroad." *Colorado Magazine* 50, 2, Colorado Historical Society, Denver, Spring 1973.

———. "William D. Haywood." *Colorado Heritage*, Issue 2, 1984.

Peterson, Richard H. "Thomas F. Walsh and Western Business Elitism: The Lifestyle of a Colorado Mining Magnate, 1896–1910." *Red River Valley Historical Review* 6, 4, Fall 1981.

Poore, C. G. "Two Views from Red Gap." *The New York Times Book Review*. March 15, 1936.

Precious Metals Digest. Malden House, Seattle, 1983.

Presidential Addresses and State Papers of Theodore Roosevelt. Part One. P. F. Collier & Son, New York, 1920.

Purinton, Chester W., Thomas H. Woods, and Godfrey D. Doveton. "The Camp Bird Mine, Ouray, Colorado, and the Mining and Milling of the Ore." *American Institute of Mechanical Engineers Transactions* 33, 1902.

Raines, Ed. "Colorado Gold: Part 2—The Discovery, Mining History, Geology and Specimen Mineralogy of Selected Occurrences in Central Colorado and the San Juans." *Rocks and Minerals* 72, 5, September–October 1997.

Ransome, Frederick Leslie. "A Report of the Economic Geology of the Silverton Quadrangle, Colorado." U.S. Geological Survey, Washington, D.C., 1901.

Rickard, T. A. "Two Famous Mines—II." *Mining and Scientific Press*, December 30, 1911.

Rosemeyer, Tom. "Camp Bird Mine, Ouray County, Colorado." *Rocks and Minerals* 65, 2, March–April 1990.

Ryland, Charles S. "Golden's Resourceful Merchant." *Denver Westerners Roundup* 28, 9, November–December 1972.

Sixteenth Street Architecture. Commission of Fine Arts, Washington, D.C., 1988.

Spring, Agnes Wright. "Theodore Roosevelt in Colorado." *Colorado Magazine* 35, 4, Colorado Historical Society, Denver, October 1958.

Stead, W. T., and Rev. E. M. Morrison. "The Congo Free State and Its Autocrat." *American Monthly Review of Reviews*, July 1903.

Sternstein, Jerome L. "King Leopold, Senator Nelson W. Aldrich, and the Strange Beginnings of American Economic Penetration of the Congo." *African Historical Studies*, African Studies Center of Boston University, Brookline, Massachusetts, 1969.

"Thomas F. Walsh." *Child and Animal Protection*, Colorado Humane Society, Denver, September 1908.

"Thomas Francis Walsh." *The National Cyclopedia of American Biography*, Vol. 15. James T. White, New York, 1915.

Titcomb, H. A. "The Camp Bird Gold Mine and Mills." *School of Mines Quarterly* 24, Columbia University, New York, November 1902.

Tribble, Edwin. "The Hope Springs Eternal." *New Republic*, April 12, 1936.

GOVERNMENT RECORDS

Congressional Record. 57th Cong., 2nd sess., 1903, Vol. 36, 1396.

———. 60th Cong., 1st sess., 1908, Vol. 42, 6715–6724.

BUSINESS REPORTS

Reports of the Operations of Camp Bird, Ltd., for the years 1903–1918. Archives, Ouray County Historical Society, Ouray, Colorado.

Travelers Official Guide of the Railways and Steam Navigation Lines in the U.S. and Canada, 2 vols. (publisher unknown), 1874, Archives, Colorado Railway Museum, Golden.

COLLECTIONS, PRIVATE PAPERS

Edward Hanley Collection, Colorado Historical Society, Denver

Evalyn Walsh McLean Collection, Manuscript Division, Library of Congress, Washington, D.C.

Agnes Wright Spring Collection, Colorado Historical Society, Denver

Charles S. Thomas Collection, Colorado Historical Society, Denver

Thomas F. Walsh Collection, Special Collections, E. S. Bird Library, Syracuse University, Syracuse, New York

Arthur Redman Wilfley Papers, Archives, University of Colorado at Boulder Libraries, Boulder

UNPUBLISHED DOCUMENTS

Beatty, A. Chester. "Report on the Camp Bird Mine." February 1902, Archives, Colorado School of Mines, Golden.

"History of the Uncompahgre Project." Undated, Archives, Uncompahgre Valley Water Users' Association, Montrose, Colorado.

Kennedy, Margaret. "The Family History." Undated, in the possession of Kathleen O'Brien, Worcester, Massachusetts.

BAPTISMAL, MARRIAGE, AND BURIAL RECORDS

Bru Boru Heritage Center, Cashel, Ireland

Mount Olivet Cemetery, Golden, Colorado

INTERVIEWS

O'Brien, Kathleen, Worcester, Massachusetts, September 2000

O'Brien, Michael, Clonmel, Ireland, August 2001

Ratmansuyu, Ratmoko, Washington, D.C., September 2000

Ryan, Mary, Dublin, Ireland, July 2000

INSCRIPTIONS

Grave of Bridget Scully Walsh, Kilmurray Cemetery, Ballyneale Parish, County Tipperary, Ireland

INDEX